VEGETARIAN DISHES FROM AROUND THE WORLD

VEGETARIAN DISHES FROM AROUND THE WORLD

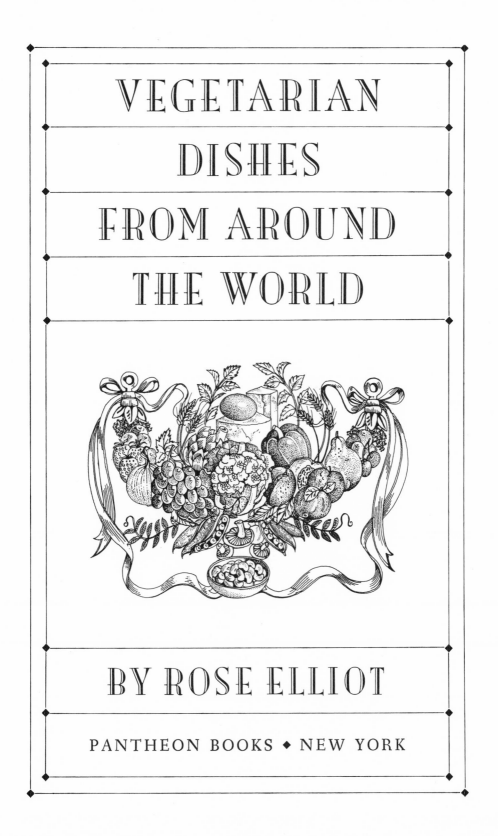

BY ROSE ELLIOT

PANTHEON BOOKS ◆ NEW YORK

Library of Congress Cataloging in Publication Data
Elliot, Rose.
Vegetarian dishes from around the world.
1. Vegetarian cookery.   I. Title.
TX837.E47   641.5'636   81-18943
AACR2
ISBN 0-394-52258-8
ISBN 0-394-74997-9 (pbk.)
Designed by Elissa Ichiyasu
Manufactured in the United States of America
First American Edition

CONTENTS

INTRODUCTION

ALTHOUGH I WAS BROUGHT UP AS A VEGETARIAN, when I started to cook for people who were used to eating meat I found that, unlike me, they did not relish with delight the thought of nut roast. So I began to look for alternatives that they would enjoy more. I soon realized that nearly every country has in its national cuisine at least one or two traditional dishes that do not contain meat or fish yet are still good to look at, good to eat, and very satisfying. Over the years I have gradually built up a collection of these recipes and this book is the result; it contains over 250 recipes from more than 30 different countries.

From Britain there are a couple of traditional cheese dishes, including Welsh rabbit; a creamy leek pie; and pease pudding, which I've included because, although really intended as an accompaniment to meat, it is nutritious enough to eat as a main course and probably often was when times were hard. It's good with vegetables and one of the piquant sauces—mint sauce or applesauce—which the British do so well. The real strength of the British contribution lies in the baking: there are some excellent breads, scones, and cakes, including Madeira cake and Dundee cake; and some quite surprisingly superb puddings such as trifle, gooseberry fool, and *crème brûlée*, which sounds and tastes as though it ought to be French, but isn't.

France itself has any number of delectable vegetarian dishes. The French just seem to have the knack of putting together a few simple yet high-quality ingredients and finishing up with something that's exactly right. Add to this a love of and respect for vegetables and you come up with such wonderful mixtures as red cabbage cooked with butter, chestnuts and red wine; or eggplant stuffed with mushrooms, parsley, and cheese. This book contains many examples of this type of flair as well as those great French vegetarian classics, omelettes, soufflés and savory flans, with their mouthwatering combination of crisp pastry and creamy filling. Then there are the dishes that to me exemplify the thrifty, inventive side of French cookery: the light, stuffed crêpes and the golden choux-pastry ring, or *gougère*, which help make the precious vegetables go further. Finally there are one or two slightly frivolous cakes and some good simple puddings.

Italy, with its pizza, pasta, and rice dishes, is another country that has a great deal to offer the vegetarian, and it's just the type of food that is so useful and popular—cheap and tasty, quick to make and quick to eat. I've often thought it strange that Italian cuisine, which is the oldest in Europe, should in many ways be the one with the most contemporary appeal and practicality. There is certainly plenty of scope for the vegetarian: as well as cereal and pasta dishes there are also vegetable dishes, including a rich-tasting eggplant casserole and stuffed onions; then there's that cheesy golden bake, *gnocchi alla Romana*, as well as delicate spinach *gnocchi* and tasty fritters. From Italy also come some refreshing desserts, including again the one with perhaps the most appeal for today, ice cream.

German cookery is rather like that of Great Britain in that it seems to be very much orientated toward meat, but there are some interesting vegetable dishes and I particularly like the German way of mixing fruit with vegetables: white beans or carrots with apples; potato pancakes with cranberry or applesauce. The Germans also have a split pea purée rather like the British pease pudding except that they add vegetables, which makes a good variation. And they use dried fruits for a compote that makes a pleasant winter dessert.

Austria does not seem to be a very rich source of vegetarian dishes— here again the emphasis is on meat—but the Austrians do have a good way of serving those light little cheesy dumplings, *gnocchi*, in a velvety mushroom sauce, and also of course that marvelous almond and raspberry tart, *linzertorte*.

Much of the cookery of Spain and Portugal includes fish or meat in one form or another, but I have allowed myself the indulgence of including a vegetarian version of perhaps the most famous Spanish dish of all, *paella*. Although fish is usually among the ingredients, it's a very variable dish and so I hope a vegetarian version will be considered valid. In addition, there are that well-known cold Spanish soup, *gazpacho*; some simple stuffed vegetables; a red kidney bean dish from

Portugal; and from Spain perhaps one of the most luxurious desserts of all, chocolate and orange mousse.

Some versatile cheese dishes are to be found in the cuisine of both Holland and Switzerland, including one of the best cheese dishes of all, surely a classic, cheese fondue. I have attributed this to Switzerland, although I believe a rather similar dish is made in Holland and in my recipe I have taken the liberty of suggesting Dutch Edam cheese as a good alternative to the more expensive Gruyère and Emmenthal! Also from Switzerland come what I consider to be a particularly appealing cheese flan, a couple of vegetable dishes, and a moist fruit bread.

The main contribution from Scandinavia seems to be in the dessert section. From Denmark there's red fruit pudding made from raspberries and red currants, and the rice and almond pudding that is traditionally served at Christmas. I've included an apricot and almond pudding from Sweden, and recipes with rhubarb and prunes from Norway and with apples from Finland. But the Scandinavians also have some unusual ways of serving vegetables to make them a bit special. I especially like the two Finnish mushroom recipes and the Norwegian recipes for cabbage and new potatoes. And then of course there are open sandwiches—ideal for a buffet meal—and Danish pastries, for which I've developed a whole-wheat version.

Although the countries of Eastern Europe are not vegetarian, they do have a number of national dishes that do not contain meat and so are ideal for vegetarians. In Rumania, for instance, there is a mixed vegetable stew called *ghiveci*; while this can sometimes contain meat it by no means always does, and so I have given an all-vegetable version of that dish, plus a protein-rich cheesy dip. Then from Bulgaria there are a couple of stews, one based on lentils and the other made from red kidney beans; from Hungary come vegetable stews enlivened with sour cream and paprika, and from Poland a vegetable and bean salad that is pretty to look at and very filling.

Russian cookery offers the vegetarian an ingenious dip with smoky mock caviar; then there's a beet soup, or borsch, and some little curd cheese tartlets, *vatrushki*, to eat with it as well as a protein-rich dessert, that traditional Easter dish made from curd or cream cheese, called *pashka*.

I love the easy-going, inventive feel of American cookery; it's exciting and it's fun. Americans seem to be particularly good with salads— to them we owe coleslaw and Waldorf salad, and a number of cooked vegetable dishes, including glazed sweet potatoes and corn fritters; and perhaps the best chilled soup of all, vichyssoise, which was invented by a chef in America, although admittedly he was French. But then one of the strengths of American cookery seems to be the way it can contain the cuisines of so many different nationalities and yet retain a recognizable character of its own. There are also some particularly interesting desserts; I've included those American favorites, cheesecake and pumpkin pie, and also a less well-known flan, raisin and sour cream pie.

The cookery of South America and the Caribbean features several vegetarian dishes: a red bean and rice dish from the Caribbean, as well as pumpkin soup and banana fritters; and from South America, chilled avocado soup and that creamy avocado dip, *guacamole*; also an unusual hot potato salad with a peanut and chili dressing, which sounds strange but works well. In South America, as in India, unleavened breads are an important part of the diet; here they are called tortillas and are usually made from cornmeal. You will find a recipe for making these, two recipes for stuffing and baking them, as you would crêpes, and also recipes for making them into *tostadas* and for using them as a base for salad mixtures.

The national cereal of North Africa is couscous, which consists of pellets of semolina (or other grains) and is served with spicy sauces. These sauces generally contain meat of some type, but nearly always have chick peas in the mixture too, which in fact provide excellent protein and can thus replace the meat altogether without reducing the nutritional content of the dish. I have therefore given a vegetarian version based on chick peas, vegetables, and spices. Cooling side salads are served with couscous meals, and there are some typical mixtures in the salads section.

I think the Middle East offers some of the best vegetarian dishes of all. There are dreamy dips, smooth chick pea *hummus*, of course, as well as some less well-known ones made from eggplant and sesame paste and from dried beans. These make first courses or fillings for sandwiches or for the pocket-shaped Middle Eastern bread, pita, of which I've evolved a whole-wheat version. Then there are some unusual salads, among them the famous bulgur wheat, tomato, and parsley one called *tabbouleh*, and a cold cooked spinach one, which sounds odd but which is particularly cooling on a hot day. But perhaps the most important Middle Eastern contribution to vegetarian cookery is the stuffed vegetables that look so appetizing: tomatoes stuffed with rice, little stuffed eggplants, stuffed vine leaves baked in tomato sauce. There are some splendid pies, too; I think the spinach pie, with its smooth filling and flaky crust is one of the best. And when it comes to desserts, there's an easy uncooked yogurt tart, a honey cheesecake, and a chilled ground rice and rosewater pudding, all of which are nutritious and therefore useful in menu planning as well as being good to eat.

India has a large proportion of vegetarians in its population, and thus as you might expect, one of the best sources of vegetarian food—and what colorful, tasty food it is! I think there are few foods as appetizing as a really well-cooked curry or spicy rice dish, and you will find a number of recipes for these including *khitchari*, that mixture of lentils and rice from which our present-day kedgeree originated. The Indians are also excellent at making unleavened breads, and these are perfect accompaniments not only to curries but also with salads and dips as a change from ordinary bread. One of these unleavened bread mixtures is also rolled out thinly, wrapped around a vegetable filling, and then deep-fried to make *samosas*, little Indian pastries.

China is another country that has plenty to offer the vegetarian. The Chinese were making their own versions of textured protein from wheat flour long before it was ever thought of in the West. I have included a sweet and sour recipe using this wheat protein, or wheat gluten, as well as a recipe using that other high-protein vegetable product, *tofu*, which is made from soya beans and which you can sometimes buy very cheaply in Chinese shops. I have also included a couple of the crunchy stir-fried vegetable dishes that the Chinese do so well.

I think most people like to try something new sometimes, and there are occasions when even the most dedicated meat eater wants a change, so I hope this book will prove interesting and helpful and that you will be tempted to cook the recipes and will enjoy the results.

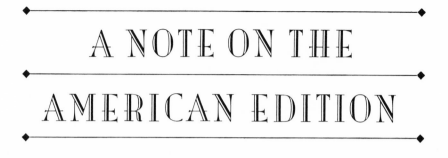

A NOTE ON THE AMERICAN EDITION

Having this american edition of my cookbook published is one of the most thrilling things that has happened to me, and I do hope that you will be as pleased with it as I am!

I should like to thank my agent, Vivienne Schuster, and Wendy Wolf and her team at Pantheon Books, especially Lorraine Alexander Veach, for making it possible. I must say I did not realize before how much "translation" is necessary to make an English cookbook practical and useable for American cooks. Not only do we call some ingredients, methods, and utensils by totally different names, but the prepackaged quantities in which certain foodstuffs can be bought and even the sizes of some of your standard baking pans (or "tins" as we call them here) are different.

So we have had a lot of fun as well as hard work converting, re-testing, and, in some cases, re-writing this book. I hope that the result will be a thoroughly accurate and understandable edition that you'll find really helpful. Happy Cooking!

NOTE ON SPECIAL
INGREDIENTS

Most of the recipes are self-explanatory, and nearly all the ingredients are easy to get; when something scarce or exotic is called for, I've tried to give substitutes where possible so that, even if you can't get that item, you can still make the dish. But here are just one or two notes that might be helpful.

FATS AND OILS

You will notice that I generally suggest butter in the recipes, because very often that is the fat traditionally used and therefore the one that gives the most authentic flavor. "Sweet creamery" (unsalted) butter is generally preferably and especially in dessert recipes, but "lightly salted" may also be used as long as you remember its salt content and adjust for it when it's appropriate or desirable to do so, depending on taste or dietary constraints. You could substitute a pure vegetable margarine if you prefer, and of course make it an unsaturated one if you wish.

I still cannot make up my mind whether butter or polyunsaturated margarine is better from the health point of view; opinions differ depending on which expert you consult. Butter has more fat but is pure; margarine contains chemical additives. Personally I hedge my bets by using butter at the table and in some cookery and a polyunsaturated margarine in cakes and baking. I also use corn oil, which is low in saturated fat, for frying, while I prefer olive oil, which is neutral, for salad dressings. If you want to use a shortening (high in saturated fat) for pastry, choose a pure vegetable one.

Although I remain open-minded about the butter versus polyunsaturated margarine controversy, I think the most important thing is to keep a check on the amount of *any* fat used in cooking (including the fat content in cream and egg yolks) and to try to plan a day's—and a week's—meals carefully, balancing eggs, cheese, and other fats with plenty of cereal and vegetable protein, low-fat dairy products such as cottage cheese, farmer's cheese, buttermilk, and yogurt, vegetables, and salads.

FLOUR

The flour I normally use is plain 100% whole wheat, which I find excellent for nearly all my cooking. If you're new to whole-wheat flour, it's often helpful to begin by mixing it with a proportion of unbleached, all-purpose flour; I've given suggestions for this in the recipes where applicable. I also use unbleached all-purpose flour for all sauces that require a flour thickening.

You will notice, in the recipes where whole-wheat flour is sifted, I say "add the sifted flour and the residue of bran left in the sieve" or something similar. People sometimes ask me why I bother to sift the flour and then add the bran that's been sifted out. The flour is sifted to aerate it and make it lighter, not to remove the bran, so, having sifted the flour, the bran can then be put back.

SUGAR

This is another controversial subject, and my own feelings are that it's not so much the color of the sugar that makes a dish more or less nutritious as it is the quantity used. Brown sugar "feels" healthier to use, but I've found this tends to make me a bit more lavish with it! I use brown sugar in breads and in cakes such as Dundee cake, parkin and chocolate brownies, also sometimes in shortbreads and cookies. But there are times when I prefer to use a small quantity of white refined sugar or honey because of their particular flavor and appearance. This is especially true, I feel, when a delicate vanilla flavor is called for, and for this I think there is nothing better than vanilla sugar, which is so easy to make. All you do is break a vanilla pod in half and bury the halves in a canister of refined sugar, scooping up the sugar as it is used.

SALT

I'm afraid I'm very addicted to sea salt, which I know is more expensive than ordinary table salt, but I like it because it's natural and pure. The trouble is it also makes food taste so much better that once you've used it you won't want to settle for anything else.

HERBS AND SPICES

It's often the use of a herb or spice that makes food taste of a particular country: dill immediately gives a Scandinavian or Eastern European flavor, paprika a Hungarian one. I've tried, however, to keep the recipes as simple and straightforward as possible (while still, I hope, safeguarding their authenticity), and the only spice that I think you could have difficulty in obtaining is fresh gingerroot (unless there is a large Asian community where you live). But it's much easier to find than it used to be, and I've discovered that the root, carefully wrapped, will keep beautifully in the freezer. You can grate it straight from the freezer, so it's worth buying a few knobbly pieces of root when you see it, especially if you have to go some distance to get it.

BEANS, PEAS, AND LENTILS

These days it's usually not difficult to find dried beans, peas, and lentils, and I've been delighted to see dried red kidney beans, chick peas, and lentils appearing in my local supermarket alongside the more familiar split red lentils and lima (or butter) beans. Instructions for using these foods appear in the individual recipes, but as a general rule it's worth remembering that, if you rinse dried beans and peas after soaking and before cooking, it helps to make them more digestible. Also it's best *not* to add salt to the cooking water as this can toughen the skin before the inside is cooked. Salt also tends to draw a food's nutrients out into the cooking liquid where it can then, quite literally, evaporate. In the recipes, I've given approximate cooking times for the dried peas and beans, but these can vary according to how long they have been stored, so it's best to keep an eye on them and adjust the timing a little if necessary; do make sure the beans, peas, and lentils are thoroughly cooked.

MENU PLANNING

PLANNING A VEGETARIAN MEAL IS NOT COMPLI-
cated or difficult—all you have to do is to decide on your source of
protein and build the rest of the meal around that. So you could
have something like, say, cheese soufflé with new potatoes and green
beans followed by a refreshing tangy orange salad. If you wanted a
first course as well, you could have a stuffed tomato salad or mushrooms *à la Grecque*; or a dip such as mock caviar with crisp Melba
toast; or a vegetable purée soup, like French tomato soup or lettuce
soup. As you can see there is plenty of scope!

Other examples of this type of simple menu planning based around
a protein-rich main course are: Zucchini stuffed with cheese and onion,
with tomato sauce; served with new potatoes (or cooked rice) and
spinach or baby carrots; preceded by pumpkin soup, if you like; and
perhaps followed by an exotic fruit salad or banana fritters. Or from
Italy, a gorgeous tomato and mushroom pizza with green salad, with
perhaps stuffed cucumber as a starter and pineapple sherbet for
dessert. There are plenty of high-protein dishes like these in the book
and plenty of opportunities for many different combinations. Although
I've given suggestions for more than one course, if you want to be
simpler and more economical, the appetizers and desserts can of course
be left out as long as you've included some protein in the main course.

I think, however, that part of the pleasure and satisfaction of vegetarian cookery come from the opportunity it affords to be very fluid and
creative in meal planning enabling you to enjoy dishes that you
probably wouldn't otherwise try. Take, for instance, luscious French
red cabbage stuffed with chestnuts and baked in red wine. This really

makes a lovely main dish but it only contains a minimal amount of protein; however, there's no reason why the protein should always be in the main dish. You can make a beautifully balanced meal by serving a protein-rich first course, such as the creamy chick pea and vegetable salad, *aigroissade*, or little individual cheese soufflés; or a nutritious dip, such as feta cheese and herb spread or *hummus*, served with fingers of hot buttered or Melba toast; or just plain cheese and crackers.

You could boost the protein level still further if you wanted to by concluding the meal with little coffee custards or *coeurs à la crème*.

Here are some of the ways in which you can provide protein for the meal when it is not in the main dish.

- *Serve a protein appetizer*—e.g., any soup, dip, or vegetable dish containing lentils, nuts, cheese, milk, or egg.
- *Offer a milk-based or cheesy sauce with the meal.* This is particularly good with some of the stuffed vegetable dishes, such as the tomatoes *à la Provençale* or stuffed onions.
- *Provide grated cheese for people to add to their meal.* This is a useful and simple way of increasing the protein with some pasta dishes or vegetable stews, such as ratatouille or the mixed vegetable stew from Bulgaria.
- *Garnish the dish with slices of hard-boiled egg.* Again, if you like egg, this is a good simple way of adding protein to vegetable casseroles, salads, curries, or rice dishes.
- *Whenever appropriate, serve the meal with rice and even add some nuts, sunflower seeds, or sesame seeds to increase the protein further.*
- *Have a protein-rich vegetable or salad with the meal.* This is a nice, easy way of adding nourishment. Potatoes Anna, layered with cheese, are good, or baked potatoes with a dollop of a smooth low-fat cheese like ricotta or cottage cheese, or the German white beans with apples.
- *Provide protein with a nutritious dessert.* Perhaps this is one time when you can indulge with a relatively easy conscience! Examples of such desserts are ice cream (homemade, with egg custard), yogurt with fruit and nuts or yogurt tart, *crème brûlée*, coffee *ricotta* pudding, cheesecake, rice pudding, or even crackers and a creamy dessert cheese.

As you will see some of these ideas are really very simple, while others take more time and organization, but I think you'll agree they are quite feasible and practical—and it really is fun to experiment with creative menus.

Here are just a few examples of how this meal-planning works—
there are lots more ideas with the recipes.

Stuffed tomato salad
Cheese Fondue with French bread
Pear bread (birnbrot)

Chick pea soup
Paella with Spanish green salad
Chocolate and orange mousse

Individual cheese soufflés
Stuffed eggplant with wine sauce
Gratin dauphinoise
Green beans
Fresh peach salad

Bean dip with fingers of hot toast
Stuffed vine leaves
Tomato salad
Greek honey pie

Avocados vinaigrette
Mushroom soufflé
Green salad
Linzertorte

Mock caviar with hot toast
Russian beet soup with little cheese tartlets
Fresh fruit

French onion soup
Tomatoes à la Provençale with
noodles and green beans
Crème brûlée

Hummus
Tomatoes stuffed with rice
Green salad with Gruyère cheese (or you
could serve cheese sauce)
Orange fruit salad

Red cabbage and chestnut casserole
Baked potatoes filled with cottage cheese,
or sour cream and chopped chives
Little coffee custards

Chilled cucumber soup
Red pepper stew with brown rice
Green salad with Gruyére
Chilled yogurt

Biriani
Curry sauce
Tomato side salad
Chopped hard-boiled eggs, roasted peanuts,
poppadums, mango chutney
Rice pudding

White bean salad with bread and butter
Ratatouille with potatoes Anna
Crêpes Suzette

If you follow the suggestions I've given in the book, you certainly needn't worry about missing out on any essential nutrients. The dairy foods, cheese, eggs, milk, and milk products such as yogurt are as rich in protein as meat, whilst the other forms of protein—nuts and seeds, beans and cereals—are all nourishing if you mix ingredients from two or more of the categories for any given meal. You needn't worry that you'll be undernourished!

VEGETARIAN DISHES FROM AROUND THE WORLD

SOUPS

Vegetarian Stock
Borsch (Beet Soup)
Cheese and Onion Soup
Chestnut Soup
Chick Pea Soup
Chilled Avocado Soup
Chilled Cherry Soup
Chilled Cucumber Soup
Cacik
Gazpacho
Split Pea Soup
Lentil Soup
Lettuce Soup
Mushroom Soup
Onion Soup
Potato Soup
Pumpkin Soup
Tomato Soup
Vichyssoise
Watercress Soup
Yellow Split Pea Soup

A BOWL OF HOMEMADE SOUP MAKES A VERY WELcoming start to a meal. It can even become the main part of the meal if it's a filling soup: one of our favorite weekend lunches in winter is a good lentil soup with hot rolls and cheese and fresh fruit. There are, of course, other hearty soups to choose from besides lentil; French onion soup, with its cheesy bread topping is another favorite, and vivid beet soup, or Borsch, from Russia is cheering to look at as well as filling to eat on a cold day.

Lighter soups made from puréed vegetables, as well as some chilled soups for serving before other, more substantial dishes are ideal. I know some people find the idea of chilled soups rather strange, but they make a beautifully refreshing start to a summer meal. Both the chilled avocado soup and the chilled cucumber soup are also particularly easy to make if you have a blender or food processor. Personally I consider one or the other machine to be almost essential for soup making, but you could use a *Mouli-légumes* or some other food mill for nearly all the soups in this section if you prefer.

In most of the soups, the thickening comes from the vegetables themselves after they have been puréed. This usually seems to be sufficient, especially if a little potato is included in the ingredients. Quite often I purée half or three-quarters of the mixture to give the soup a thick, smooth base, and leave the rest as it is to supply some texture and add interest, but this is something you can vary according to how you feel and the effect you want to achieve.

You will notice in the recipes that sometimes I suggest using vegetable stock, sometimes just water, and sometimes a choice. I think some soups—like French onion soup, for instance—need stock to give a good flavor: you can use homemade vegetable stock, or vegetarian stock cubes or powder from a health-food shop. There are other soups, however, particularly the simple vegetable soups for which it's less important to use stock; sometimes I think you can even get a better effect by using just water, which allows the full flavor of the vegetables to come through; so don't feel guilty if you haven't got any stock.

I've also found it a mistake to think that the longer soups cook the tastier they'll be. This may be true of meat soups, but with vegetable soups once the vegetables are tender there's no point in further cooking. The soup tastes fresher if it's not overcooked.

Soups are fun to serve because it doesn't take much extra trouble to make them look really pretty. A few fresh green herbs snipped over a pale soup, a swirl of cream on a deep-colored tomato or beet soup, or some crunchy little croutons topping a smooth-textured soup take only moments to add and make the soup look and taste extra good.

VEGETARIAN STOCK

This is the soup base I use most often. It is a light and delicately flavored alternative to the beef and chicken broths that many people automatically turn to when preparing a homemade soup, and, needless to say, it contains none of the fat or salt (particularly a problem in canned broths and stocks) of the meat bases. *Makes 2 quarts.*

1 onion, peeled and roughly sliced
1 celery stick, roughly chopped
1 large carrot, scrubbed and
  roughly chopped
1 medium-size potato, scrubbed
  and roughly chopped
2 or 3 sprigs of parsley
2 quarts (2 liters) water

Put all the vegetables and the parsley into a large saucepan and cover with the water. Bring to the boil, then turn down the heat and leave to simmer for 1½–2 hours, covered. Strain through a sieve.

You can vary the flavor by adding other herbs and perhaps a bay leaf or several cloves of garlic (which only need halving, not peeling). You can make this up and keep it in your freezer as a reserve for those occasions when the urge for a bowl of piping hot homemade soup sneaks up on you.

BORSCH (BEET SOUP)

RUSSIA

This soup looks very warming and appetizing, its rich ruby red swirled with sour cream. Although borsch, to give it its Russian name, is usually made with beef stock and may contain meat as well, there are numerous versions throughout Russia; the only consistent ingredient is the beets, and so I don't think my vegetarian one is too far-fetched. In Russia, borsch is often accompanied by little cottage- or curd-cheese tartlets, *vatrushki*, which turn it into a complete lunch or supper. *Serves 4–6.*

2 *large onions*	*1 can (8 oz/240 g) tomatoes*
2 *large carrots*	*1 pound cooked beets (not pickled)*
2 *stalks celery*	*Sea salt (to taste)*
¼ *pound (115 g) cabbage*	*Sugar (to taste)*
2 *tablespoons vegetable oil*	*⅔ cup (160 ml) sour cream*
4 *cups (1 liter) water or vegetable*	*(optional)*
stock	*Fresh dill or chives (optional)*

Peel and chop the onions; scrape and dice the carrots and slice the celery and cabbage. Heat the oil in a good-size saucepan and add the prepared vegetables; stir them so that they all get coated with the oil, then leave them to fry over a gentle heat for about 10 minutes, stirring from time to time. Stir in the water or vegetable stock and tomatoes, and bring to a boil. Cover the saucepan and leave the soup to simmer for about 20 minutes, until all the vegetables are tender. (I sometimes use a pressure cooker for this, in which case it takes about 5 minutes.)

If you are using fresh beets, once they are cooked and cooled, carefully peel them (canned beets will already be peeled). Dice the beets, add them to the soup, and season to taste with salt and a little sugar. Bring the soup to the boil again, then lower the heat and let it simmer gently for 3–4 minutes. You can serve the borsch like this, but I prefer to purée about half of it in the blender, which makes the soup slightly thicker and smoother while allowing it to retain a some-what chunky texture. If you add the sour cream, whisk it lightly with a fork to make it creamy, then swirl a little into each bowl. Sprinkle with chopped dill if you've got some; or you can use chopped chives.

◆——————◆——————◆

CHEESE AND ONION SOUP

ITALY

Although the ingredients used in this soup are very similar to those in French onion soup, the result is quite different: This soup is white with a smooth texture, and the cheese is stirred in just before serving to thicken and flavor it. If you've got time to make them, homemade croutons are a very nice garnish. It's a filling, protein-rich soup, lovely before a salad meal, or with a buttery pasta and green salad. *Serves 4.*

1½ pounds (675 g) onions
3¾ cups (930 ml) water
2 tablespoons (30 ml) butter
Sea salt
Freshly ground black pepper
1–1½ cups (250–650 ml) grated
cheese (a hard, flavorful cheese,
such as Gruyère or aged
Cheddar)
¼ cup (60 ml) grated Parmesan
cheese
Croutons (optional)

Peel and chop the onions and put them into a large saucepan with the water to simmer gently until tender (15–20 minutes). Purée this mixture, then return it to the rinsed-out saucepan and add the butter and a little seasoning. When you're ready to serve the soup, reheat it until bubbling hot. Take it off the heat and stir in the cheeses. Check the seasoning and serve immediately.

If you reheat the soup once the cheese has been added, don't let it boil or it might get stringy. Also be careful not to over-season the soup before you add the cheese, as the cheese itself will most likely contain considerable salt.

CHESTNUT SOUP

ITALY

The starchy texture and slightly sweet flavor of chestnuts go well with hot vegetables and make this a very warming winter soup. You can use fresh chestnuts if you've got time to prepare them, but I must admit I usually use the dried ones, which you can get easily now in health-food shops and some supermarkets. *Serves 4–6.*

1½ pounds (675 g) fresh
　chestnuts, or dried chestnuts
1 large onion
2 large carrots
1 turnip
2 celery stalks
2 tablespoons butter
4 cups (1 liter) stock or water
1 tablespoon fresh chopped parsley
Sea salt
Freshly ground black pepper

If you're using fresh chestnuts, make a little cut in them with a sharp knife, then simmer them in boiling water until the cut opens (about 10 minutes). Remove the skins with a sharp-pointed knife; keep the chestnuts in the water until you're ready to peel them because the skins will firm up as they cool. If you're using dried chestnuts, soak them in cold water for an hour or so, then simmer them gently in plenty of water until they're really tender. I find this takes a good hour or more. Drain the cooked, dried chestnuts, saving the liquid.

Peel and chop the onion, carrots, and turnip; wash and dice the celery. Melt the butter in a large saucepan and fry the onion for 5 minutes; then add the rest of the vegetables and cook for another 5 minutes before pouring in the stock. (If you're using dried chestnuts, add enough water or stock to the reserved cooking liquid to make 4 cups (1 liter). Simmer the soup for about 40 minutes, until the chestnuts and vegetables are tender. Stir in the parsley and season the soup to taste with salt and pepper.

CHICK PEA SOUP

SPAIN

I think chick peas have a very special savory sort of flavor, and here they are used to make a tasty soup. If possible, allow time for them to soak before cooking as this does speed up the cooking time. This is a useful soup for serving before the Spanish *paella* or stuffed peppers because it supplies plenty of protein. *Serves 4.*

8 ounces (240 g) chick peas	*1 bay leaf*
1 onion	*Sea salt*
2 carrots	*Freshly ground black pepper*
4 tablespoons (50 g) butter	*Croutons*
1 tablespoon (15 ml) lemon juice	

Soak the chick peas in cold water for several hours or overnight, then drain and rinse them. Put them into a saucepan with plenty of cold water and simmer gently until they are tender—this can take as long as an hour or even more. Then drain the chick peas, reserving the liquid. Measure this and add enough water or stock to make 2 pints (1.2 liters).

Peel and chop the onion; scrape the carrots and dice them. Melt half the butter in a large saucepan and fry the onion and carrot for 5 minutes, letting them get golden brown. Stir them often so that they don't stick, then add the chick peas, liquid, lemon juice, and bay leaf, and simmer the soup gently until the vegetables are tender—about 20 minutes. Take out the bay leaf and purée the soup. Put it into a clean saucepan, stir in the remaining butter, and season to taste. Serve topped with croutons.

CHILLED AVOCADO SOUP

MEXICO

This soup is a good way of making two avocados feed six people. It's very easy to make (with a blender) and comes out a creamy, very pale green. It's best not to make this soup more than about 45 minutes in advance, as the lemon juice is not a total guarantee against discoloration. *Serves 6.*

2 large ripe avocados (make sure they feel slightly soft all over when you hold them in the palm of your hand)
1 tablespoon (15 ml) lemon juice

3¾ cups (930 ml) ice-cold milk
Sea salt
Freshly ground black pepper
2 tablespoons chopped chives

Cut the avocados in half, then twist the two halves apart and remove the pits. Carefully peel and cut the avocados into chunks. Put them, along with lemon juice and milk into your blender jar and blend at medium speed until the mixture is smooth. Season to taste with salt and pepper. Chill the soup until it's needed; it's a good idea to chill the soup bowls, too.

When you're ready to serve, ladle the soup into the bowls and sprinkle generously with chopped chives.

CHILLED CHERRY SOUP

HUNGARY

No one finds it odd to start a meal with melon; a fruit soup simply takes this practice a stage further! Anyway, this black cherry soup looks so delicious with its topping of sour cream that I don't think you'll have much trouble persuading people to try it. I usually use frozen or canned morello cherries, but of course fresh ones would be better if you can get them. *Serves 6.*

1 pound (450 g) frozen or fresh
    cherries
3¾ cups (930 ml) water
8 ounces (240 g) sugar
2 tablespoons arrowroot
¼ pint (150 ml) dry red wine

or 2 cans (16 ounces/480 g each)
    black cherries

A little lemon juice (optional)
A little sour cream

Pit the cherries by halving them and digging out the pits with a sharp knife. This is an essential first step—unless, of course, you're using a pitted frozen or canned variety.

If you're using fresh or frozen cherries, put them into a saucepan with the water and sugar and heat gently to dissolve the sugar, then bring to a boil and simmer gently until tender. If you're using canned cherries just put them into a saucepan and bring them to the boil. Mix the arrowroot with a little cold water to make a smooth paste, then stir some of the hot cherry liquid into the arrowroot mixture. When blended, add it to the cherries and liquid in the saucepan and simmer for 2–3 minutes. Take the saucepan off the heat and pour the soup into a bowl. When it's cool, stir in the wine; chill before serving. Taste and add a little more sugar, if desired or possibly a drop or two of lemon juice if you've used canned cherries and need to sharpen the flavor slightly; it should be sweet but refreshing.

CHILLED CUCUMBER SOUP

BULGARIA

Yogurt, cucumber, walnuts, and dill sound like rather a strange mixture, but actually the combination of smooth, creamy yogurt and chewy walnuts with refreshing cucumber and dill works well, and this soup makes a lovely protein-rich first course for a summer meal. The Bulgarian name for this soup is *tarator*. *Serves 4.*

1 large cucumber
1 clove garlic, peeled and crushed
  in a little salt
2 cups (500 ml) plain yogurt
¼ cup (60 ml) walnut pieces
Sea salt

Freshly ground black pepper
1 tablespoon chopped fresh dill
  weed or parsley (or 1 teaspoon
  dried dill weed and 2 teaspoons
  chopped fresh parsley)

Peel the cucumber (if you leave the skin on it can make the soup taste rather bitter), then cut it into rough chunks. Put the chunks into the blender with the garlic, yogurt, walnuts, about half a teaspoon of sea salt and a grinding of pepper, and blend until you've got a smoothish purée. Taste the mixture and add some more salt and pepper if you think it needs it, then pour the soup into a bowl and chill it thoroughly.

To serve, ladle the soup into individual bowls and sprinkle each portion with the chopped green herbs.

◆———◆———◆

CACIK

TURKEY

This soup is similar to the preceding one but milder in flavor—no walnuts, garlic, or dill, just mint and parsley. It's very refreshing, especially delicious in hot weather, and also beautifully low in calories, so ideal for dieters. *Serves 4.*

1 cucumber
2 cups (500 ml) plain yogurt
8 sprigs of mint

4 sprigs of parsley
1 teaspoon sea salt
4 sprigs of mint to garnish

Peel the cucumber, cut it into rough chunks, and put them into the blender jar with the yogurt. Wash the mint and parsley and remove the stalks; add the leaves to the cucumber and yogurt together with the salt. Blend at medium speed until you've got a smooth purée. Transfer the purée to a bowl and chill thoroughly. Check the seasoning and add more seasoning if necessary—chilling tends to dull the flavor. Remember, too, that dill is often said to respond to the body's need (or desire) for salt, so take this into account when adjusting the seasoning. Serve the soup in individual bowls with a sprig of mint floating on top.

If you want a richer-tasting soup for a special occasion, you can replace some of the yogurt with light cream—but this will make the soup richer in calories, too!

GAZPACHO

S P A I N

Most people are familiar with this chilled Spanish "salad soup," and there are many versions of it. The method I've evolved is very quick and easy: You just purée canned tomatoes in your blender and stir in chopped fresh vegetables and herbs. If you keep a can of tomatoes in the fridge in the summer, you can make this soup in a matter of moments. It's nice served with crunchy fresh croutons. *Serves 6.*

1 large onion, peeled and cut into rough chunks
2 large cloves garlic, peeled and crushed in a little salt
1 can (28 ounces/480 g) tomatoes
4 tablespoons olive oil
2 teaspoons wine vinegar
1½ teaspoons sea salt

Freshly ground black pepper
1 cucumber
1 small green or red pepper
1 tablespoon chopped fresh chives
1 tablespoon chopped fresh mint
A few cubes of homemade croutons

Put the onion and garlic into the blender jar together with the tomatoes, olive oil, vinegar, salt, and a grinding of pepper; blend to a purée. (If you haven't got a blender grate the onion finely and pass the tomatoes through a vegetable mill, then mix them together and add the garlic, oil, vinegar, and other seasoning.) Chill the mixture.

Just before you want to serve the soup, peel the cucumber and remove the seeds from the pepper, chopping both into small pieces. Stir the cucumber and pepper into the soup, together with the freshly chopped herbs, then ladle the soup into individual bowls and serve the croutons separately.

SPLIT PEA SOUP

HOLLAND

I must admit that this soup is a bit of an adaptation: It usually contains ham, which is cut up and added at the end, but this vegetarian version tastes good and makes a lovely, warming winter soup. It's useful for serving before a main course that may include some protein, but it's also nice for lunch or supper served with wholewheat bread, cheese, and fruit. *Serves 4.*

1 cup (250 ml) green split peas
  (available presoaked)
4½ cups (1.2 liters) water
1 onion
2 medium-size potatoes
2 celery stalks

2 small leeks
½ teaspoon dried savory or
  marjoram
Sea salt
Freshly ground black pepper

Wash the split peas and put them into a large saucepan with the water. Peel and slice the onion and potatoes; wash and slice the celery and leeks. Add all these vegetables to the liquid, bring to the boil, and simmer gently until the peas are tender—about 40 minutes. Stir in the savory or marjoram and season the soup carefully with salt and pepper. You can serve the soup as it is, but I think it's best to purée at least half of it in the blender to make a good base, and leave the remainder to give some texture.

LENTIL SOUP

MIDDLE EAST

I think this is one of the most comforting soups of all and, since you don't have to prepare lots of vegetables, it's also one of the easiest to make. It takes about 5 minutes to get everything into the saucepan, followed by 15–20 minutes gentle simmering, then a quick blend in the blender, and it's ready. Quite often when we get in late and the children are milling around me in a hungry way, I make the soup in a pressure cooker, which cuts the cooking time to 5 minutes. (If you do use a pressure cooker, add a couple of tablespoons of oil to the mixture to prevent the water from frothing up as it comes to the boil.)

This soup makes quite a filling meal on its own with bread and fruit, or serve it before the low-protein Middle Eastern dishes such as rice-stuffed tomatoes or stuffed vine leaves to make a well-balanced meal. *Serves 4.*

8 ounces (240 g) split lentils
4 cups (1 liter) stock or water
1 large onion, peeled and chopped
2 cloves garlic, peeled and crushed

1 teaspoon ground cumin
2 tablespoons butter
Salt and pepper

Wash the lentils, then put them into a large saucepan with the stock or water, onion, garlic and cumin; bring to the boil and simmer gently for 15–20 minutes, until the lentils are cooked. Purée the soup until smooth, then add the butter and seasoning to taste and reheat the soup gently. This makes a thickish soup, but you can of course thin it down with a little milk or water if you want to.

LETTUCE SOUP

FRANCE

I like this soup because it's such a good way of using up those outer lettuce leaves you feel so guilty about throwing away. It's also got a nice fresh summery flavor. For a special occasion it's lovely with the light cream added, but for everyday you can leave it out and use extra milk instead. *Serves 4.*

1 onion
1 pound (450 g) potatoes
Outside leaves of 2 or 3 heads of
   romaine
2 tablespoons butter
2½ cups (625 ml) water

2 cups (500 ml) milk
⅔ cup (160 ml) light cream
Sea salt
Freshly ground black pepper
Nutmeg

Peel and chop the onion and potatoes. Wash the lettuce leaves and cut them up. Melt the butter in a large saucepan and sauté the onion and potato gently for 5 minutes, but don't brown them. Then add the lettuce leaves and stir them for a minute or two so that they get all buttery. Add the water and milk and let the soup simmer gently for 15–20 minutes, until the vegetables are cooked.

Purée the soup and stir in the cream if you're using it. Season it with salt, pepper, and a grating of nutmeg. Reheat it but don't let it boil after you've added the cream.

MUSHROOM SOUP

FRANCE

Little button mushrooms give a delicate, pale, creamy result. If you want to make the soup really special, add a tablespoonful of sherry just before serving. *Serves 4.*

½ pound (225 g) fresh mushrooms	*3 tablespoons flour*
Small piece of onion, peeled	*About 2½ cups (625 ml) milk*
1 bay leaf	*Sea salt*
1 clove garlic, peeled and sliced	*Freshly ground black pepper*
A few parsley stalks	*Freshly ground nutmeg*
2½ cups (625 ml) stock	*Cayenne pepper*
4 tablespoons butter	*1 tablespoon sherry (optional)*

Wash the mushrooms and remove the stalks. Put the stalks into a medium-size saucepan together with the onion, bay leaf, garlic, parsley stalks, and stock and bring to the boil, then leave to simmer for 10 minutes to extract the flavors. Strain the liquid into a measuring cup and add enough milk to make 3¾ cups (930 ml). Discard the mushroom stalks, etc.)

Melt three tablespoons of the butter in the saucepan and stir in the flour. After a moment or two, when it looks bubbly, pour in a half cup of the milk mixture and stir over a fairly high heat until it has thickened. Repeat the process with the rest of the milk four more times. Now chop or slice the mushrooms, sauté them lightly in the remaining butter, and add them to the thickened milk, together with the salt, pepper, a grating of nutmeg, a pinch of cayenne pepper, and the sherry if you're using it. Let the soup simmer for 3–4 minutes to give the flavors a chance to blend before serving.

ONION SOUP

F R A N C E

Although French onion soup is usually made with brown meat stock, I've found that it's possible to make a surprisingly rich-tasting vegetarian version. The important part is the preliminary careful sautéeing of the onions in the butter—and the sherry, if you can spare it, makes all the difference too. This soup is splendid served as a protein-rich starter before a light vegetable main course; it's also filling enough to make a lovely late night supper with just a little fruit to follow. *Serves 4.*

1½ pounds (675 g) onions
3 tablespoons butter
1 tablespoon flour
3¾ cups (930 ml) vegetable stock
 or water
3 tablespoons cheap sherry
Sea salt

Freshly ground black pepper
Slices of whole-wheat or French
 bread
Butter (for spreading on bread)
1–1½ cups (125–175 g) grated
 cheese

Peel the onions and slice them into fairly fine rings. Melt the butter in a large saucepan and sauté the onions slowly for 15–20 minutes until they're golden, stirring them from time to time; then mix in the flour and cook for a few seconds before adding the stock or water, sherry, and a seasoning of salt and pepper. Bring the mixture to the boil, then let it simmer gently with the lid on the saucepan for 30 minutes. Just before the soup is ready warm heatproof soup bowls and lightly toast and butter a slice of bread for each; put the toast, whole or roughly broken, into the bowls. When the soup is ready, check the seasoning, then ladle it into the bowls, scatter the grated cheese on top, and place the bowls under your oven's broiler to melt the cheese; serve immediately.

If you have enough room, I find it's a help to stand the bowls on a baking sheet—then they're easier to withdraw from the broiler when ready. Alternatively you can put all the soup in a large ovenproof dish or soup tureen; in this case you'll probably need to use the oven to melt the cheese. Or another way of doing it is to prepare the bread and cheese separately under the broiler and then pop them on top of the soup just before you serve it!

POTATO SOUP

FRANCE

This is a velvety soup with a delicate flavor. You can make it even better by adding a little cream at the end for special occasions, but it's very good just as it is. *Serves 4.*

½ pound (225 g) onions
¾ pound (350 g) potatoes
2 tablespoons butter
1¼ cups (310 ml) milk

2½ cups (625 ml) water
1 teaspoon sea salt
Freshly ground black pepper
Fresh chives (optional)

Peel and chop the onion; peel the potatoes and dice them. Melt the butter in a large saucepan and add the onions; sauté for 5 minutes, stirring often, until transparent (do not brown). Add the potato and cook for a further 2–3 minutes, until the potato looks nice and buttery; then stir in the milk, water, and sea salt. Bring the soup to a boil and let it simmer gently for 20–30 minutes, until the vegetables are tender. Purée the soup to a smooth, creamy consistency; then return it to the rinsed out saucepan and check the seasoning. Reheat the soup gently. It's nice served with a scattering of chopped chives on top to provide a little color.

PUMPKIN SOUP

JAMAICA

Pumpkin makes a very delicious soup, golden in color with a delicate yet distinctive flavor. It's lovely sprinkled with chopped parsley and served with garlic bread at Halloween. *Serves 6.*

2¼ pounds (1 kg) pumpkin
(this weight includes the skin
and seeds); or 2 cups canned
pumpkin
2 large onions
2 large cloves garlic
2 tablespoons butter

4 cups (1 liter) vegetable stock
Sea salt
Freshly ground black pepper
⅔ cup (160 ml) light cream or
whole milk
Fresh parsley

Cut the skin off the pumpkin, and scoop out and discard the seeds; cut the flesh into even-size pieces. Peel and chop the onion; peel and crush the garlic.

Melt the butter in a heavy saucepan and cook the chopped onions for about 5 minutes. Add the garlic and pumpkin, and cook for a further 5 minutes. Add the stock and some salt and pepper; bring to the boil and simmer until the pumpkin is tender—this takes about 15 or 20 minutes. Purée the soup in the blender and then stir in the light cream or milk. Reheat the soup gently. Serve in individual bowls garnished with chopped parsley.

TOMATO SOUP

FRANCE

This is a wonderful light soup with a buttery tomato flavor. I think it's best when you can make it with fresh tomatoes in the late summer, but I use canned tomatoes in the winter and it's still very good. *Serves 4–6.*

1 onion	*Sea salt*
¾ pound (350 g) potatoes	*Freshly ground black pepper*
2 tablespoons butter	*Sugar*
1 pound (450 g) tomatoes or	*Chopped fresh green herbs—*
1 can (16 ounces/480 g)	*basil is best if you can get it;*
4½ cups (1.2 liters) water	*otherwise use chives or parsley*

Peel and chop the onion; peel and cube the potatoes. Melt the butter in a large saucepan and sauté the onion for about 5 minutes, until it's beginning to soften but not brown; then put in the potato and stir over the heat for a minute or two until it is well coated with butter. With fresh tomatoes, wash and quarter them—there's no need to skin them as the soup is first puréed then strained at the end. If you're using canned tomatoes drain them and keep the juice. Add the tomatoes to the vegetables in the saucepan, mix them together and then pour in the water (or reserved tomato juice and water) to make 4½ cups (1.2 liters) in all. Bring to the boil and let the soup simmer for 20–30 minutes, until the vegetables are tender. Purée the soup and then pour it through a sieve into a clean saucepan. Season it with the salt, pepper, and sugar, which helps to bring out the flavor of the tomatoes. Reheat and serve with a sprinkling of finely chopped fresh green herbs.

VICHYSSOISE

USA

I've often thought it surprising that you can make such good chilled soup from what are really winter vegetables—leeks and potatoes! It's rather a pity really that these vegetables start coming into season just when the days are getting crisp and you're thinking more of soups to warm you up than cool you down. But vichyssoise is so creamy and delicious that it always seems to be popular. If the weather gets really cold you can always serve it hot, which I think is every bit as good. *Serves 6.*

1 onion	*1 teaspoon sea salt*
2 tablespoons butter	*2½ cups (625 ml) milk*
½ pound (225 g) potatoes	*Freshly ground black pepper*
1½ pounds (675 g) leeks	*⅔ cup (160 ml) light cream*
2½ cups (625 ml) water	*2 tablespoons chopped chives*

Peel, chop, and sauté the onion in the butter for about 5 minutes in a large saucepan, but don't let it get at all brown. While the onion's cooking, peel the potatoes and cut them into smallish chunks. Cut the bottom half inch and most of the green top off the leeks, slit them down the side, open them out, and rinse them *thoroughly* under the cold tap; then cut them up into small rings. Add the potato and leek to the onion and mix so that everything gets coated in the butter, then let it all cook gently for another 4–5 minutes, but be very careful not to brown the vegetables. Stir in the water and sea salt, and bring to the boil; then put a lid on the saucepan and leave the soup to simmer for 20–30 minutes, until the vegetables are tender. Purée the soup, adding some of the milk if you like to make the process easier; then pour the soup into a bowl or jug that will fit into your refrigerator and add the remaining milk. Taste and season the soup and then chill it.

You can stir the cream into the soup before you serve it, or swirl some over the top of each bowlful and sprinkle with the chopped chives. It looks very pretty—palest green with the darker chives on top. It's a good idea to check the seasoning after you've chilled the soup, adding some more salt and pepper if necessary, as chilling seems to dull the flavor a little.

WATERCRESS SOUP

FRANCE

I think this is one of the best soups because it's got such a lovely flavor and the ingredients are easy to get and don't need much preparation. My own special tip is to cook only the watercress stalks with the potatoes, adding the chopped leaves at the end, just before you serve the soup. This makes the soup look and taste very fresh and inviting. *Serves 6.*

2 bunches watercress	*1¼ cups (310 ml) milk*
1 onion	*Sea salt*
1 pound (450 g) potatoes	*⅔ cup (160 ml) light cream or*
2 tablespoons butter	*whole milk*
2½ cups (625 ml) water	

Wash the watercress carefully, separating the tough stalks from the leaves; chop the stalks roughly and keep the leaves on one side for later. Peel and slice the onion and potatoes. Melt the butter in a large saucepan and add the onion, cooking gently for 5 minutes (but don't brown it). Add the potato and watercress stalks. Stir the vegetables over a gentle heat for a minute or two so that they are all coated with the butter. Pour in the water and milk, bring the mixture to the boil, and let it simmer gently for about 15 minutes, or until the potato is soft. Put the soup in the blender jar, together with the watercress leaves and a little salt, and blend until smooth. Return the soup to the saucepan and stir in the cream or milk and check the seasoning; reheat the soup gently.

Although the cream gives the final touch to the recipe and makes it suitable for extra special occasions, you can make a nice everyday version without it—just increase the quantity of milk to 2 cups (500 ml).

YELLOW SPLIT PEA SOUP

CZECHOSLOVAKIA

This is quite a simple soup but it has a good flavor and is lovely on a cold day. The split pea purée is thickened slightly with a roux of butter and flour, which gives the soup a nice smooth texture and a buttery taste. *Serves 4–6.*

8 ounces (240 g) yellow split peas
2 quarts (2 liters) water
2 tablespoons butter
1 large or 2 medium onions,
   peeled and finely chopped

1 clove garlic, peeled and crushed
4 tablespoons whole-wheat flour
Sea salt
Freshly ground black pepper

Put the spliit peas into a saucepan with the water and let them simmer gently for 40–50 minutes, until they're tender; then purée them. Melt the butter in the rinsed-out saucepan and cook the onion until it's golden, then stir in the garlic and flour. Cook for a minute or two, then gradually pour in the split pea purée, stirring until you have a smooth mixture. Let the soup simmer for 5–10 minutes and then season the mixture with salt and pepper to taste. This makes quite a thick soup; if you want it thinner you can always add more liquid.

You will need to use a large saucepan for boiling the split peas because of the way they bubble up as they cook. Adding a couple of tablespoons of oil to the cooking water helps, or if your saucepan isn't quite big enough you can cook the peas using only 4½ cups (1.2 liters) of water, adding the rest when you purée the soup.

SAUCES AND SALAD DRESSINGS

I FIND THAT THESE SAUCES AND SALAD DRESSINGS are useful in practice and go with the other foods in this book. Some of them, such as the milk-based White Sauce, Cheese Sauce, and the sweet Egg Custard, are an easy and delicious way of including more protein in a meal. Others, particularly the fruit sauces and the English Mint Sauce, are good for adding piquancy and color to a meal and seem to go with many vegetarian dishes just as well as with the meat ones with which they are traditionally served.

APPLESAUCE

GREAT BRITAIN

This sauce is also very popular in Germany, where it's often served with crisp potato fritters—a delightful combination—and in the USA, where it's frequently eaten with pork dishes (chops, ham, etc.). It's also good with bean and lentil dishes. *Serves 4–6.*

½ pound (225 g) cooking apples
1 tablespoon butter
1–2 tablespoons granulated or
 brown sugar
Sea salt

Peel and core the apples, and then cut them up into smallish pieces. Put the apples into a heavy-based saucepan with the butter and about half the sugar. Cover the saucepan and set it over a fairly gentle heat, stirring occasionally, for about 10 minutes, until the apple has softened and collapsed to a soft purée. Beat the mixture a bit with a wooden spoon and taste it. Add a little more sugar and some salt if necessary; those who prefer a more tart taste will want to keep the seasonings to a minimum. I think this sauce is nicest served warm. For variety, you may want to add a few raisins or a sprinkling of cinnamon or nutmeg.

CHEESE SAUCE

This cheese sauce, *sauce Mornay*, is useful both for incorporating into other dishes before baking or broiling them and for serving over vegetables to make them into a more filling meal. Strictly speaking, this sauce should be made with half Gruyère cheese and half Parmesan. The Gruyère makes it creamy and the Parmesan gives it a good flavor, but both are expensive and for day-to-day cooking I use a cheaper substitute (such as domestic Swiss, cheddar, or Gloucester) plus a good seasoning of mustard, cayenne, and freshly ground black pepper. *Makes 1½ cups.*

2 tablespoons butter	1 teaspoon mustard powder
2 tablespoons all-purpose flour	Cayenne pepper
1 bay leaf	Sea salt
1¼ cups (310 ml) milk	Freshly ground black pepper
¼ cup grated cheese	

Melt the butter in a medium-size saucepan and stir in the flour; cook for a few seconds, stirring, until the flour bubbles round the edges. Add the bay leaf, turn up the heat, and pour in about a half cup of the milk. Stir hard until the sauce is very thick and smooth, then repeat the process with the remaining milk so that you finish with a smooth, medium-thick sauce. Take the saucepan off the heat and blend in the grated cheese, mustard, a tiny pinch of cayenne pepper, and salt and pepper to taste. Don't let the sauce get too hot once the cheese has been added or it may stick to the pan or burn.

CRANBERRY SAUCE

Red cranberry sauce with its sweet yet slightly astringent taste is one of the most delicious parts of the traditional American Thanksgiving dinner, and of the British Christmas. It goes surprisingly well with such vegetable dishes as the German potato fritters and the sweet corn pudding from the USA. *Makes 2 cups.*

| 1 package (12 ounces/360 g) | 1½ cups water |
| whole cranberries | 1–1½ cups sugar |

Sort out the cranberries and remove any bruised ones; take off any little stems. Wash the berries and put them into a saucepan with the water. Cover and cook gently, until the berries begin to pop and are tender—7–10 minutes on rather a high heat. Add the sugar and simmer for another few minutes. This makes quite a thick mixture; you can thin it with a little more water (or some red wine) if you like.

CURRY SAUCE

This spicy sauce is useful for serving with Indian rice dishes like *biriani* or with the spicy little Indian pastries, *samosas*. It also provides the basis of a quick curry—you just add some vegetables, simmer them in the sauce until they're tender, and then serve with fluffy boiled rice. *Serves 4–6.*

1 large onion	2 teaspoons ground coriander
2 tablespoons oil, butter, or ghee	1 bay leaf
1–2 cloves garlic	1¼ cups (310 ml) water
1 can (8 ounces/240 g) tomatoes	Sea salt
½ teaspoon ground ginger	Freshly ground black pepper
1 teaspoon ground cumin	

Peel and chop the onion and sauté it in the butter, oil, or *ghee* in a fairly large saucepan for 10 minutes, until it's tender but not browned. Peel and crush the garlic, and add it along with the tomatoes, spices, and bay leaf to the onion, mixing them around so that they all get coated with the fat. Pour in the water and bring to the boil; then turn the heat down, partially cover the saucepan, and leave the mixture to simmer for about 20 minutes. Taste and season with salt and pepper. Take out the bay leaf and purée the sauce if you want it smooth; or serve it as it is if you prefer some texture.

POURING EGG CUSTARD

ENGLAND

This is a sweet sauce, a real egg custard that is delicious with desserts when you don't want to have cream; it's useful too as a way of adding protein to the meal. *Serves 4–6.*

2 eggs	*1¼ cups (310 ml) milk*
1 tablespoon sugar	*Vanilla extract, to taste*

Whisk the eggs in a medium-size bowl. Put the sugar into a saucepan with the milk and scald. Remove from the heat and *very gradually* pour onto the beaten eggs. Transfer this mixture back into the saucepan and stir over a low-to-moderate heat for a minute or two, until the sauce thickens. This will happen very quickly and you need to be ready to take the saucepan off the heat immediately. If, in spite of all your care, it does overheat and curdle, I've found it's usually all right again if I purée it in the blender—the standard remedy for any lumpy sauce! Flavor with a few drops of the vanilla or with grated orange or lemon rind. Serve this sauce hot or cold.

◆———◆———◆

GRAVY

GREAT BRITAIN

I have to admit that this is not quite a traditional British gravy (that's usually made with the fat and juices from meat), but I hope you'll agree that this vegetarian version is also very tasty. You can buy vegetarian stock cubes and powder from health-food shops and these make a good base for the gravy, as does Marmite (available in gourmet shops) or one of the other vegetable yeast extracts. The preliminary browning of the flour is important because this gives the gravy a lovely nutty flavor and dark color. *Serves 6.*

1 onion
2 tablespoons vegetable oil
2 tablespoons all-purpose flour
1 clove garlic
2 cups (500 ml) well-flavored
    vegetable stock

A bouquet garni or a bay leaf and
    ½ teaspoon mixed herbs
Sea salt
Freshly ground black pepper

Peel and finely chop the onion and sauté it in the oil in a saucepan for 5 minutes, then stir in the flour and continue to cook until the flour and onion are well browned. Add the garlic, stock, and herbs. Bring to the boil and let the mixture simmer for 10–15 minutes without a lid on the saucepan. Take out the herbs and season the gravy well with salt and pepper. You can serve the gravy as it is, with the bits of onion in it, or strain or purée it to give a smooth consistency. For a special occasion it's delicious with a tablespoon of sherry stirred in.

◆——◆——◆

MAYONNAISE

FRANCE

If you use a blender to make mayonnaise it really is a quick and easy process. I find that mayonnaise keeps very well in a jar in the refrigerator. *Makes 1¼ cups.*

1 whole egg
¼ teaspoon salt
¼ teaspoon dry mustard
2 or 3 grindings of black pepper
2 teaspoons wine vinegar

2 teaspoons lemon juice
1 cup (250 ml) olive oil or a
    mixture of olive oil and another
    good-quality oil such as corn
    oil or sunflower oil

Break the egg straight into the blender jar and add the salt, mustard, pepper, vinegar, and lemon juice. Blend for a minute at medium speed until everything is well mixed, then turn the speed up to high and gradually add the oil, drop by drop, through the hole in the lid of the jar. When you've added about half the oil, you will hear the sound change to a *glug-glug* noise and then you can add the rest of the oil more quickly, in a thin stream. If the consistency of the mayonnaise seems a bit on the thick side, you can thin it with a little more lemon juice.

MINT SAUCE

ENGLAND

Sharp-tasting yet sweet as well, mint sauce is a lovely accompaniment to many lentil and bean dishes. *Serves 4–6.*

2 tablespoons fresh mint leaves,   1 tablespoon boiling water
    washed and chopped   4 tablespoons cider vinegar
1 tablespoon sugar

If you've got a blender, just put the mint leaves into the blender jar with all the other ingredients and blend until the mint is all finely chopped. Pour into a sauce boat to serve.

If you'd rather make the sauce by hand, put the mint leaves into a bowl, add the sugar, boiling water, and cider vinegar, and mix well.

TOMATO SAUCE

ITALY

With canned tomatoes and a blender, this sauce really couldn't be easier and is one of my standbys. I find it best not to let the tomatoes cook for very long; this way the sauce seems to have a much fresher flavor. *Serves 4–6.*

1 onion   1 can (16 ounces/480 g) tomatoes
2 tablespoons vegetable oil   Sea salt
1 clove garlic   Freshly ground black pepper

Peel and chop the onion and sauté it gently in the oil in a medium-size saucepan, until it's soft but not browned—about 10 minutes. Peel the garlic, crush it in a little salt with the flat side of the blade of a knife, and add it to the onions along with the tomatoes.

Purée the mixture, and then put it back in the saucepan and reheat it. Taste the sauce and season with salt and pepper.

That's the basic recipe, but you can vary it in lots of ways. Try putting a bay leaf with the onions to flavor the onions as they soften, or add a little chopped fresh or dried basil, thyme, or powdered cinnamon to the finished sauce. Or stir a couple of tablespoons of red wine into the mixture before you reheat it. Another addition I sometimes make, and which I'm rather ashamed to admit, is a little Heinz tomato ketchup; used discreetly, it perks up the flavor without being at all obvious!

◆——◆——◆

VINAIGRETTE DRESSING

FRANCE

The secret of a good vinaigrette lies almost entirely in the quality of the ingredients. If you use a really fine olive oil, a good red wine vinegar, sea salt, and freshly ground black pepper—and remember the proportions three or four parts oil to one of vinegar—you really can't fail! *Serves 4–6.*

1 tablespoon wine vinegar	*Sea salt*
3 or 4 tablespoons olive oil	*Freshly ground black pepper*

Mix together the vinegar and 3 tablespoons of oil. Add a good seasoning of salt and pepper—remember the dressing will be weakened by being served with other ingredients so it needs to be well seasoned. Taste the dressing and, if it's too vinegary, add the remaining oil until you get the flavor just right. Pour the dressing into a small jug or bowl and blend it again before you serve it. A small wire whisk is particularly handy to ensure the complete blending of oil and vinegar, which separate so easily. This dressing is also nice with a tablespoon of chopped herbs added, or a little mustard, depending on what you're going to serve it with; a generous dollop of brown mustard (whisked in) will make the consistency creamy and smooth. It's fun to experiment once you've got the basic mixture right.

WHITE SAUCE AND VARIATIONS

FRANCE

Strictly speaking, a proper *sauce Béchamel* is made from milk that has been delicately flavored by being heated in a saucepan with a clove, a piece of onion, a slice of carrot, and a bay leaf; covered and left to infuse; and then strained. I must admit that for normal cookery I generally use ordinary milk plus a bay leaf, and rely on good seasoning for the flavoring, but if you do go to the trouble to infuse the milk first, the sauce will be that much more delicate and delicious.

If you make your roux of equal parts of butter and flour, and then add the milk in batches and let the sauce thicken over a moderate heat before adding more, by the time you've added all the milk the flour will have cooked sufficiently and the sauce will be ready to be seasoned.

Sauce making is easy if you can remember the basic quantities. I find it difficult to hold figures in my head so I remember just one quantity and relate everything to that. Two tablespoons each of butter and all-purpose flour, and 1 cup (250 ml) liquid make a medium-thick sauce—the type you would use to cover cauliflower or stuffed crêpes, commonly called a coating sauce. If you want it thicker or thinner you can decrease or increase the amount of butter and flour: 3 tablespoons each gives a thickish pouring sauce; 1 tablespoon each gives a thin pouring sauce. If you go the route of altering the amount of milk, you alter your final sauce yield in the process. *Makes about 1 cup.*

2 *tablespoons butter or margarine*	1 *bay leaf*
2 *tablespoons all-purpose flour*	*Sea salt*
1 *cup (250 ml) milk—ordinary*	*Freshly ground black pepper*
milk or milk that you have	*Nutmeg*
flavored as above	

Put the butter or margarine into a medium-size saucepan and melt it gently over quite a low heat; then stir in the flour and add the bay leaf. Let the flour cook for a few seconds, then turn up the heat, pour in one-third of the milk and blend carefully until you've got a very thick, smooth sauce; then add another third of the milk. At first the sauce will look lumpy but don't worry: continue stirring over a medium heat and soon the sauce will be beautifully smooth again.

Repeat the process with your final batch of milk. Then when the sauce is smooth turn down the heat and season the sauce to taste with salt, pepper, and a grating of nutmeg. It's now ready to serve, but if you want to make it look extra good and glossy for a special occasion you can beat in an extra tablespoon of butter at the last minute. If you're making the sauce in advance and want to prevent a skin's forming on the surface of the sauce, you can dot this extra butter over the surface, then beat it in when you reheat it. Alternatively a circle of buttered waxpaper pressed down onto the surface of the sauce also stops a skin from forming.

MUSHROOM SAUCE

This is good with vegetables and for serving with pasta and *gnocchi*. To make it, wash and finely slice ¼ pound (115 g) button mushrooms and add them to the basic white sauce. Some people sauté the mushrooms lightly in butter before adding them to the sauce but I prefer this less rich version.

WHITE ONION SAUCE

Another useful variation, good when you want to add more flavor to a meal. Make it by peeling, finely chopping, and sautéeing an onion in the butter before adding the flour. I think this is nice flavored with a pinch of ground cloves.

PARSLEY SAUCE

For this fresh-tasting variation add 1 or 2 tablespoons of finely chopped parsley to the white sauce. Or, take the stalks off a few sprigs of parsley and put the sprigs into a blender jar with the sauce; blend for a few seconds.

◆——————◆——————◆

WINE SAUCE

This sauce always makes a meal taste special. You can either use a cheap wine for the sauce, or buy a little extra of what you plan to drink with the meal and use some of that to make the sauce. *Serves 6.*

1½ cups (375 ml) stock
1½ cups (375 ml) dry red wine
1 bay leaf
A piece of onion, peeled
1 clove garlic, peeled and sliced
A pinch of dried thyme
½ teaspoon black peppercorns

2–3 parsley stalks
1 tablespoon red currant jelly
Sea salt
Freshly ground black pepper
3 tablespoons butter, softened
2 tablespoons all-purpose flour

Put the stock and red wine into a saucepan with the bay leaf, onion, garlic, thyme, peppercorns, and parsley stalks and bring to the boil. Let the mixture boil vigorously for 10–15 minutes so that the amount of liquid reduces by half. Strain the liquid into a clean saucepan and mix in the red currant jelly and salt and pepper to taste. Next make a *beurre manié:* mash half the butter with the flour to make a paste and add this, in small pieces, to the still-warm sauce, mixing well after you've added each piece. Put the sauce back over the heat and stir it gently until it has thickened slightly. Then let the sauce simmer gently for a few minutes to cook the flour. Check the seasoning again and beat the remaining butter into the sauce just before serving, to make it look glossy and appetizing.

If you want to prepare the sauce in advance, after you've added the *beurre manié* and simmered the sauce for a few minutes, take it off the heat and dot the remaining butter over the surface of the sauce to prevent a skin's forming. When you're ready, heat the sauce gently and stir the butter in.

DIPS AND SPREADS

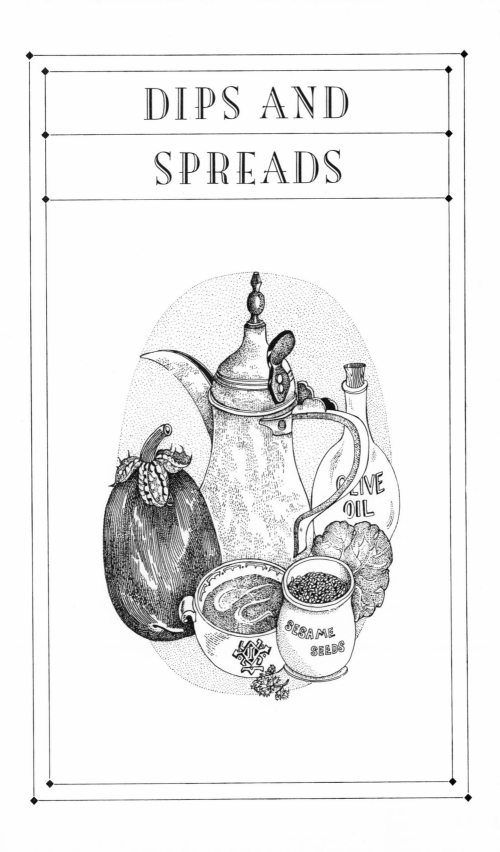

Aïoli with Crudités

Eggplant and Sesame Cream

Avocado Dip

Bean Dip

Cream Cheese and Sour Cream Dip

Feta Cheese and Herb Spread

Hummus

Liptauer Cheese

Mock Caviar

THESE DIPS AND SPREADS ARE REALLY THE VEGE-
tarian alternative to meat pâtés and appetizers. If you serve them with something crisp, like fingers of hot buttered toast, they make a delicious first course; or for a party you can spread them on little crackers and garnish them with pieces of olive, pickle, or parsley.

One of these dips and a bowl of homemade soup and some hot rolls or toast make a welcoming late supper or winter lunch. In the summer they're also nice served very cold from the fridge with a crisp salad.

Some of the dips contain protein, which makes them useful for serving as an appetizer when you want to increase the nutritional value of a meal, or for putting in sandwiches for packed lunches.

As with soups, I think you really need a blender or food processor for making dips; you can get such a deliciously smooth and creamy texture that way.

In my view dips should have a slightly salty, tangy flavor to whet the appetite, so they need careful seasoning, and it's worth using good-quality olive oil and wine vinegar if possible.

The sesame cream, or *tahini*, that's used in two of the recipes can be bought from health-food shops. It's very nourishing, indeed, and an excellent source of calcium. It's quite expensive but keeps for ages.

◆———◆———◆

AÏOLI WITH CRUDITÉS

FRANCE

Crisp raw vegetables dipped in smooth garlic-flavored mayonnaise make a delicious appetizer or can become a full side dish with a lentil or vegetable soup and some whole-wheat bread or rolls.

If you want to serve *aïoli* but hesitate on account of all the calories it contains, you might like to do what I usually do and use half mayonnaise and half plain yogurt; or add some garlic to the dressing recipe for the Russian Cucumber Salad with sour cream and hard-boiled eggs and use that instead of the mayonnaise. It tastes surprisingly like mayonnaise but contains no oil.

The *crudités* can be a gloriously colorful selection of whatever fresh vegetables are available as seasons change: crunchy red radishes served whole with some of the green part still attached; bright orange carrots cut into matchsticks; red or green pepper deseeded and cut into strips;

tiny crimson cubes of beet; sprigs of pearly cauliflower; small, very fresh mushrooms; baby green Brussels sprouts served whole, or bigger ones (as long as they're firm) cut into halves or quarters; scallions, shiny white and just trimmed; pieces of crunchy fennel bulb; juicy cucumber in chunks; crisp leaves of endive or sticks of celery; quarters of firm red tomatoes. *Serves 4–6.*

FOR THE CRUDITÉS:

A selection of about 4 or 5 different types vegetables.

FOR THE AÏOLI:

1 egg
2–4 cloves garlic, peeled and
  crushed
¼ teaspoon sea salt
¼ teaspoon dry mustard

¼ teaspoon pepper
2 teaspoons wine vinegar
2 teaspoons lemon juice
1 cup (250 ml) salad oil

Break the egg into the blender jar and add the garlic, salt, mustard, pepper, vinegar, and lemon juice. Blend at medium speed for about 1 minute. Then turn the speed to high and gradually add the oil, drop by drop, through the top of the lid. When about half the oil has been added and you see the consistency of the mixture change, you can add the oil more quickly in a thin stream. If the mixture is very thick you can thin it by adding a little more lemon juice; if you're doing the yogurt version, add the yogurt now, stirring it gently into the mayonnaise. Spoon the *aïoli* into a bowl and place it on a large plate or small tray with the *crudités* arranged around it. People can then help themselves.

EGGPLANT AND SESAME CREAM

MIDDLE EAST

In this paste, *baba ghannooj*, the intense, subtle flavor of the eggplant goes well with the rich, earthy taste of the sesame cream. The texture is substantial without being at all heavy. I think it's nice with fingers of crisp toast or some warm pita bread. It makes a good light lunch served with lentil soup. *Serves 4–6.*

2 medium eggplant—about
  1 pound (450 g)
2 heaping tablespoons sesame
  cream (tahini)
1 tablespoon lemon juice
1 large clove garlic, peeled and
  crushed

Sea salt
Freshly ground black pepper
Crisp lettuce leaves
Olive oil
Sesame seeds, if available
Fresh parsley and chives

Prick the eggplant and bake them on a baking sheet in a fairly hot oven—400° F (200° C). But you don't have to heat the oven specially; the eggplant will bake with something else and adapt to any temperature from about 325° F (160° C) to 450° F (230° C). They'll take about 20–30 minutes, depending on the temperature, and are done when they can be pierced easily with the point of a sharp knife. Let them cool, then remove the skins and stalks. Chop the flesh as finely as you can and then mix it with all the other ingredients, or put the eggplant into the blender or processor with the sesame cream, lemon juice, and garlic and blend until fairly smooth. You will probably have to do this in several short bursts, stopping the machine and stirring the mixture in between, as it is fairly thick. Season the mixture with salt and pepper to taste and then chill it.

To serve, spoon the mixture into little dishes and smooth the tops, or arrange a bed of lettuce leaves on small plates and spoon the mixture on top. Pour a little olive oil over the paste, sprinkle with some whole sesame seeds, if you have them, and snip some parsley and chives over the top of everything.

◆——◆——◆

AVOCADO DIP

MEXICO

In Mexico this creamy pale-green avocado mixture, *guacamole*, would probably be served as a sauce or as a filling for tortillas, but I think it makes a lovely appetizer either served on a bed of crisp lettuce or with crunchy Melba toast. It's also a good way of making two avocados feed six people. *Serves 6.*

2 large ripe avocados
2 tablespoons lemon juice
1 clove garlic
Sea salt

Tabasco sauce
Freshly ground black pepper
Paprika

Cut the avocados in half, twist the halves in opposite directions to separate them, and remove the seeds. Carefully peel off the skins—they should come away quite easily if the avocados are really ripe. Put the avocado into a bowl, sprinkle it with lemon juice, and mash it with a fork. Peel the garlic and crush it in a little salt with the flat side of the blade of a knife; add the garlic to the avocado together with a drop or two of Tabasco (go carefully as it's hot) and some pepper. Taste and add more salt, pepper, and Tabasco as desired. Decorate with paprika to give a nice touch of scarlet against the pale green.

Guacamole is best made just before you need it; don't keep it waiting more than 1 hour or the avocado will begin to discolor.

BEAN DIP

MIDDLE EAST

You're supposed to use *ful medames*, an Egyptian bean, for this dip, but these are hard to get and I find it tastes good with other types of bean, such as the fava. This is a protein-rich dish, so it makes a good appetizer before a salad or vegetable meal. It is also useful as a sandwich filling or as a spread for little crackers or fingers of buttered pumpernickel toast. *Serves 4.*

1 cup (250 ml) dried fava beans
    or whole lentils
2 tablespoons olive oil
1 tablespoon lemon juice
1 clove garlic, peeled and crushed
1 tablespoon finely chopped
    parsley

Sea salt
Freshly ground black pepper
Sugar
4 pitted ripe olives

Cover the beans generously with boiling water and leave them to soak for 4–5 hours if possible (not so long if you're using lentils);

then drain and rinse them, put them into a good-size saucepan with plenty of cold water, and simmer them over a gentle heat until they're tender: 1¼–1½ hours for beans, 30–45 minutes for lentils. Drain the beans or lentils, reserving the liquid. Pass the beans through a vegetable mill or mash the lentils with a fork; then mix in the olive oil, lemon juice, garlic, parsley, salt and pepper, and, if necessary, enough of the reserved cooking liquid to make a thick creamy paste. Taste the mixture and add a little sugar if you think it needs it.

Spoon the paste into 4 small ramekin dishes, smooth the surface, and decorate each with an olive. Serve chilled.

◆———◆———◆

CREAM CHEESE AND SOUR CREAM DIP

USA

An American friend gave me this recipe, which she serves on Thanksgiving Day as a first course. Like the *aïoli*, it's superb with a colorful selection of crisp fresh vegetables for dipping into the creamy mixture. The recipe as I've given it makes a rich, luxurious-tasting dip; for a less caloric version you could use *ricotta* instead of the cream cheese; and, for an even less caloric dip, you could use plain yogurt in place of the sour cream. *Serves 6.*

FOR THE DIP:

1 package (8 ounces/240 g) cream cheese
2 cups (16 ounces/500 ml) sour cream
1 clove garlic, peeled and crushed
2 tablespoons finely chopped chives
Sea salt
Freshly ground black pepper

FOR THE CRUDITÉS:

A selection of about 5 different vegetables of contrasting colors, like those described for the *aïoli* on page 35.

Put the cream cheese into a bowl and break it up with a fork. Stir in the sour cream, garlic, and chives; mix to a smooth consistency. Season with salt and pepper. Spoon the dip into a serving dish and chill it until required. Arrange the colorful vegetables around the dip, and let everyone help themselves to a spoonful of the creamy mixture and some crisp *crudités*.

FETA CHEESE AND HERB SPREAD

RUMANIA

You can serve this spread in a pâté dish or, if you want to be more Rumanian, heap it up into a cone shape in the center of a serving dish and surround it with tangy ripe olives, whole radishes, crunchy scallions, and quartered tomatoes. It is also excellent served with un-salted crackers. (Remember, *feta* cheese is very salty.) *Serves 4 as an appetizer.*

4 ounces (120 g) feta cheese
8 tablespoons unsalted butter,
  softened
1 tablespoon chopped chives
1 tablespoon chopped green
  fennel, if available

1 tablespoon chopped fresh
  parsley
Pinch each of paprika and
  caraway seeds

Crumble the cheese finely. Put the butter into a bowl and cream it with a wooden spoon, then gradually beat in the crumbled cheese, herbs, and spices. Chill the spread before serving.

HUMMUS

MIDDLE EAST

If I, as a vegetarian, told you that one of my favorite dishes consisted of a purée of chick peas and sesame cream you might well be forgiven for thinking it was some strange vegetarian concoction, certainly too adventurous to be tried. Yet the dish I've described is of course *hummus*, one of the best known and most popular dips in the Middle

East. It's interesting too, because it contains two complementary proteins and is thus nutritious as well as delectable. The sesame cream, *tahini*, can be bought from health-food shops. It tastes like rather earthy, slightly bitter peanut butter, but once you come to appreciate the flavor you may become "addicted" to it. *Serves 4 as a main course, 8 as an appetizer.*

8 ounces (240 g) chick peas	*Sea salt*
½ cup (125 ml) olive oil	*Paprika*
3 cloves garlic, peeled and crushed	*Lemon wedges*
¼ cup (60 ml) lemon juice	
4 tablespoons sesame cream	
(tahini)	

Soak the chick peas in plenty of cold water for several hours, then drain and rinse them. Put them into a saucepan, cover them with fresh cold water, and let simmer for 1–1½ hours, until they're tender; then drain them, reserving the cooking water. You can pass the chick peas through a vegetable mill, then mix in half the olive oil and all the other ingredients, but I find the easiest way to make *hummus* is to use the blender or food processor. Put the chick peas into the jar or container with half the olive oil, the garlic, lemon juice, sesame cream, and some salt, and blend to a smooth, fairly thick purée. You may need to add some of the cooking liquid to bring the mixture to a nice creamy consistency. Chill the *hummus* and then serve it on a flat dish (individual or large, depending on how it's fitting into your meal plan), with the rest of the olive oil spooned over the top and a good sprinkling of paprika. Garnish with lemon wedges. *Hummus* is particularly good served with plenty of soft bread—pita bread if you can buy or make it (see page 281); this is the usual accompaniment in the Middle East.

LIPTAUER CHEESE

HUNGARY

This mixture of cheese, soft butter, and flavorings is popular in Austria, Hungary, Yugoslavia, and Holland. It makes a good appetizer when served with hot toast. You don't need extra butter, and it spreads easily, which makes it convenient for sandwiches or on little crackers. *Serves 4–6.*

4 tablespoons butter, softened
1 cup (8 ounces/240 g) ricotta or
  cottage cheese
1 teaspoon paprika

1 teaspoon chopped capers
1 tablespoon chopped chives
½ teaspoon Dijon-style mustard
Salt and pepper

Beat the butter until it's soft and light; then gradually mix in the ricotta or cottage cheese until well blended. Add the paprika, capers, chives, and mustard, then season to taste with salt and a grinding or two of black pepper. Put the mixture into a small bowl or pottery crock and serve it chilled.

MOCK CAVIAR

RUSSIA

This popular Russian dip is made from eggplant. It has a luscious, slightly smoky taste and a lovely creamy consistency, which goes beautifully with rye bread or whole-wheat toast. It makes a perfect appetizer when you're entertaining adventurous friends! *Serves 4–6.*

1 large eggplant—about 1 pound
  (450 g)
1 large clove garlic, peeled and
  crushed

3 tablespoons olive oil
1 tablespoon lemon juice
Sea salt
Freshly ground black pepper

Before you make this dip you need to char the eggplant in order to give the dip its slightly smoky flavor. The easiest way to do this is to put the eggplant under the broiler, turning it from time to time so that it gets evenly burnt. Then carefully scrape off the skin (you don't need this!) and mash, chop, or purée the eggplant. Put this purée into a bowl and stir in the garlic, oil, lemon juice, and a seasoning of salt and pepper. Mix everything well and then spoon the mixture into a small dish—or individual dishes—and chill until required.

SALADS

Avocado and Carrot Salad

Beet and Horseradish Salad

Bulgur Wheat, Tomato, and Parsley Salad

Lima Bean Salad

Cabbage Salad with Mint and Pomegranate

Cauliflower and Apple Salad

Celeriac Salad

Chick Pea and Vegetable Salad

Coleslaw

Cucumber Salad with Sour Cream and Hard-Boiled Eggs

Stuffed Cucumber Salad

Cucumber and Yogurt Salad

Fennel and Cucumber Salad

Green Salad

Spanish Green Salad

White Bean Salad

Lentil Salad

Mushroom Salad

Mushrooms à la Grecque

Mediterranean Salad

Orange and Radish Salad

Potato Salad

Hot Potato Salad with Peanut Dressing

Kidney Bean Salad

Red Cabbage Salad

Rice and Artichoke-Heart Salad

Spinach Salad

Cooked Spinach Salad

Three-Bean Salad

Tomato Salad

Tomato, Cheese, and Olive Salad

Stuffed Tomato Salad

Vegetable and Bean Salad

Waldorf Salad

THE SALADS IN THIS SECTION CAN BE DIVIDED INTO two types: those that contain protein and those that don't (and I've mentioned this in the individual recipes). Most of the protein salads can be made into complete meals, perhaps with some bread and another lighter salad, like a green or tomato salad, to accompany them. The lima bean salad from the Middle East; the white bean salad, chick pea and vegetable mayonnaise, and *salade Niçoise* from France; and the vegetable and bean salad from Poland are all examples of this type of substantial salad. These protein salads are also useful for serving as a first course if the main dish is rather low in protein, as a vegetable casserole might be; or they can be served with the main dish as a side salad. The tomato, cheese, and olive salad and the green salad with Gruyère cheese are particularly good on the side.

The non-protein salads make excellent side salads, too, and these I serve alongside main dishes that contain plenty of protein, such as cheese flans or stuffed crêpes. They are often quicker to prepare than a cooked vegetable, and very refreshing. Some of these salads also make good first courses; I particularly like the stuffed tomato salad from Switzerland, which is good before a fondue, and the spicy mushrooms *à la Grecque* from France, which are good before a soufflé.

AVOCADO AND CARROT SALAD

MIDDLE EAST

This mixture of pale green, buttery avocado, crisp orange carrots, and sweet raisins is very pleasant. If you serve the salad with some bread and butter and soft cheese or hard-boiled egg wedges, it makes a good lunch or supper. *Serves 2 as a main course, 4 as a first course.*

1 large ripe avocado	*Juice of 1 orange*
A little fresh lemon juice	*⅓ cup (80 ml) seedless raisins*
½ pound (225 g) coarsely grated	*Parsley sprigs*
carrot	

Cut the avocado in half and remove the seed. Carefully peel off the outer skin of each half, using a sharp knife—it should come away quite easily if the avocado pear is really ripe. Cut the avocado into long, thin slices and sprinkle them with lemon juice, making sure that the cut surfaces are completely coated.

Mix together the grated carrot, orange juice, and raisins. Arrange the avocado slices on individual plates, top with the grated carrot mixture, and garnish with the parsley.

BEET AND HORSERADISH SALAD

AUSTRIA

A curiously pleasant mixture of flavors and textures, this salad makes a good accompaniment to cold savory dishes. *Serves 4.*

1½ pounds (700 g) cooked beets	*1 tablespoon sugar*
1 apple	*2 tablespoons wine vinegar*
1 teaspoon caraway seeds	*1–2 tablespoons horseradish sauce*

Peel and dice the beets and the apple. Put them into a bowl with the caraway seeds, sugar, vinegar, and horseradish sauce, and mix them all together, lightly. Chill before serving.

BULGUR WHEAT, TOMATO, AND PARSLEY SALAD

MIDDLE EAST

In this Middle Eastern salad, *tabbouleh*, parsley is used rather like a vegetable to provide the basis of the dish, and it's surprising what a big bunch you'll need to make a quarter pound. If you haven't got enough, you can use a bunch of watercress or tender young spinach leaves instead. The bulgur wheat is quite easy to get in health-food shops. *Serves 4.*

1½ cups (225 g) bulgur wheat	Juice of 1 lemon
¼ pound (125 g) parsley	1 clove garlic, peeled and crushed
A few sprigs mint leaves	in a little salt
1 onion	Sea salt
3 tomatoes	Freshly ground black pepper
2 tablespoons olive oil	

Cover the wheat with boiling water and leave it to soak for 15 minutes; then drain it thoroughly and put it into a bowl. Meanwhile, wash the parsley and mint, and chop them up fairly finely. Peel and chop the onion and tomatoes, then add them to the wheat, together with the oil, lemon juice, and garlic. Mix everything together and season with salt and pepper to taste.

Spoon the mixture onto a flat serving dish and press it down with the back of a spoon. Serve it chilled. You can sprinkle a little extra olive oil over the top if you like, to make it look shiny. Or simply serve it in a salad bowl or heaped up on crisp lettuce leaves.

LIMA BEAN SALAD

MIDDLE EAST

Serve this substantial, protein-rich dish with a fresh vegetable salad, such as the Middle Eastern cabbage salad (below) or a platter of lettuce and juicy sliced tomatoes, along with whole-wheat bread rolls or pita bread. *Serves 4.*

1 cup (250 ml) dried lima beans	1 tablespoon lemon juice
6 scallions	3 tablespoons olive oil
2 tablespoons chopped fresh	Sea salt
parsley	Freshly ground black pepper

Cover the lima beans with water and leave them to soak for several hours if possible (or according to package instructions). Then drain and rinse the beans and simmer them gently in plenty of water until they're tender; drain them thoroughly (the liquid makes good stock). Put the beans into a bowl.

Wash and trim the scallions, retaining as much of the green part as seems reasonable, then chop them up and add them to the lima beans, along with the parsley, lemon juice, oil, and a seasoning of salt and pepper. Stir the mixture gently, being careful not to break up the beans; then leave it to cool. I think this salad is nicest served really cold.

If you prefer to use frozen lima beans, you'll need two 10-ounce (300 g) packages, prepared according to package instructions.

◆——◆——◆

CABBAGE SALAD WITH MINT AND POMEGRANATE

MIDDLE EAST

Those large green cabbages make a good basis for winter salads when lettuce is scarce and expensive, but I think they need additional ingredients to make them really interesting. Here in this Middle Eastern salad the cabbage is flavored with mint and topped with a flush of red pomegranate seeds. When you can't get fresh mint I find you can do very well by omitting some of the lemon juice from the recipe and replacing it with the same amount of bottled mint sauce, which makes a nice dressing for other salads, too. *Serves 4–6.*

1 pound (450 g) green cabbage (about a quarter of a medium-size cabbage)
1 clove garlic
Sea salt
2 tablespoons lemon juice
3 tablespoons oil

Freshly ground black pepper
2 tablespoons chopped fresh mint, if available
1 pomegranate
A few sprigs of fresh mint, if available

Shred the cabbage finely with a sharp knife or in a food processor and then rinse and drain well. Peel the garlic and crush it in a little salt with the blade of a knife; put it into a large bowl and gradually add the lemon juice, oil, and a grinding of black pepper, stirring until it's all well blended. Put the cabbage into the bowl together with the mint and mix everything gently in order to coat the cabbage with the dressing and distribute the mint throughout.

To prepare the pomegranate, cut it in half and carefully ease out the juicy red seeds using the point of a sharp knife or a pointed skewer or cocktail stick, catching the juice on a plate as you work. Arrange the cabbage salad on a shallow dish with the pomegranate seeds and juice poured over the top. Garnish with a few sprigs of fresh mint.

If you prepare the cabbage an hour or more before you need it, you will find that it will soften considerably in the dressing; do not, however, add the pomegranate until just before serving.

CAULIFLOWER AND APPLE SALAD

USA

This is useful for serving as a side salad with cooked dishes, particularly those containing cheese, and it's quick and easy to make. *Serves 4.*

1 small cauliflower	*Juice of 1 orange*
2 large sweet apples	*Sea salt (optional)*

Wash the cauliflower, break it into florets, and slice fairly finely. Wash and dice the apples (unpeeled), discarding the cores. Mix the cauliflower and apple together in a large bowl; pour in the orange juice and toss the salad so that everything is coated with the juice. Season with a very little salt if you like.

You may want to add a tablespoonful or so of oil to the dressing, but I think orange juice makes a very refreshing dressing on its own.

CELERIAC SALAD

FRANCE

Celeriac, that knobbly root with the delicious celery flavor, makes a good salad. The skin is brown and the flesh white, and you may have to ask your grocer to stock it, as it is not always easy to find in the U.S. Persevere, however, you'll find your efforts worthwhile. In some ways I prefer celeriac to celery itself, although the texture is not as crisp. It's very nice prepared the French way in a mustardy vinaigrette (the famous *remoulade*), and makes a pleasant side salad to accompany either a hot or cold protein dish. *Serves 4.*

1 smallish celeriac—about	1 tablespoon wine vinegar
1 pound (450 g)	3 tablespoons olive oil
½ teaspoon dry mustard	1 bunch watercress, washed and
½ teaspoon sugar	trimmed
¼ teaspoon sea salt	Paprika
Freshly ground black pepper	

Peel the celeriac and cut it into quarters. Keep the pieces under cold water while you make the dressing, as celeriac quickly discolors. Put the mustard, sugar and salt into a shallow dish with a good grinding of black pepper and the vinegar. Mix to a paste and then gradually stir in the oil. Grate the celeriac by hand or in a food processor, and put it straight into the dish, turning it over in the dressing as you do so to coat it well and prevent discoloration. I think it's best to use a fairly coarse grater, as it gives the salad a nice texture. Taste the mixture and add a little more seasoning if you think it needs it. If possible let the salad rest for 30 minutes or so to give the celeriac a chance to soak up the flavor of the dressing; then pile it into a serving dish, arrange the watercress around the edge, and sprinkle the top with a little paprika.

CHICK PEA AND VEGETABLE SALAD

FRANCE

This combination of chick peas, tender young vegetables, and smooth garlic-flavored mayonnaise, called *aigroissade*, is delicious. It makes a beautiful protein-rich appetizer or main salad dish served with crisp lettuce or watercress. You can use plain mayonnaise for the dressing, but I prefer this lighter version. *Serves 4 as a main course, 6–8 as an appetizer.*

1 cup (250 ml) dried chick peas	1–2 large cloves garlic
1½ pounds (675 g) tender new	⅔ cup (160 ml) mayonnaise
vegetables—potatoes, carrots,	⅔ cup (160 ml) plain yogurt
green beans, shelled lima beans	Sea salt
—cooked, drained, and cooled	Freshly ground black pepper
1 can (14 ounces/420 g) artichoke	A little chopped fresh parsley
hearts, drained	

Cover the chick peas with cold water and leave them to soak for several hours; then drain and rinse them, put them into a saucepan with a good covering of water, and simmer for 1–1½ hours, until they're tender. Drain the chick peas thoroughly (the cooking water makes good stock for soups and sauces).

Cut the cooked vegetables and the artichoke hearts into chunky pieces and put them into a bowl with the chick peas. In another bowl mix together the garlic, mayonnaise, and yogurt. Add this to the vegetables in the bowl, turning them over gently until coated with the creamy mixture. Season carefully with salt and pepper. Cool, then chill the salad. Serve it heaped up in a serving dish, or spoon the salad onto crisp lettuce leaves arranged on individual plates. Sprinkle the top with chopped parsley to give a pleasant color contrast. It's nice with warm soft rolls, French bread, or pita bread.

◆———◆———◆

COLESLAW

USA

"Cole" is the general term for all members of the cabbage family and coleslaw is a delicious cabbage salad mixture. It's best made with firm 'salad' cabbage in the winter and in the summer a compact, hearty cabbage such as Primo. Coleslaw is a marvelous crunchy side salad, especially when it accompanies a hot main course. *Serves 4.*

¾ pound (350 g) green cabbage	*3–4 tablespoons mayonnaise*
2 medium-size carrots	*Sea salt*
1 small onion	*Freshly ground black pepper*

Wash and very finely shred the cabbage; scrape or peel and coarsely grate the carrots; skin and finely slice the onion. Put all the prepared vegetables into a bowl and stir in the mayonnaise so that you have a nice creamy mixture. Season the salad with a little salt and pepper, to taste.

This is the basic coleslaw, but you can vary it by adding other ingredients such as chopped red or green peppers, raisins, chopped dates, roasted peanuts, sunflower seeds, bean sprouts, sliced apple or other fruits, and green herbs. You can also use half mayonnaise and half plain yogurt for a less rich, lower-calorie version.

CUCUMBER SALAD WITH SOUR CREAM AND HARD-BOILED EGGS

R U S S I A

This refreshing salad makes a good protein-rich appetizer when served with thinly sliced brown bread and butter. Or it can be served on lettuce as a side salad. Traditionally, the dressing is made with sour cream, but yogurt can also be used as a low-calorie substitute. *Serves 4.*

1 large cucumber
Sea salt
Whites of 4 hard-boiled eggs
1 tablespoon chopped fresh dill
    weed, or ½ teaspoon dried dill

and 2 teaspoons chopped
    parsley
4 crisp, nicely shaped lettuce
    leaves

FOR THE DRESSING:

Yolks of 4 hard-boiled eggs
2 teaspoons wine vinegar
1 teaspoon sugar
1 teaspoon dry mustard

Sea salt
Freshly ground black pepper
⅔ cup (160 ml) sour cream or
    plain yogurt

Wash the cucumber and remove the peel if you want to; then slice the cucumber into thin rounds, put them into a colander, sprinkle with salt, and weight them down. Leave them for 30 minutes to draw out the excess water. Meanwhile chop the egg whites and leave them to one side. To make the dressing, put the egg yolks into a medium-size bowl with the vinegar, sugar, mustard, salt, and pepper and mash them all together. Add the sour cream or yogurt, a little at a time, and mix well to smooth, creamy consistency. Season to taste. Rinse and drain the cucumber rings and mix them with the egg white and dill. Chill and serve.

STUFFED CUCUMBER SALAD

ITALY

This is an unusual dish with a fresh, tangy flavor. It makes a good protein-rich appetizer or can be the basis of a simple lunch. If you don't like onions, use chopped chives or scallion greens instead. *Serves 2 as a main course, 4 as an appetizer.*

1 large cucumber	*1 tablespoon olive oil*
⅔ cup (160 ml) water	*½ teaspoon dry mustard*
2 tablespoons wine vinegar	*1 small onion, peeled and minced*
Sea salt	*Sprigs of watercress*
Freshly ground black pepper	*A few radishes*
2 hard-boiled eggs	

Trim the cucumber and then cut it into 4 equal chunks. Peel the chunks, halve them lengthwise. Scoop out the seeds and discard them, leaving a cavity for the stuffing. Put the pieces of cucumber into a saucepan with the water, wine vinegar, and a little salt and pepper. Simmer gently for about 5–7 minutes, or until tender. Drain and cool the cucumber.

To make the filling, peel the eggs and mash them with a fork; then mix in the olive oil, mustard, onion, and salt and pepper to taste. Arrange the cucumber in a serving dish and spoon the filling neatly into the cavities. Decorate the dish with the watercress and radishes.

CUCUMBER AND YOGURT SALAD

MIDDLE EAST

The combination of cucumber, yogurt, and herbs is very refreshing, making this a good salad to serve on a hot day, either accompanying a main dish or as an appetizer. *Serves 4–6.*

1 cucumber	*2 teaspoons chopped fresh dill or*
Sea salt	*fennel if available*
1 tablespoon chopped fresh	*1 cup (250 ml) plain yogurt*
parsley	*Freshly ground black pepper*
1 tablespoon chopped fresh chives	

Wash the cucumber and slice it finely or grate it fairly coarsely. Put the pieces into a colander, sprinkle them with salt, weight them down, and leave for about 30 minutes to draw out the excess moisture. Then rinse and squeeze the cucumber to extract as much liquid as possible. In a large bowl, combine the cucumber with all the other ingredients and season to taste.

This salad is nicest served really cold so chill it for an hour or so if you can. You can serve each portion of the salad spooned over a crisp wedge of lettuce heart, or serve in small bowls, with fresh, warm whole-wheat rolls.

◆———◆———◆

FENNEL AND CUCUMBER SALAD

ITALY

Raw fennel, with its crisp texture and slightly aniseed flavor, combines well with cool, juicy cucumber and makes a refreshing first course or side salad. *Serves 4–6.*

1 cucumber	*2 fennel bulbs*
Sea salt	

FOR THE DRESSING:

1 tablespoon lemon juice	*1 tablespoon chopped fresh mint*
1 tablespoon olive oil	*1 teaspoon sugar*

Wash and dice the cucumber and put it into a colander, sprinkling each layer with a little salt. Put a saucer on top and weight it down for about 30 minutes; then rinse and pat dry. Meanwhile wash the fennel and trim off the root ends and tough stalks but keep any tender stems and little bits of feathery leaf. Cut the fennel into neat slices and put them into a bowl.

For the dressing put the lemon juice, oil, mint, and sugar into a bowl and beat them together until blended. Add the cucumber and the dressing to the fennel and mix everything together gently and thoroughly.

To serve, arrange lettuce leaves in the base of one large salad bowl, or put a single leaf on each individual serving dish, and spoon the salad on top.

GREEN SALAD

FRANCE

A well-made green salad goes with so many dishes; it's quick and easy to make and ideal for entertaining. You can serve it as a first course, with the main dish, or, as is often done in France, at the end of the meal, as a palate-cleansing course on its own (and before the cheese course, if you're having one). *Serves 4.*

1 large head of lettuce   *1 bunch watercress*

FOR THE DRESSING:

1 clove garlic   *Freshly ground black pepper*
1 tablespoon wine vinegar—   *Fresh green herbs—parsley*
* red or white*   * and chives, and others such as*
3 tablespoons olive oil   * tarragon, chervil, and fennel, if*
Sea salt   * available*

Wash and dry the lettuce (preferably romaine or boston, *not* iceberg, which has very little nutritive value) and watercress, discarding tough stalks and damaged leaves. Keep the salad in a plastic bag in the refrigerator until you're almost ready to serve it. While the lettuce is crisping, make the dressing; you can make it in a screw-top jar but I think it's easier to put the ingredients directly into the salad bowl and mix them in that. Peel the garlic, cut it in half, and rub the salad bowl thoroughly with the cut surfaces, if you like a delicate garlic flavor. For a stronger taste, crush the garlic in a little salt with the blade of a knife, dice it finely and put it into the salad bowl. Add the vinegar, oil, some salt and pepper, and mix well. Scatter the herbs on top of the dressing and leave in a cool place until just before the meal; then add the lettuce and watercress, gently tearing them into manageable pieces. Toss the salad in the dressing at the last moment so that it won't go soggy (I usually do this at the table).

A green salad is easy to make but its success depends on the quality of the ingredients: really crisp lettuce and watercress, the best wine vinegar and olive oil, sea salt and freshly ground black pepper. Make sure that you dry the salad carefully or the water clinging to the leaves will dilute the dressing and spoil it.

For a delicious and simple variation, toss ¼ pound (125 g) diced or grated Gruyère (or any other hard, tangy cheese, such as Parmesan or aged Cheddar) into your salad just before serving.

SPANISH GREEN SALAD

SPAIN

This salad makes a tasty accompaniment to such dishes as the vegetable *paella* and the Portuguese kidney-bean stew. *Serves 4.*

1 large head of lettuce	*Freshly ground black pepper*
1 bunch watercress	*1 large tomato*
1 tablespoon lemon juice	*1 large onion, preferably Spanish*
1 tablespoon olive oil	*A few Spanish olives*
Sea salt	

Wash and dry the lettuce (once again, romaine or boston are preferable to iceberg) and watercress, discarding any damaged leaves and tough stems. Gently tear the lettuce leaves into even-size pieces and put them into a bowl with the watercress.

Make the dressing by mixing together the lemon juice, olive oil, and a seasoning of salt and pepper. Add this to the lettuce and watercress in the bowl and toss the salad gently, so that all the leaves are coated in the dressing and glossy-looking; arrange the salad in a mound on a large plate. Slice the tomato into thin rounds; peel and thinly slice the onion; arrange these on top of the green salad, along with a few olives. Serve at once.

WHITE BEAN SALAD

F R A N C E

Served with one or two other salad dishes, such as a green salad or a tomato salad, and some nice soft whole-wheat rolls, this makes a delicious light meal. It's also good as a first course. The important thing is to cook the beans only until they're tender but before they start to break up; they get firmer as they cool and if they're at all underdone it makes for a very chewy salad. I think the mustard and sugar in the dressing go well with the beans but the chopped fresh herbs really make all the difference and enable you to vary the flavor. If you can't get any fresh green herbs, one or two chopped scallions (including as much of the green part as possible) are also good. Serves 4.

8 ounces (240 g) dried white, or
   navy beans
1 teaspoon sugar
1 teaspoon dry mustard
1 tablespoon wine vinegar
4 tablespoons olive oil

Sea salt
Freshly ground black pepper
3 tablespoons chopped fresh green
   herbs—parsley, chives, mint,
   chervil, tarragon, or fennel

Soak the beans in plenty of cold water for 2–3 hours. Drain and rinse them, put them into a saucepan with plenty of cold water, and let them simmer gently for 1–1¼ hours, or until they're very tender but not soggy. Drain. Put the sugar, mustard, vinegar, and oil into a salad bowl and mix together; season with salt and pepper, then stir in most of the herbs and the hot beans. Toss the beans gently in the dressing until they're well coated. Cool to room temperature and then chill. Serve sprinkled with the remaining herbs.

LENTIL SALAD

F R A N C E

You should try to buy whole lentils for this salad because they hold their shape when they're cooked. Combined with a good fruity olive oil, lemon juice, and some crisp onion rings they make a delicious salad, which if served with whole-wheat rolls, French bread, or pita bread, and a green salad, makes a complete meal. *Serves 4.*

8 ounces (240 g) dried lentils
1 tablespoon lemon juice
3 tablespoons olive oil

Sea salt
Freshly ground black pepper
1 onion

Soak the lentils in water for a couple of hours or so if possible, then drain and rinse them, put them into a saucepan with fresh water, and simmer them gently until tender—about 45 minutes. Drain the lentils thoroughly (keep the cooking liquid, it makes good stock) and put them into a bowl with the lemon juice, olive oil, and some salt and pepper. Peel the onion and cut it into thin rounds; then add these to the lentils and mix everything gently together. Cool, then chill the salad. It looks nice in a white bowl, which contrasts with the rich brown lentils.

MUSHROOM SALAD

FINLAND

This salad differs from mushrooms *à la Grecque* (see following recipe) in that the mushrooms are not cooked, so you need to use very fresh button mushrooms. *Note:* If it's important to you that the mushrooms be pure white, you'll probably wind up with mushrooms to which a preservative has been added. Otherwise, I would suggest the more mottled beige, but firm, mushrooms, free of chemicals. *Serves 4 as a first course.*

½ pound (225 g) fresh button
   mushrooms
1 tablespoon lemon juice
Sea salt
Freshly ground black pepper

2 tablespoons lightly whipped
   heavy cream, or sour cream, or
   plain yogurt
Lettuce leaves
Fresh chives

Wash the mushrooms, pat them dry, and slice thinly. Put the slices into a bowl and sprinkle them with the lemon juice and a light sprinkling of salt and pepper. Add the heavy cream, sour cream, or yogurt and stir gently. Chill, then check the seasoning. To serve the salad, spoon it onto lettuce leaves on individual plates and sprinkle with chopped chives.

The mushrooms will give off some liquid after you've sprinkled them with the lemon juice and salt, and this will blend with the cream to make a thin dressing. If you would prefer a thicker dressing, sprinkle the lemon juice and salt on the mushrooms an hour or so before the meal, then drain off the juice that will have accumulated and fold the mushrooms into the cream just before serving them, checking the seasoning. (The mushroom liquid makes good stock.)

MUSHROOMS À LA GRECQUE

FRANCE

These coriander-flavored mushrooms make an excellent appetizer before a non-spicy main meal. *Serves 4.*

1 pound (450 g) small, fresh	*2 tablespoons lemon juice*
mushrooms	*Freshly ground black pepper*
4 tablespoons olive oil	*Sea salt*
2 teaspoons ground coriander	*Lettuce leaves*
1 bay leaf	*Fresh parsley*
2 cloves garlic, peeled and crushed	

Wash the mushrooms and sauté them in the olive oil with the coriander, bay leaf, and garlic for about 2 minutes, stirring all the time. Turn the mushrooms straight into a large bowl to prevent further cooking; then add the lemon juice and a grinding of black pepper. Cool the mixture to room temperature and then chill it. Check the seasoning before serving. Mound the mushrooms on lettuce leaves on individual plates and sprinkle with chopped parsley. They're also nice served in a bowl as part of a selection of different salads for a buffet lunch or supper.

MEDITERRANEAN SALAD

FRANCE

This is my vegetarian version of a *salade Niçoise*, as it contains neither tuna fish nor anchovies. Mine is a mixture of the other usual ingredients—tomatoes, cooked green beans, black olives, and hard-boiled eggs—all bound together in a good vinaigrette. Purists serve the traditional *salade Niçoise* with all the ingredients in separate little clumps on a bed of lettuce, but I like it best served in a glossy, colorful heap. It makes an excellent main dish for lunch or supper, served with a good country bread. *Serves 4.*

1 *large head of romaine*
1 *pound (450 g) tomatoes*
6 *hard-boiled eggs*
1 *pound (450 g) cooked green beans*

12 *pitted ripe olives*
2 *tablespoons chopped fresh parsley*

FOR THE DRESSING:

1 *large clove garlic, peeled and crushed*
2 *tablespoons wine vinegar*

6 *tablespoons olive oil*
Sea salt
Freshly ground black pepper

Wash and dry the romaine. Spread the leaves out on a flat serving dish. Slice the tomatoes, quarter the hard-boiled eggs, and cut the green beans (steamed so that they're still slightly crunchy) into even-size lengths. Put them all into a bowl together with the olives and parsley.

To make the dressing, put the garlic into a bowl and gradually mix in the wine vinegar; then add the oil and some salt and pepper, and beat it all together until it's smooth. Pour the dressing over the green bean and tomato mixture and toss it gently so that all the ingredients are coated with the dressing without being broken up. Heap the salad on top of the lettuce leaves and serve at once.

ORANGE AND RADISH SALAD

NORTH AFRICA

Bright red radishes and golden sections of orange make a colorful salad especially good in early summer when lettuce is still scarce but the first radishes have appeared and there are plenty of juicy oranges in the shops. *Serves 4.*

2 bunches radishes	*Sea salt*
6 large oranges	*1 bunch watercress*

Wash the radishes and cut them into thin slices. Using a sharp knife, cut and pull the skin and pith from the oranges. Separate the sections and remove the membranes. Mix the oranges with the radishes and season to taste with a very little salt. Chill, then serve the salad with a border of watercress.

POTATO SALAD

USA

For this salad you need firm potatoes that won't break up and go mushy when you mix them with the mayonnaise. In the summer new potatoes are ideal, but in the winter I use King Edwards or Desirée. As with the chick pea and vegetable salad (see p. 50) and the Waldorf salad (p. 71), I prefer to use a mixture of mayonnaise and yogurt, which is lighter and less fattening, but of course you could use just mayonnaise. You could also use the dressing given for the Russian cucumber salad on p. 52, or a vinaigrette as the French and German versions of this salad prescribe. *Serves 4.*

1½ pounds (675 g) potatoes	*2 tablespoons fresh green herbs—*
Sea salt	*parsley, chives, tarragon, fennel*
2 rounded tablespoons mayonnaise	*—whatever is available*
2 rounded tablespoons plain	
* yogurt*	

Scrub the potatoes and cook them in their skins in boiling water until they're tender. You may salt the water if you wish, but this does draw out some of the nutrients as the vegetables cook. Let them cool enough to handle, and then slip the skins off using a small pointed knife. (Cooking the potatoes in their skins like this really does make a surprising difference to the flavor.) Cut the potatoes into chunky pieces and put them into a bowl with the mayonnaise, yogurt, and herbs. Toss the mixture gently with a spoon until all the potatoes are coated with the dressing, but be careful not to break them up. Check the seasoning, adding pepper and salt if necessary.

Cool to room temperature and then chill the mixture and serve it heaped up on a dish: this salad looks particularly good in a shallow glass bowl or on a bed of crisp lettuce on a flat plate.

◆———◆———◆

HOT POTATO SALAD WITH PEANUT DRESSING

SOUTH AMERICA

This is one of those dishes which sounds very strange but tastes really good. It's a mixture of hot and cold, bland and spicy, and it is rich in protein too. You can use ordinary salted peanuts but if you can get the plain roasted kind from a health-food shop they're better. *Serves 4.*

½ pound (225 g) roasted unsalted
   peanuts
⅔ cup (160 ml) milk
½ cup (125 ml) finely grated
   cheese
½–1 teaspoon chili powder, or a
   small green chili

1½ pounds (675 g) potatoes
1 head of lettuce
1 bunch of watercress
4 tomatoes
1 onion

First put the peanuts and milk into your blender jar and blend until thick and fairly smooth (add a little more milk if necessary to give the consistency of whipped cream). Turn the mixture into a bowl and stir in the grated cheese. Add chili powder to taste; or, if you're using a fresh chili, remove and discard the seeds and chop the flesh very finely.

Add it to the mixture a little at a time, tasting to get the right degree of hotness.

Cut the potatoes into even-size pieces and then boil them until they're just tender; drain. Wash the lettuce, watercress, and tomatoes; peel the onion. Slice the onion and tomatoes into thin rounds.

To serve, spoon the hot potatoes into the center of a serving dish (or individual plates) and arrange the lettuce, watercress, tomatoes and onion around the edge. Spoon the peanut sauce over the potatoes and serve at once.

◆——◆——◆

KIDNEY BEAN SALAD

U S A

This salad looks particularly appetizing, with its shiny red beans and slivers of white onion. You can make it spicier if you want to by adding some chili powder and cumin to the dressing. It makes a lovely lunch with homemade whole-wheat bread and soup or green salad. *Serves 4.*

8 ounces (240 g) dried red kidney
    beans, soaked, cooked, and
    drained; or use 1 can (16
    ounces/480 g) and 1 can (8
    ounces/240 g) red kidney
    beans, drained

1 small onion, peeled and cut into
    thin slices
Fresh parsley if available

FOR THE DRESSING:

1 clove garlic, peeled and crushed
Sea salt
½ teaspoon dry mustard
½ teaspoon sugar

Freshly ground black pepper
1 tablespoon tomato paste
1 tablespoon red wine vinegar
3 tablespoons olive oil

Put the beans into a bowl with the onion. For the dressing, put the mustard, sugar, and garlic into a small bowl with a little salt and a grinding of pepper. Mix with the tomato paste and vinegar, and then gradually add the oil until everything is blended. Pour this dressing over the beans, tossing them gently until they're all coated and look glossy. Check the seasoning and add more salt, pepper, or sugar if necessary.

This salad looks pretty in a glass or white china bowl with chopped parsley sprinkled over the top.

RED CABBAGE SALAD

POLAND

This is a hearty winter salad, and the warm mauve color adds a cheerful touch on a cold day.

It goes well with a protein-rich dish such as a cheese flan, and is an eye-appealing addition to any buffet lunch or supper.

You can leave out the caraway seeds if you don't like them, though they do give a lovely spicy flavor. I don't think the raisins are very authentic, but we like them and I'm giving you the version I usually make but you can leave them out, too, if you prefer! *Serves 4.*

1 pound (450 g) red cabbage
2 apples
⅓ cup (80 ml) raisins
1 tablespoon lemon juice or red wine vinegar

2–3 tablespoons oil
2–3 teaspoons caraway seeds
Sea salt
Freshly ground black pepper

Wash the cabbage and then grate or shred it as finely as you can. I think it's best grated because then it's soft enough to blend well with the other ingredients and isn't too chewy. Wash and dice the apples (unpeeled) and discard the cores; wash the raisins, then add both fruits to the cabbage together with the lemon juice or vinegar, oil, caraway seeds, and a little salt and pepper. Stir well so that everything is thoroughly mixed together.

RICE AND ARTICHOKE-HEART SALAD

FRANCE

This makes a complete meal if you serve it with a soup or one or two other vegetable salads, such as a bowl of crisp lettuce and herbs or a juicy tomato salad. A green salad with Gruyére cheese or the tomato salad with cheese and olives will supply the extra protein needed; or the salad can be garnished with wedges of hard-boiled egg. Alternatively, you could start or end the meal with a protein dish, such as a lentil soup or homemade ice cream. *Serves 4.*

1¼ cups (310 ml) brown rice
2½ cups (625 ml) water
1 can (14 ounces/420 g) artichoke
  hearts, drained
Sea salt
1 clove garlic
1 tablespoon wine vinegar
3 tablespoons olive oil

Freshly ground black pepper
1 tablespoon chopped fresh
  parsley
1 tablespoon chopped fresh chives
Extra parsley to garnish
3 hard-boiled eggs, quartered
  (optional)

Put the rice into a heavy-based saucepan with the water and half a teaspoon of salt and bring to the boil; then put a lid on the saucepan, turn the heat down low, and leave the rice to cook very gently for 40–45 minutes, or until the rice is tender and all the water has been absorbed. If there is still a little water, put the lid back on the saucepan and leave it to stand (off the heat) for 10–15 minutes.

While the rice is cooking slice the artichoke hearts, and peel and crush the garlic in a little salt with the blade of a knife. Dice the garlic and mix it in a small bowl with the vinegar, olive oil, and a grinding of pepper. Stir this mixture gently into the hot rice, together with the parsley, chives, and sliced artichoke hearts, using a fork to avoid mashing the rice. Check the seasoning and then leave the mixture to cool at room temperature.

Serve the salad in a shallow dish with a sprinkling of chopped parsley and the hard-boiled eggs, if you're using them, tucked around the edge.

SPINACH SALAD

U S A

This is different from the Middle Eastern cooked spinach salad (see p. 66) because here tender young spinach leaves are used uncooked, and they make a surprisingly good mixture. This recipe is often called

"American Salad" in Europe. This version dispenses with the usual crisp bacon garnish and uses tomatoes instead. They're combined with fresh mushrooms and tossed in a garlic-flavored French dressing. *Serves 4.*

½ pound (225 g) very fresh tender
  spinach

2 tomatoes
¼ pound (115 g) fresh mushrooms

FOR THE DRESSING:

1 clove garlic
Sea salt
1 tablespoon red wine vinegar

3 tablespoons olive oil
Freshly ground black pepper

Wash and dry the spinach thoroughly, and then tear it into rough pieces, discarding any tough stems. Wash and slice the tomatoes and mushrooms.

Peel the garlic and crush it in a little salt with the blade of a knife. Dice and put the garlic into a large bowl—you can use the bowl in which you're going to serve the salad—and add the vinegar, then gradually the oil. Season with a little pepper and then put in the spinach, tomatoes, and mushrooms, and toss them lightly. Serve at once.

◆——◆——◆

COOKED SPINACH SALAD

MIDDLE EAST

I know some people find the idea of a salad made from cold cooked spinach very off-putting, but I think the mixture of the soft, dark-green spinach, the fruity olive oil, and the sharp-tasting lemon juice is delicious. There are different versions of this salad throughout the Middle East. Yogurt can be included in the dressing or served with the salad, as in this recipe; cooked chick peas can be added, providing a pleasant contrast of color and texture as well as protein. I also like it with a topping of slivered almonds sautéed in butter until golden and crisp. *Serves 4.*

2 pounds (900 g) fresh spinach	1 clove garlic
1 tablespoon lemon juice	1 cup (250 ml) plain yogurt
3 tablespoons olive oil	Fresh mint, parsley or chives; or
Sea salt	⅓ cup (80 ml) slivered almonds
Freshly ground black pepper	sautéed in butter

Wash the spinach well and either steam it or cook it in just the water clinging to it. Drain thoroughly and leave to cool. Chop the cooled spinach and put it into a bowl with the lemon juice, olive oil, and some salt and pepper, tossing it gently so that the oil and lemon juice are well distributed.

Peel and crush the garlic and then mix it with the yogurt. Put the spinach salad onto a flat plate and spoon some of the yogurt mixture on top; garnish with chopped green herbs or the almonds. Serve the rest of the yogurt separately.

THREE-BEAN SALAD

U S A

This attractive salad shows off the contrasting shapes and colors of three different types of bean: red kidney beans, navy or other white beans, and chick peas. Other beans could of course be used; the aim is to have as much variety as possible. It's advisable to soak and cook the red kidney beans separately as the color can stain the others slightly pink, but you can cook them all in one saucepan if you wish, although you will still run the risk of some discoloration. *Serves 4 as a main course, 6–8 as an appetizer.*

¾ cup (180 ml) dried red kidney beans	2 tablespoons wine vinegar
½ cup (125 ml) dried navy or other white beans	6 tablespoons olive oil
½ cup (125 ml) dried chick peas	Sea salt
2 tablespoons chopped fresh green herbs	Freshly ground black pepper

Soak the red kidney beans in water in one bowl and the other two types together in another; then drain, rinse, and cook them in fresh water until they're tender, again keeping the red ones separate if possible. Drain the beans well, put them all into a bowl together, and add the herbs (you don't need to cool the beans). Mix the vinegar, oil, and some salt and pepper in a small bowl, and then stir this into the bean mixture, tossing the beans until they're thoroughly coated. Leave the mixture to cool, stirring it from time to time; then chill it.

Three-bean salad looks pretty served in a shallow glass bowl or white dish to show off the colors of the beans, or it can be spooned over crisp lettuce leaves and garnished with extra chopped fresh green herbs if you prefer.

TOMATO SALAD

FRANCE

One of the joys of late summer is getting firm, fragrant, orange-red tomatoes and then using them extravagantly, as in this juicy salad, which I like to serve with pasta dishes. *Serves 4.*

1½ pounds (675 g) tomatoes	*1 tablespoon olive oil*
1 small onion	*Sea salt*
1 teaspoon red wine vinegar	*Freshly ground black pepper*

Wash the tomatoes and cut them into slices. Peel and finely slice the onion. Put the tomato and onion into a bowl and gently stir in the vinegar and oil. Salt and pepper to taste. Serve as soon as possible.

TOMATO, CHEESE, AND OLIVE SALAD

FRANCE

If you serve this as a side salad with a plain pasta or rice dish it will supply the extra protein ideally desired; accompanied by bread or rolls, it also makes a delicious lunch, simple yet good. The type of cheese you use is up to you; Brie or Camembert is delicious. *Serves 4 as a side salad, 2–3 for lunch.*

1 pound (450 g) firm tomatoes	*Sea salt*
1 onion	*Freshly ground black pepper*
8 pitted ripe olives	*6 ounces (180 g) soft white cheese*
2 tablespoons olive oil	*such as Brie or Camembert*
1 tablespoon wine vinegar	

Wash the tomatoes and cut them into fairly thin slices; peel and finely slice the onion. Put these two into a bowl with the olives, oil, vinegar, and salt and pepper to taste, and mix lightly together. Just before you want to serve it, cut up the cheese and add it to the salad. This looks good in a shallow glass bowl or white china dish. If possible, don't make this salad more than about 30 minutes in advance or the juices will run and it could be a bit too wet.

STUFFED TOMATO SALAD

SWITZERLAND

Stuffed tomato salad from Switzerland makes a refreshing first course in late summer when tomatoes are large and cheap; or it can make a light salad lunch after a substantial soup. *Serves 6.*

6 good-size tomatoes—about	*1 tablespoon mayonnaise*
1 pound (450 g)	*1 tablespoon plain yogurt*
Sea salt	*Freshly ground black pepper*
2 apples	*Lettuce leaves*
4 stalks of crisp, tender celery	

Halve the tomatoes around their middles and, using a teaspoon, scoop out the centers (you won't need them for this recipe but may wish to reserve them for other uses). Sprinkle a little salt inside each tomato half and leave them upside down on a plate or in a colander to drain off any excess liquid.

Wash the apples and celery, then dice them and add the mayonnaise, yogurt, and a little salt and pepper to taste. Clean any excess salt out of the tomatoes, pat them fairly dry, and arrange them, right way up, on a bed of lettuce. Spoon the celery and apple mixture into the tomato halves, and serve.

VEGETABLE AND BEAN SALAD

POLAND

This salad, *salata mehania*, from Poland makes a lovely and filling meal. It's nice with homemade brown bread or pita bread. You can really use any dried beans but I prefer the red kidney beans as they're nice and colorful. *Serves 4–6.*

1 cup (250 ml) green peas
1 cup (250 ml) green beans
¾ cup (180 ml) dried red kidney
 beans, soaked, cooked, and
 drained; or use 1 can (16
 ounces/480 g)
½ pound (225 g) cooked potatoes,
 cubed
¼ pound (115 g) fresh mushrooms
1 celery heart
½ pound (225 g) firm cabbage,
 red or green

2 tablespoons chopped chives, if
 available
1 clove garlic
Sea salt
Freshly ground black pepper
½ teaspoon dry mustard
½ teaspoon sugar
1 tablespoon wine vinegar
3 tablespoons olive oil

Steam the peas and green beans together until they're just tender; then drain them. Put them into a bowl with the kidney beans and potatoes. Wash and slice the mushrooms and celery; wash and shred the cabbage. Add these all to the bowl, together with the chives.

Peel the garlic and crush it in a little salt; then dice it and put it into a small bowl with a grinding of pepper, the mustard, sugar, and vinegar. Mix well, then gradually stir in the oil and pour over the vegetables in the bowl, tossing them lightly so that they are well coated. Serve the salad in a glass bowl or on a base of crisp lettuce on a flat plate.

WALDORF SALAD

U S A

This salad contains a very pleasant mixture of flavors and textures; crisp celery, sweet apple, and crunchy walnuts bound together in a creamy mayonnaise (I use half mayonnaise, half plain yogurt). The only problem is the color, which can be rather dull, so I try to use red-skinned apples that don't need peeling. Served on crisp lettuce leaves, Waldorf salad makes an excellent lunch, and is also delicious as a protein-rich first course. *Serves 4 as a main course, 6–8 as a first course.*

1 celery heart—about ½ pound (225 g) after it's been trimmed
2 red-skinned apples—about ½ pound (225 g)
1–1½ cups (250–375 ml) walnuts, roughly chopped

3–4 rounded tablespoons mayonnaise
3–4 rounded tablespoons plain yogurt
Sea salt

Wash the celery thoroughly and slice it finely. Wash and quarter the apples, remove the cores, and dice the unpeeled fruit. Put the apple and celery into a bowl and add the walnuts. Stir in enough mayonnaise and yogurt to bind everything lightly and give a creamy consistency. The salad looks nice in a shallow glass bowl and garnished with a few extra pieces of walnut, or heaped onto crisp lettuce leaves.

If you don't like the slightly bitter flavor of walnuts, you can of course use other nuts for this salad. My family likes it best made with whole roasted hazelnuts: I spread them on a dry baking tray and roast them in a moderate oven—350° F (180° C)—for about 20 minutes, or until the skins will rub off easily; then I cool them and remove the skins by rubbing the nuts gently in a soft dry cloth before mixing them with the apple and celery. You could also use roasted peanuts or toasted almonds.

VEGETABLE
SIDE DISHES

Brussels Sprouts with Cheese

Cabbage with Sour Cream

Stir-Fried Chinese Cabbage

Carrots with Apples

Carrots à la Vichy

Cauliflower in Tomato Sauce

Zucchini with Fresh Herbs

Fennel Baked with Cheese

White Beans with Apples

Mushrooms in Sour Cream

Spicy Okra

Creamed Onions and Peas

Glazed Parsnips

Peas Braised with Lettuce

Potatoes Anna

Baked Potatoes

Potatoes Baked with Cream

New Potatoes Baked in Butter

Roast Potatoes

Pumpkin Baked with Butter and Garlic

Stewed Red Cabbage

Salsify with Parsley, Butter, and Lemon

Creamed Spinach

Baked Creamed Turnips

Glazed Sweet Potatoes

THESE RECIPES ARE FOR THE VEGETABLES THAT you serve alongside the main dish, and some of them make good hot appetizers, too. They are mostly fairly simple ideas for making ordinary vegetables a bit different, or for preparing some of the more exotic vegetables (like okra, fennel, or pumpkin). One or two of the recipes contain protein—the Brussels sprouts with cheese, white beans with apples and potatoes Anna, for instance—which makes them another useful option for increasing the nourishment of a meal.

BRUSSELS SPROUTS WITH CHEESE

HOLLAND

This is really a very simple recipe for Brussels sprouts and one that's good for a dinner party because it can be prepared ahead. *Serves 4.*

1½ pounds (675 g) Brussels
   sprouts
Sea salt
A little butter

1–1½ cups (250–375 ml) finely
   grated Edam cheese
Freshly ground black pepper

Preheat oven to 325° F (160° C). Wash and trim the sprouts. Leave them whole if they're tiny; otherwise halve or quarter them—that way they cook well and don't get soggy. Put ½ inch (12 mm) water into a saucepan and bring to the boil; add the sprouts, bring up to the boil again and cook for 2 minutes. Drain the sprouts immediately. Butter an ovenproof dish quite generously and add the sprouts; sprinkle the grated cheese over them and then grind a little pepper on top. Dot with a little more butter, cover with foil or a lid, and bake the sprouts in the oven for about 20 minutes, or until the cheese has melted and they're piping hot.

If you want to keep the sprouts warm before serving, I find they will stay nice and fresh-looking for quite a long time if you prepare them as above and put them in a lower oven—say 300° F (150° C).

CABBAGE WITH SOUR CREAM

NORWAY

If you cook cabbage until it's just tender, then drain it well and stir in some sour cream, you get a delicious mixture: simple yet good enough for a special occasion. In Norway, caraway seeds would probably be added too, but these are optional. *Serves 4.*

1½–2 pounds (675–900 g) firm
   cabbage, washed and shredded
Sea salt
½ cup (125 ml) sour cream

Freshly ground black pepper
1 teaspoon caraway seeds
   (optional)

Put about 1 inch (2.5 cm) water into a large saucepan, together with a pinch of salt; bring to the boil, and then add the cabbage. Let the cabbage simmer gently, covered, for about 7–10 minutes, until just tender. Drain the cabbage well and stir in the sour cream, a good grinding of pepper, and the caraway seeds if you're using them. Reheat for a minute or two, just to warm through the sour cream, then serve.

STIR-FRIED CHINESE CABBAGE

CHINA

Chinese cabbage, or Chinese leaves, as it's sometimes called, is quite often found in the shops now and makes a lovely cooked vegetable dish that's very quickly prepared. I like to stir-fry the cabbage in the Chinese way; it's good with either an ordinary Western-style meal or as part of a Chinese meal. *Serves 4.*

1 Chinese cabbage, about
   1½ pounds (675 g)
1 small onion, peeled and
   chopped
2 tablespoons oil
1 clove garlic, crushed
1 piece of fresh ginger, if
   available, peeled and grated to

make 1 teaspoonful; or use
   ½ teaspoon powdered ginger
1 teaspoon soy sauce
½ teaspoon cornstarch
1 tablespoon cold water
Sugar
Sea salt
Freshly ground black pepper

Wash the cabbage and shred it—not too finely. Sauté the onion, without browning it, in the oil in a large saucepan for about 7 minutes. Add the garlic and ginger and sauté for another 2 or 3 minutes. Take the saucepan off the heat and leave to one side until just before you want to serve the cabbage. Mix the soy sauce, cornstarch, and water in a small cup and keep this to one side, too.

When you're ready for the cabbage, reheat the onion in the large saucepan. When it's really hot put in the cabbage and sauté it over a fairly high heat for about 2 minutes, stirring all the time. It will quickly soften. Give the cornstarch mixture a quick stir and then pour it into the saucepan with the cabbage and continue stirring over the heat for about 30 seconds, until the juices have thickened. Check the seasoning, then serve immediately. The cabbage should still be rather crisp and crunchy.

◆———◆———◆

CARROTS WITH APPLES

GERMANY

Fruit, both dried and fresh, is used a good deal in German cookery, resulting in some delicious sweet-sour mixtures. Here the soft, slightly sharp cooking apples contrast well with the firm sweet carrots. Like the white beans with apples, this is a useful recipe to serve with a dish that would normally be accompanied by an applesauce. *Serves 4.*

1½ pounds (675 g) carrots	*Sea salt*
2 pounds (900 g) cooking apples	*Freshly ground black pepper*
1 large onion	*Sugar*
2 tablespoons oil	

Peel the carrots and cut them into even-size pieces; cook them in a little boiling water until they're nearly tender; then drain them, reserving the cooking liquid. While the carrots are cooking, peel and slice the apples and the onion. Add the apple to the cooked, drained carrots in the saucepan, together with 4 tablespoons of the reserved cooking liquid, and cook over a gentle heat, covered, for 5–7 minutes, until the apple has reduced to a soft pulp. Meanwhile sauté the onion in the oil until it's crisp and beginning to brown. Season the carrot and apple mixture to taste. Serve with the fried-onion topping.

CARROTS À LA VICHY

FRANCE

Although you're supposed to use baby carrots for this recipe, I find it's a marvelous way of making larger carrots taste extra special. Some people use Vichy water for cooking the carrots or put a pinch of bicarbonate of soda in with them for a more authentic-tasting result, but I don't think this makes much difference and I just use ordinary tap water. Personally I think it's the butter, sugar, and chopped parsley that work the magic, not the water! *Serves 4.*

1 pound (450 g) carrots　　*1 tablespoon butter*
¼ cup (60 ml) water　　*Sea salt*
1 tablespoon sugar　　*Fresh parsley*

Scrape the carrots and cut them into matchsticks. Put the water, sugar, butter, and salt into a heavy-bottomed saucepan and bring to the boil. Add the carrots, cover, and simmer very gently for about 10–15 minutes, until the carrots are tender and all the water has been absorbed. Watch them carefully to make sure they don't burn. Serve them sprinkled with a little chopped parsley.

CAULIFLOWER IN TOMATO SAUCE

GREECE

This is an easy and attractive way of preparing and serving cauliflower, and makes a nice alternative to the traditional white sauce or cheese sauce. *Serves 4.*

1 onion, peeled and chopped	Sea salt
2 tablespoons oil	Freshly ground black pepper
1 clove garlic, peeled and crushed	1 medium-size cauliflower,
1 can (16 ounces/480 g) tomatoes	washed and broken into florets
⅔ cup (160 ml) water	Fresh parsley

Cook the onion gently in the oil for 10 minutes, until soft but not browned. Put the onion in your blender jar along with the garlic, tomatoes, and water, and purée. Put this mixture into a fairly large saucepan and add some salt and pepper. Bring the mixture to the boil and then add the cauliflower and simmer gently, covered, for 10–15 minutes, until the cauliflower is just tender. You can take the cauliflower out of the saucepan using a perforated spoon and serve the sauce separately, but I usually serve them together with a little chopped parsley sprinkled over the top.

ZUCCHINI WITH FRESH HERBS

FRANCE

This is a good way to serve zucchini early in the season when they're young and tender and you want to make the most of their delicate flavor. *Serves 4–6.*

1½ pounds (675 g) zucchini	1 tablespoon finely chopped fresh
Sea salt	chives
2 tablespoons butter	Freshly ground black pepper
1 tablespoon finely chopped fresh	
parsley	

Wash the zucchini, trimming the ends, and cut into ¼ inch (6 mm) slices; then cook them in ½ inch (12 m) boiling water for 5–7 minutes, until they're just tender but not soggy. Drain the zucchini well and add the butter, parsley, chives, pepper, and a little salt to taste if necessary.

FENNEL BAKED WITH CHEESE

ITALY

It's quite easy to find crisp white bulbs of Florentine fennel these days, and it makes an interesting vegetable dish. Fennel is very nice steamed and served with just a little butter and black pepper, or you can boil it and then bake it with cheese, as in this recipe, which gives a tasty golden result. *Serves 4–6.*

2 large bulbs of fennel—about
  1½ pounds (675 g) together
1 cup (240 ml) water
Sea salt

2 tablespoons butter
Freshly ground black pepper
½ cup (125 ml) grated cheese

Preheat oven to 400° F (200° C). Trim the fennel and slice the bulbs into quarters or eighths. Put the water and a little salt into a saucepan; bring to the boil and put in the fennel and simmer for 20–30 minutes, or until tender. Take the fennel out of the saucepan with a slotted spoon and arrange it in a shallow buttered dish. While you're doing this, let the water in which the fennel was cooked boil away vigorously until it has reduced to just a couple of tablespoons or so of well-flavored liquid. Pour this liquid over the fennel, then dot with the butter, grind some pepper over the top, and finally sprinkle with the grated cheese. Bake the fennel, uncovered, for 20–30 minutes, until it's heated through and golden brown on top.

WHITE BEANS WITH APPLES

GERMANY

You might think this is an unlikely combination, but it works well. The apples collapse, bathing the beans in a soft sweet-sour sauce. The recipe can also be made with pears, but I think it's nicest with apples. Obviously, with the protein-rich beans, it's useful for serving with a low-protein main dish. I like it with crisp German potato pancakes or Swiss *rösti. Serves 4.*

8 ounces (240 g) dried white, or
  navy beans
1 pound (450 g) cooking apples
4 tablespoons butter or margarine

2 tablespoons sugar
Sea salt
Freshly ground black pepper

Cover the beans with plenty of cold water and leave them to soak for several hours or overnight. Then drain off the water and rinse the beans under cold running water; put them into a large saucepan, cover them generously with more cold water, and simmer gently until they're tender—about 1 hour. Drain off the cooking liquid—it won't be needed for this recipe but it's nutritious and worth keeping for soups or sauces.

Peel, core, and dice the apples. Melt the butter in a fairly large saucepan and gently sauté the apples in it, until they're soft but not browned. Then add the beans and cook gently until they're heated through. Stir in the sugar and salt and pepper to taste.

MUSHROOMS IN SOUR CREAM

FINLAND

In Finland and Sweden whole families go into the woods in the autumn to gather baskets of fresh earthy-smelling mushrooms, and they have quite a number of different ways of cooking them. This is one of the simplest but makes a luxurious vegetable dish to go with a plainer main course, or it can be served as a delicious appetizer, with fingers of hot toast. *Serves 2–3 as a side-dish vegetable, 4–6 as an appetizer.*

1 medium-size onion
1 pound (450 g) mushrooms
2 tablespoons butter
½ cup (125 ml) sour cream

Sea salt
Freshly ground black pepper
Fresh parsley

Peel and finely chop the onion; wash the mushrooms. Cut the mushrooms into even-size pieces. Melt the butter in a fairly large saucepan and sauté the onion, without browning, for about 5 minutes; then add the prepared mushrooms and cook for a further 4–5 minutes, until they are tender. If they make a lot of liquid, boil them vigorously for a minute or two, without a lid on the saucepan, to evaporate it. Then stir in the sour cream and salt and pepper, and heat through gently. Serve at once and sprinkle with chopped parsley.

SPICY OKRA

INDIA

Okra is an intriguing vegetable, a plump green pod with a soft, glutinous texture and delicate flavor when it's cooked. It's nice as an accompaniment to curries or Caribbean rice dishes. *Serves 4.*

½ *pound (225 g) fresh okra; or*
  10 ounces (300 g) frozen okra,
  thawed
1 medium-size onion, peeled and
  chopped
2 tablespoons butter
1 can (8 ounces/240 g) tomatoes

1 clove garlic, peeled and crushed
2 teaspoons ground coriander
1 tablespoon garam masala, *or*
  curry powder
Sea salt
Freshly ground black pepper
2 teaspoons lemon juice

Trim the fresh okra or drain off the liquid if you're using the frozen variety. Sauté the onion in the butter for about 10 minutes, until it's soft and golden; then add the tomatoes, garlic, coriander, garam masala, and a pinch of salt. Bring to the boil and add the okra, letting it simmer gently for 15–20 minutes (until it's tender). Check the seasoning and add a little lemon juice to taste.

CREAMED ONIONS AND PEAS

USA

An American friend gave me the recipe for this creamy vegetable dish, which she serves her family at Thanksgiving. *Serves 6.*

¾ *pound (350 g) pearl onions*
Sea salt
20 *ounces (600 g) frozen peas*
3 *tablespoons butter*
3 *tablespoons (45 ml) all-purpose*
  flour

1 ½ *cups (375 ml) milk*
Freshly ground black pepper
Grated nutmeg
Ground cloves

Peel the onions with a small sharp-pointed knife and then boil them in a little water for 15–20 minutes, or until they're almost tender; drain them, reserving the liquid. Defrost the peas by putting them in a colander and rinsing them under hot water.

Melt the butter in a large saucepan and add the flour; cook the roux for a minute or two and then pour in the milk in three batches, over a high heat, stirring each time until the mixture is smooth before adding more. When all the milk has been incorporated and you have a smooth sauce, taste it and season with the salt, pepper, nutmeg, and cloves. Carefully stir in the onions and peas and cook gently for 5 minutes to heat them through. Serve at once.

GLAZED PARSNIPS

FRANCE

This French way of cooking parsnips gently with butter, sugar, and just a little liquid leaves them glistening in a buttery syrup that enhances their natural sweetness. You can apply this method to other root vegetables, including, carrots, turnips, and sweet potatoes. *Serves 4.*

1 ½ *pounds (675 g) parsnips*
¾ *cup (180 ml) water or stock*
2 *tablespoons butter*

1 *tablespoon soft brown sugar*
½ *teaspoon sea salt*
Freshly ground black pepper

Peel the parsnips and cut them into small even-size pieces, discarding the central core if it is at all tough, though it should be all right if the parsnips are small. Put the parsnips into a heavy-bottomed saucepan with the liquid, butter, sugar, salt, and a grinding of black pepper. Cover and simmer over a gentle heat for about 20 minutes, until the pieces of parsnip are tender and the liquid has reduced to a syrupy glaze.

PEAS BRAISED WITH LETTUCE

FRANCE

If you can get fresh young peas they are superb cooked in this manner: sweet, tender, and juicy. But it's also a marvelous way to make frozen peas taste really good—and it's so simple to do. *Serves 4.*

20 ounces (600 g) frozen peas or	*2–3 sprigs of mint or parsley*
2 pounds (900 g) fresh peas	*½ teaspoon sea salt*
About 6 outer lettuce leaves	*½ teaspoon sugar*
2 tablespoons butter	

Put the frozen peas into a colander and run them under the hot tap to rinse off the ice. Or, if you're using fresh peas, shell them and then rinse them in cold water. Wash the lettuce leaves, tear them gently into small pieces, and put them in a heavy-bottomed saucepan. Put the peas in on top, then the butter, in pieces, and the mint or parsley, salt, and sugar. Cover and set over a moderate heat; when you hear the liquid start to bubble, turn the heat down a bit and cook gently until the peas are tender—3 minutes for frozen peas, 10–15 minutes for fresh. Remove the parsley or mint sprigs before serving.

I find you don't need to add any water if the lettuce leaves are freshly washed when they're put into the saucepan, and they really do give the peas a lovely flavor. You can also add some chopped scallions, to make a pleasant variation.

POTATOES ANNA

FRANCE

This is a potato dish that cooks slowly in the oven and won't spoil. It's rather like another famous, creamy potato dish, *gratin dauphinois*, except that it's turned out like a cake for serving. You don't have to add cheese, but I often do because it improves the flavor and increases the protein content of the dish, if that is appropriate to your meal plan. *Serves 4–6.*

4 tablespoons butter　　　　　　*Salt and pepper*
1½ pounds (675 g) potatoes　　*Fresh parsley*
1½ cups (375 ml) grated cheese

First line an 8-inch (20 cm) cake pan by pressing a piece of foil into the base, extending it up the sides a little. Preheat the oven to 325° F (160° C).

Melt the butter in a small saucepan and then use some of it to brush the inside of the foil-lined cake pan. Peel the potatoes and slice them into thin rounds. Put the rounds into a colander and rinse them thoroughly under cold water; then drain them and pat them dry with a clean cloth. Arrange a layer of potatoes in the bottom of the pan and then sprinkle it with some of the grated cheese and a little salt and pepper; add another layer of potatoes and continue in this way, ending with a generous layer of grated cheese. Pour the remaining butter over the top and cover with foil. Bake in the oven for about 2 hours, or until the potatoes can be pierced easily with the point of a knife. Slip a knife around the sides of the tin to loosen the potatoes. Place a warmed plate over the pan and turn out. Remove the foil. Sprinkle a little chopped parsley over the top.

◆———◆———◆

BAKED POTATOES

GREAT BRITAIN

There are a number of ways to prepare baked potatoes. You can rub the skins with butter or oil before you bake them, which makes the skin soft and flavorful; or you can just wash, prick and bake them as they are (with the skins still wet), in a hot oven; this way the skins will get lovely and crisp and crunchy. *Serves 4.*

4 medium-size baking potatoes
A little butter, if desired

Preheat oven to 450° F (230° C). Scrub the potatoes and cut out any blemishes. Make two or three small cuts or fork pricks on each potato to allow the steam to escape. (Rub each potato in a little oil or butter if you're using this method.) Then put them in a baking pan and place them in the oven. Bake the potatoes for 1–1¼ hours, or until they feel tender when squeezed slightly. Serve them at once.

If you're going to have to keep them waiting, it's best to use this soft-skinned approach. The potatoes can be cooked at a lower temperature, too, if more convenient—anything from 325° F (160° C) is all right, but of course they then take longer to cook.

Baked potatoes can really make a meal. Of course they're delicious served with grated cheese and a bowl of mixed salad, or you can make quite a festive meal by offering a choice of salads and several different toppings for the potatoes: *hummus*; the sour cream dip or the goat cheese and herb spread; and bowls of different-colored grated cheeses.

POTATOES BAKED WITH CREAM

FRANCE

In this dish, *gratin dauphinois*, potatoes are sliced very thin, layered in a shallow casserole with cream and butter, and baked in a slow oven until they're meltingly tender. I find it a useful dish for entertaining because it doesn't need any last-minute attention and will keep warm in the oven for a long time without spoiling.

If you want to increase the protein content of this dish, you can add some layers of grated cheese, preferably Gruyère, but I think the flavor is better without. Incidentally you can make a nice economical family version by using whole milk instead of light cream. My own favorite but unauthentic variation is to substitute tomato juice for the cream. *Serves 4–6.*

1 clove garlic, peeled and halved	*Freshly ground black pepper*
2 tablespoons butter	*Nutmeg*
1½ pounds (675 g) potatoes	*1¼ cups (310 ml) light cream*
Sea salt	

First prepare a shallow ovenproof dish by rubbing the inside with the cut clove of garlic, then buttering it generously with about half the butter. Preheat oven to 325° F (160° C).

Next peel the potatoes, then slice them very finely. Put the potato slices into a colander and rinse them thoroughly under the cold tap to remove some of the starch; pat them dry on paper towels. Arrange a layer of the potato slices in the prepared dish; season with salt, pepper, and a little grating of nutmeg; then add another layer of potato slices, continuing in this way until all the potato is used. Pour the cream evenly over the top and dot with the remaining butter. Cover with a piece of foil and bake in the preheated oven for 1½–2 hours, until the potatoes feel tender when pierced with the point of a knife. Remove the foil and serve the potatoes straight from the dish.

Usually I find I'm baking this dish in the oven with other things and so have to compromise a little over the temperature; it's all right at a hotter temperature if you use the lowest rack of the oven.

NEW POTATOES BAKED IN BUTTER

NORWAY

This is such an easy way to cook new potatoes, but it really seems to conserve their delicate flavor so that they come out tender and buttery. In Norway they would probably be garnished with a sprinkling of chopped fresh dill, which is a very popular flavoring in Scandinavia, but chopped parsley or chives will do just as well. *Serves 4.*

1½ pounds (675 g) new potatoes	*3 tablespoons butter*
—try to choose ones that are all	*1 teaspoon sea salt*
the same size, the smaller the	*Freshly ground black pepper*
better	*Fresh dill, parsley, or chives*

Preheat oven to 325° F (160° C). Wash and scrape the potatoes or just scrub them thoroughly and leave the skins on. Put them into an ovenproof casserole with the butter, salt, and a little grinding of black pepper. Cover the casserole and place it in the oven for about 45 minutes, or until the potatoes are tender when pierced with a sharp knife. Serve the potatoes sprinkled with chopped herbs.

If you want to cook something else in the oven at the same time and need to have it hotter, the potatoes will be all right if they're put on the lowest rack.

ROAST POTATOES

GREAT BRITAIN

Quite a number of vegetarian dishes have a fairly soft consistency and so, I think, need to be served with something crisp. These crunchy golden potatoes are a popular and delicious way of providing that textural contrast. *Serves 4.*

2 pounds (900 g) potatoes
Sea salt

Vegetable oil—I like corn oil best for this

Preheat oven to 425° F (220° C). Peel the potatoes and cut them into even-size pieces. With medium-size potatoes I usually cut them into four or six pieces as I think it's nicer to have a serving of two or three small crisp potatoes than one larger one. Cook the potatoes in boiling water for 5–6 minutes; then drain them thoroughly.

While the potatoes are boiling, pour about ¼ inch (6 mm) corn oil into a roasting pan and place it on the top rack of the oven. Put the hot, drained potatoes into the hot oil—if the oil is really hot enough it should hiss and splutter as they go in. *Be careful.* Turn the potatoes over in the oil so that they are well coated in it, and return to the oven. After about 25–30 minutes, take a look at the potatoes and if they're nice and golden underneath turn them over to give the other side a chance to crisp. I find they take about 45 minutes. If they seem to be racing along and you're afraid they'll be done before you're ready, turn the oven down to 325° F (160° C). Remove the potatoes with a perforated spoon, let them rest for a moment on paper towels, and serve them in a hot dish.

PUMPKIN BAKED WITH BUTTER AND GARLIC

FRANCE

Pumpkin is a vegetable I find difficult to resist. I don't know whether it's something to do with the time of the year and the magic of Halloween, or whether it's their glorious warm apricot color and pretty rounded shape, but I always seem to end up buying one. This is my favorite way of cooking pumpkin as a vegetable (it's also good for zucchini). *Serves 4.*

2 pounds (900 g) pumpkin
1 large clove garlic or 2 small ones
Sea salt

4 tablespoons butter
Freshly ground black pepper

Preheat oven to 350° F (180° C). Cut the pumpkin into smallish even-size pieces. Peel the garlic and crush it into a paste with a little salt, then mix it with the butter. Use half this garlic butter to grease an ovenproof dish generously, then put in the pumpkin and top with the remaining butter and a good grinding of black pepper. Cover and bake in the oven for about 40 minutes, or until the pumpkin is tender, stirring it once or twice during the cooking so that the butter is well distributed throughout.

STEWED RED CABBAGE

GERMANY

This vegetable dish needs no last-minute attention; it turns out moist and juicy, can be reheated if necessary, and still tastes good. It's a lovely, warming dish for winter, but it's also good cold, as a salad.

There are similar recipes for red cabbage in many other European countries and in Scandinavia. In France chestnuts are sometimes added and I've given a recipe for this delicious variation in the stews and casseroles section of the book. In Russia the red cabbage might be served with sour cream, which is a lovely addition, and in Denmark red cabbage is part of the traditional Christmas feast. *Serves 6.*

1½ pounds (675 g) red cabbage
2 large onions
2 large cooking apples
3 tablespoons oil

⅓ cup (80 ml) raisins or sultanas
1 tablespoon sea salt
1 tablespoon brown sugar
1–2 tablespoons lemon juice

Prepare the cabbage by shredding it fairly fine with a sharp knife, discarding the hard core. Put the cabbage into a large saucepan, cover it with cold water, and bring it to the boil. Take it off the heat and turn the cabbage into a colander to drain.

Meanwhile peel and chop the onions and apples, and sauté them lightly in the oil in a large saucepan for 5–10 minutes. Add the cabbage together with the raisins or sultanas, salt, sugar, and lemon juice. Stir well to coat the cabbage with the oil and mix everything together; then put a lid on the saucepan and leave the cabbage to cook very gently for 1½ hours, stirring from time to time, until it's very tender. Or you can put the cabbage into an ovenproof casserole, cover, and bake it in the oven at 325° F (160° C), for about 2 hours.

You can make the cabbage spicier if you want to by adding some cinnamon, caraway seeds, or ground cloves to the basic mixture—lots of variations are possible.

SALSIFY WITH PARSLEY, BUTTER, AND LEMON

FRANCE

Salsify—or oyster plant—looks like a long, rather dirty root when you see it in the shops, but when it's peeled and cooked its delicate flavor makes it ideal as a hot first course. It's also nice served in a well-flavored cheese sauce and baked in little individual dishes; or mixed with a good vinaigrette while still warm, and served cold as a first course or salad. *Serves 4–6.*

2¼ pounds (1 kilo) salsify, or oyster plant—this might seem a lot but you lose a great deal in peeling
Lemon juice

Sea salt
2 tablespoons butter
2 tablespoons chopped fresh parsley
Freshly ground black pepper

Peel the roots, keeping them under cold water to preserve the color. Cut them into 1-inch (2.5 cm) pieces and put them straight into a bowl of cold water with a tablespoonful of lemon juice, again to help keep them white. When they're all prepared, bring 1 inch (2.5 cm) water to the boil in a large saucepan and cook them for about 10 minutes, or until just tender.

Drain and add the butter, a tablespoonful of lemon juice, the parsley, and salt and pepper to taste. Heat gently to melt the butter, and serve at once. Thinly sliced, buttered whole-wheat bread tastes good with this dish.

CREAMED SPINACH

S W E D E N

People who don't normally like spinach might enjoy it prepared this way because of the creamy sauce. You can increase the protein content by garnishing the creamy spinach with chopped hard-boiled egg, which is the Finnish way of serving it. *Serves 4.*

1 pound (450 g) fresh spinach
3 tablespoons butter
3 tablespoons all-purpose flour
1½ cups (375 ml) milk

Sea salt
Freshly ground black pepper
Nutmeg

Wash the spinach very thoroughly, and repeat the process twice with fresh water each time. Put the spinach into a large saucepan. If you have just washed it you won't need to put any water in the saucepan as the spinach will be wet enough not to burn. Cook the spinach over a moderate heat. Have a lid on the saucepan but keep pushing the spinach down into the saucepan, chopping it a bit as it gets softer. It will take about 10 minutes to get really tender. Drain the spinach very well—the easiest way is to turn it into a colander and press it with a spoon to squeeze out all the liquid.

While the spinach is cooking make a sauce. Melt the butter in a medium-size saucepan and add the flour, cooking the roux for a minute or two without browning. Add a third of the milk and stir over a high heat until the mixture is thick and smooth; repeat with the rest of the milk, adding it in two batches. When all the milk is in and the sauce is thick and smooth, take it off the heat and season it with salt, pepper, and some grated nutmeg.

Mix the sauce with the spinach and check the seasoning; I think spinach needs plenty of pepper. Reheat the mixture gently, stirring all the time.

BAKED CREAMED TURNIPS

SWEDEN

This is a useful dish because you can get it ready in advance and just heat it through in the oven when you want it. The crunchy bread-crumb topping contrasts well with the soft creamy turnip. *Serves 4.*

2 pounds (900 g) turnips	*Freshly ground black pepper*
2 tablespoons butter	*Nutmeg*
2 tablespoons milk	*Soft bread crumbs*
Sea salt	*A little extra butter*

Peel the turnips and cut into even-size pieces. Put the pieces into a large saucepan, almost cover them with cold water, and then cook the vegetable gently, with a lid on the saucepan, until tender. Drain off all the water, then return the saucepan to the heat for a minute or two to dry the turnip a little. Mash the turnip until it's smooth, adding the butter, milk, and seasoning, and beating well. Lightly butter an oven-proof dish—a shallow one is best as it allows for plenty of crispy topping—and spoon the turnip mixture into it, smoothing the surface.

Sprinkle the top fairly generously with soft crumbs and dot with a few little pieces of butter. All this can be done in advance; at the appropriate time, bake the casserole in a moderate oven—350° F (180° C)—for about 40 minutes, until the inside is heated through and the top is golden brown and crisp.

GLAZED SWEET POTATOES

USA

Sweet potatoes have a sweet, chestnuty flavor that I love. You can prick them and bake them in the oven as you would a baking potato; parboil and roast them as you would ordinary potatoes; or glaze them as in this American recipe, which brings out the sweetness of the potatoes in a delicious way. *Serves 4.*

1½ pounds (675 g) sweet potatoes
2 tablespoons butter
¼ cup (60 ml) firmly packed
  brown sugar

2 tablespoons lemon juice
Sea salt

Scrub the potatoes, cut them into even-size pieces, put them in a saucepan, cover the potatoes with water, and boil gently until tender—about 15–20 minutes. Drain them and peel off the skins. Preheat oven to 400° F (200° C). Use half the butter to grease a shallow ovenproof dish generously; then arrange the potato pieces (you may mash them if you wish) in the dish and sprinkle them with the sugar, lemon juice, and a little salt, dot with the remaining butter, and place them, uncovered, in the oven. Bake them for 40–50 minutes, until they're golden brown and glazed, turning them once or twice during the cooking time (unless of course, you have chosen to mash them).

VEGETABLE
STEWS AND
CASSEROLES

Asparagus Casserole

Eggplant Bake

Cauliflower, Egg, and Potato Bake

Chop Suey

Green Pepper and Tomato Stew

Kidney Beans with Tomatoes, Onions, and Cumin

Lentil and Red Pepper Stew

Mixed Vegetable Stew

Mushrooms and Tofu

Split Pea (Pease) Pudding

Potato Bake

Potato and Mushroom Stew with Sour Cream

Ratatouille

Red Cabbage and Chestnut Casserole

Red Kidney Bean Stew

Red Peppers with Tomatoes and Onions

Corn Pudding

Tian

Split Pea Purée with Vegetables

MONG THE VERY COLORFUL AND DELICIOUS MIX-
tures in this section, some were originally intended for serving as an
accompaniment to meat, but I think they are substantial and delicious
enough to be main dishes in their own right. You might add just a
side salad and rice or potatoes.

ASPARAGUS CASSEROLE

ITALY

This savory pudding is called a *sformato* in Italy and is a cross between
a soufflé and a loaf. I think it's best served straight from the dish with
something crisp—hot garlic bread if you're serving it as a first course;
toasted triangles of bread or crunchy golden roast potatoes, and a good
tomato sauce on the side for a main course. *Serves 4 as a main dish,
6 as a first course.*

3 tablespoons butter	3 eggs
3 tablespoons all-purpose flour	2 cans (10½ ounces/315 g each)
1¼ cups (310 ml) milk	cut green asparagus spears
2–3 tablespoons grated Parmesan	1 tablespoon chopped fresh
Sea salt	parsley
Freshly ground black pepper	Triangles of toasted bread

Preheat oven to 350° F (180° C). In a heavy-bottomed saucepan melt
the butter and stir in the flour; when it's blended add the milk in three
batches, keeping the heat fairly high and stirring constantly each time,
until the mixture thickens, before adding any more. Take the saucepan
off the heat and add the grated Parmesan cheese and salt and pepper to
taste.

Beat the eggs and drain the asparagus. Mix the eggs into the sauce
and then gently stir in the asparagus and parsley. Check the seasoning,
then pour the mixture into a lightly buttered shallow ovenproof dish.
Put the dish into another dish or pan containing about 1 inch (2.5 cm)
of very hot water and place it on the center rack of the oven. Bake for
about 1 hour, or until the mixture is set, and serve with triangles of
toasted bread.

EGGPLANT BAKE

ITALY

I love eggplants, with their shiny purple skins and subtle flavor, and this Italian dish, *parmigiana*, is one of my favorite ways of cooking them. With crusty bread and a green salad it makes a good lunch or light supper; with creamy mashed potatoes or fluffy brown rice and a cooked green vegetable it is substantial enough to make a main meal. *Serves 4.*

1 pound (450 g) eggplant
Sea salt
Vegetable oil
1 pound (450 g) onions, peeled and sliced
1 cup (250 ml) dry red wine—you can leave this out but it's lovely if you've got it

3 large cloves garlic, peeled and crushed
1 can (28 ounces/840 g) tomatoes
Freshly ground black pepper
⅓–½ pound (150–225 g) cheese —sliced mozzarella plus some grated Parmesan if you want to be really authentic

Wash the eggplant(s) and slice them thinly, discarding stalk ends. Put the slices into a colander and sprinkle them with salt. Place a plate and weight on top and leave for half an hour for the bitter juices to be drawn out. Then wash the slices under cold water and pat them dry. Preheat the oven to 350° F (180° C).

Heat about 4 tablespoons of oil in a large saucepan and sauté the onions for about 10 minutes, until they're softened but not brown; then remove from the heat and stir in the wine, if you're using it, and the garlic and tomatoes. Season with salt and pepper. Heat some more oil in a skillet and quickly sauté the eggplant slices until they're soft and lightly browned—you may have to do this in two or more batches. Drain the eggplant and then lay half the slices in the base of a shallow, slightly oiled ovenproof dish. Spread with half the tomato mixture, then with half the cheese. Repeat the layers, ending with grated cheese. Bake for about 1½ hours, until crisp, golden brown, and bubbly. Serve immediately.

CAULIFLOWER, EGG, AND
POTATO BAKE

R U S S I A

In Russia sour cream would probably be used for this recipe, but as this makes it both expensive and rather rich I use a well-flavored cheese sauce instead. If you don't like eggs you could put in a layer of sliced fresh mushrooms instead—you'll need about ½ pound (225 g). Serves 4–6.

1½ pound (675 g) even-size small potatoes	6 hard-boiled eggs, sliced
1 medium-size cauliflower	Dry bread crumbs
2 cups (500 ml) cheese sauce (see recipe, page 24)	A little butter for topping

Scrub the potatoes and cook them in their skins in boiling water until they're tender; drain and cool them, then slip off the skins with a sharp knife. (Cooking the potatoes in their skins like this makes a big difference to the flavor.) Cut the potatoes into slices. Wash the cauliflower, break it into even-size sprigs, and cook these in a little boiling water for 5–7 minutes, or until they're just tender; drain well. Preheat the oven to 375° F (190° C).

Butter a large shallow ovenproof dish and line with a layer of the potato slices, followed by some of the sauce, then the cauliflower and the egg slices, then some more sauce. Continue like this until everything has been used, ending with a layer of potato and then one of sauce. Sprinkle the top with the bread crumbs, dot with a little butter, and bake for about 50 minutes, until heated through and golden brown on top.

All this needs as an accompaniment is some lightly cooked greens—firm little Brussels sprouts are ideal, or some buttered cabbage or spinach.

◆———◆———◆

CHOP SUEY

U S A

Although the list of ingredients for this dish may look rather daunting, it's actually very easy to make. Much of the preparation can be done in advance so you only have to cook the vegetables quickly at the last minute. *Serves 4.*

1 onion
1 clove garlic
1 piece of fresh ginger root, about 1 inch (2.5 cm); otherwise use ½ teaspoon ground ginger
½ pound (225 g) fresh or canned bean sprouts
¼ pound (60 ml) fresh mushrooms
1 small pepper, preferably red
1 can (15¼ ounces/458 g) sliced pineapple in its own juice (not *heavy syrup*)

8 ounces (225 g) can wheat protein, or wheat gluten, from health-food shops or Chinese-food stores
1 teaspoon soy sauce
1 tablespoon tomato paste
1 teaspoon sugar
1 tablespoon dry sherry
2 tablespoons water
1 egg
Sea salt
A little vegetable or peanut oil

Peel and chop the onion; peel and crush the garlic; peel and grate the ginger. Wash the bean sprouts if fresh. Wash and slice the mushrooms and the pepper, discarding the seeds from the pepper. Drain the pineapple and the wheat protein; cut both into small pieces. In a cup mix together the soy sauce, tomato paste, sugar, sherry, and water. Break the egg into a bowl and beat it.

When you're ready to cook the meal, heat 2 tablespoons of oil in a large saucepan or wok and sauté the onion for 5 minutes. Stir in the garlic and ginger, and cook for a few seconds before adding the bean sprouts, mushrooms, pepper, pineapple, and wheat protein. (*Tofu*, if firm and drained, is an acceptable substitute.) Stir-fry over quite a high heat for about 2 minutes, then add the soy-sauce mixture from the cup and stir well. Leave this to cook for just a minute or so; in a small skillet on an adjacent burner, quickly make an omelette with the beaten egg. Keep the omelette flat. To serve the chop suey, pile it up on a hot dish and lay the omelette on top.

Serve with lots of hot, well-cooked rice and perhaps some Chinese tea.

GREEN PEPPER AND TOMATO STEW

HUNGARY

This spicy Hungarian stew, called *lesco*, is rather similar to the Italian *peperonata*, except that it's made with green peppers and a generous seasoning of paprika. You can serve it Hungarian-style with a fried egg on top, but I think it's nicer with fluffy brown rice or warm crusty bread and soft cheese. *Serves 4.*

1 pound (450 g) green peppers
2 medium-size onions
3 tablespoons vegetable oil
2 cloves garlic, crushed

2 tablespoons paprika
1 can (16 ounces/480 g) tomatoes
Salt and pepper

Wash and slice the peppers into even-size pieces, discarding seeds and stalk. Peel and chop the onions, and fry them in the oil in a large saucepan for about 5 minutes, or until golden brown. Remove from the heat and stir in the garlic, paprika, peppers, tomatoes, and a seasoning of salt and pepper. Cover and cook gently for about 20 minutes until all the vegetables are tender. Check seasoning and serve.

KIDNEY BEANS WITH TOMATOES, ONIONS, AND CUMIN

PORTUGAL

This Portuguese mixture of glossy red kidney beans, tomatoes, onions, and cumin is spicy and delicious. *Serves 4.*

8 ounces (240 g) dried red kidney
*   beans*
6 tablespoons olive oil
Sea salt

Freshly ground black pepper
1 large onion
2 teaspoons cumin seed
1 can (8 ounces/240 g) tomatoes

Soak the kidney beans for 2–3 hours in plenty of cold water; then drain and rinse them. Put the beans into a saucepan with enough cold water to come about 1 inch (2.5 cm), above them, and add 4 tablespoons of the olive oil. Simmer the beans gently, covered, until they're very tender and most of the water has gone. Season them to taste with salt and pepper.

While the beans are cooking, peel and chop the onion and sauté it lightly in the remaining 2 tablespoons of oil. Cook the onion for about 10 minutes, until it is soft but not brown. Add the cumin seeds and stir them with the onion for a minute or two before putting in the tomatoes and some salt and pepper. Let the mixture simmer for about 10 minutes to give all the flavors a chance to blend, and then take it off the heat and mix gently with the beans. Reheat as necessary and serve with fluffy brown rice, or warm whole-wheat bread and a crisp green salad.

◆——◆——◆

LENTIL AND RED PEPPER STEW

BULGARIA

You can make this stew with all lentils or all beans but I think the mixture I've suggested gives you the best of both; the lentils thicken the sauce and give it body while the beans supply extra interest and texture. One of the nicest things about this dish is its color—it comes out a heart-warming vivid red and is really welcoming on a chilly day. Serve it with a dollop of sour cream, some crunchy baked potatoes, and a green side salad; or try creamy mashed potatoes and a cooked green vegetable. *Serves 4.*

½ cup (125 ml) lentils
½ cup (125 ml) navy beans
2 large onions
1½ pounds (675 g) red peppers—
    about 4 large ones
3 tablespoons butter

4 cups (1 liter) unsalted stock or
    water
4 tablespoons tomato paste
Sea salt
Sugar

Put the lentils and beans into a bowl and cover generously with cold water; leave them to soak for several hours or overnight, then drain and rinse them.

Peel and chop the onions; slice the peppers, discarding the cores and seeds. Melt the butter in a large saucepan and sauté the onion for about 10 minutes to soften it; then add the red peppers and cook for another 4–5 minutes before stirring in the drained lentils and beans and the stock or water. Bring the mixture to the boil and let it simmer gently, half covered, until the beans are tender, for about 1 hour.

Mix in the tomato paste, and some salt and sugar to taste. If the stew still seems a bit runny, turn up the heat and boil it for a few minutes without the lid on until it's the right consistency.

◆——————◆——————◆

MIXED VEGETABLE STEW

RUMANIA

Unlike so many stews, this one, *ghiveci*, does not contain meat but is just a gloriously colorful mixture of every sort of vegetable you can find. You can really use whatever is available.

In the early autumn I make it with the first of the parsnips, celery, and leeks, and the last of the zucchini, and serve it with baked potatoes. As the season progresses I replace the zucchini with turnip, and at the end of the cooking time I may stir in some cooked lima beans, kidney beans, or even, I'm ashamed to admit, some baked beans to make it more filling for the cold weather.

When preparing the vegetables, try to cut them up into sizes that will allow them all to cook in about the same amount of time. *Serves 4.*

2 tablespoons oil
2 large onions, peeled and sliced
2 celery stalks, washed and chopped
½ pound (225 g) carrots, scraped and sliced
½ pound (225 g) parsnips, peeled and diced
½ pound (225 g) zucchini, seeded and cut into chunks
1 pound (450 g) leeks, washed, trimmed and cut into 1-inch (2.5 cm) pieces

3 large tomatoes, peeled and quartered
1 pound (450 g) potatoes, peeled and cut into chunks
4 tablespoons all-purpose flour
2½ cups (625 ml) water or stock
2 tablespoons tomato paste
2 bay leaves
1 clove garlic, peeled and crushed
Sea salt
Freshly ground black pepper

Heat the oil in a large saucepan and sauté the onion for 5 minutes; then put in the celery, carrots, parsnips, zucchini, leeks, tomatoes, and potatoes, and cook for a further 4–5 minutes stirring them often to prevent sticking. Then sprinkle the flour over the vegetables and mix gently to distribute it. Pour in the water or stock, stirring, and add the tomato paste, bay leaves, garlic, and a seasoning of salt and pepper. Bring the mixture to the boil, then turn the heat down, leaving the stew to simmer very gently, covered, for about 25–30 minutes, or until the potatoes and other vegetables are tender. Taste the mixture and add more seasoning if necessary.

I often serve this with a bowl of grated cheese or roasted sunflower seeds (just spread the sunflower seeds on a baking sheet and bake for about 10 minutes in a moderate oven) for people to sprinkle over the top of their portion—but it's really very nice just as it is. If you don't serve the cheese or sunflower seeds, though, and you want to add protein to the meal, the best way is to serve a dessert such as yogurt, cheesecake, or even *pashka*—or just finish with a dessert cheese.

MUSHROOMS AND TOFU

CHINA

Tofu, or bean curd, is creamy white and extremely high in protein. It is sold in small squares in Chinese-food shops and now that *tofu* is gaining in popularity, even in your regular grocery store. If you can buy or mail-order dried Chinese mushrooms, they give the dish an excellent flavor, but you can use ordinary fresh mushrooms instead. *Serves 2–4 depending on the size of portions.*

6 dried Chinese mushrooms or
   fresh mushrooms
8 squares of tofu
Vegetable or sesame oil
1 onion, peeled and chopped
1 clove garlic, peeled and crushed
1 piece of fresh ginger root,
   about 1 inch (2.5 cm) long,
   peeled and grated

½ teaspoon soy sauce
½ teaspoon vegetable-flavored
   instant bouillon granules
2 tablespoons water or liquid
   drained from the dried
   mushrooms
½ cup (125 ml) slivered almonds

If you're using dried mushrooms, rinse them under the tap, put them into a small bowl, cover them with boiling water, and leave them for 1 hour. Drain the mushrooms, reserving the liquid. Cut the mushrooms into pieces. If you're using fresh mushrooms, wash and slice them. Cut the *tofu* into smallish cubes, heat a little oil in a large saucepan, and sauté the *tofu* quickly until it is lightly browned on all sides. Take it out of the oil and keep it warm. Heat a little more oil in the saucepan and sauté the onions for about 5 minutes, adding the garlic, ginger, and mushrooms. Keep cooking the mixture until the mushrooms are just tender. Stir in the soy sauce, stock powder, and water or mushroom liquid. Let the mixture bubble for a moment or two, then put in the *tofu* and cook gently for about 2 minutes, just to reheat the *tofu* and give it a chance to absorb the flavors of the sauce. Sprinkle the almonds over the mixture just before serving it.

Serve this with fluffy cooked rice and Chinese cabbage; or include it as part of a selection of Chinese dishes.

◆———◆———◆

SPLIT PEA (PEASE) PUDDING

GREAT BRITAIN

Pease pudding is one of the few vegetarian traditional British dishes. Mrs. Beeton (*Mrs. Beeton's Cookery*, a classic English cookbook) describes it as "an exceedingly nice accompaniment to boiled beef" but I think it also makes a very good main dish in its own right. It's quick to make, high in fiber and protein, low in fat and cholesterol, and very economical too. We like it with crisp roast potatoes, a vegetable such as Brussels sprouts, a savory brown gravy, and some mint sauce or applesauce, which gives a pleasant sharpness that's just right with the sweet-tasting peas. *Serves 4.*

16 ounces (480 g) dried yellow split peas	3 tablespoons butter or margarine
2 large onions	Sea salt
	Freshly ground black pepper

If possible, soak the peas in cold water for a couple of hours or so—this speeds up the cooking time—then drain and rinse them, put them into a large saucepan with a good covering of cold water, and simmer them gently, with the lid half on the saucepan, until they're tender. I find the cooking time of split peas seems to vary quite a bit: sometimes they're done in 30 minutes; other times they can take as long as an hour. Watch the water level and add more, if necessary, as they cook; when they're done drain off any excess—they should be soft but not soggy.

While this is happening, peel and chop the onions and sauté them gently in the butter until they're soft and golden, about 10 minutes. Add the onion to the split peas and season with salt and pepper. You can serve the mixture straight away or keep it warm in a covered casserole in a low oven.

You can vary pease pudding in quite a few ways. It's nice with grated lemon rind added, or chopped marjoram or sage. Caraway, cumin, and fennel seeds also go well with it—add them to the onion when it's nearly done—and a pinch of ground cloves is nice, too.

◆———◆———◆

POTATO BAKE

HOLLAND

A simple savory dish that's particularly useful for children's suppers because it's quick to make and popular. It's nice with grilled tomatoes and a green vegetable. A parsley or tomato sauce goes well with it too. *Serves 4.*

2 pounds (900 g) potatoes	2 eggs
2 tablespoons butter or margarine	⅔ cup (160 ml) milk
2 tablespoons grated Parmesan	Sea salt
cheese	Freshly ground black pepper
½ cup (125 ml) grated Edam	
cheese	

Preheat oven to 375° F (190° C). Peel the potatoes, cut them into even-size pieces, and boil them until they're tender; then drain and mash them. Add the butter or margarine, the Parmesan and half the Edam, and mix well. Beat the eggs and milk together and gradually add this to the potato mixture, stirring well. Season with salt and pepper. Spoon the mixture into a shallow ovenproof dish, sprinkling the remaining grated cheese on top, and bake for 30–40 minutes, until slightly puffed up and golden brown.

POTATO AND MUSHROOM STEW
WITH SOUR CREAM

HUNGARY

A Hungarian stew, or *paprikas*, as it's called, doesn't always contain meat but can be based on vegetables, as in this version, which makes a lovely vegetarian main dish. The protein can be supplied by serving a protein appetizer or dessert, or by garnishing the *paprikas* with wedges of hard-boiled egg or grated cheese. *Serves 4.*

2 pounds (900 g) potatoes
1 medium-size onion
1 clove garlic
3 tablespoons oil
1 tablespoon paprika
¼–½ pound (115–225 g) fresh
* mushrooms*

4 tablespoons all-purpose flour
2 cups (500 ml) vegetable stock
Sea salt
Black pepper
½ cup (125 ml) sour cream or
* plain yogurt*

Peel the potatoes and cut them into even-size chunks; peel and chop the onion; peel and crush the garlic; wash the mushrooms and cut them into halves or quarters. Heat the oil in a large saucepan and sauté the onion for about 5 minutes, or until golden; then stir in the garlic, potatoes, paprika (Hungarian has more taste), and flour; and cook for another minute or two. Add the stock and bring to the boil. Cover the saucepan and leave over a gentle heat for about 20 minutes, until the potatoes are very nearly tender; then add the mushrooms and cook for another 3–4 minutes. Season to taste with salt and pepper.

Put the sour cream or yogurt into a small bowl and gradually add to it a ladleful of the liquid from the saucepan; mix well. Slowly pour this into the saucepan and heat gently until the mixture is very hot. Serve immediately.

RATATOUILLE

F R A N C E

In the late summer when zucchini, eggplant, peppers, and tomatoes are cheap and plentiful, ratatouille makes a delicious vegetarian meal. You can serve it with lots of plain, fluffy brown rice and a crisp green salad with fresh herbs in it; with a protein first course such as individual cheese soufflés; little coffee custards or ice cream for dessert; or crisp whole-wheat biscuits and Brie cheese. *Serves 4.*

1 pound (450 g) zucchini	*2 finely chopped red or green*
1 pound (450 g) eggplant	*peppers*
Salt	*4 tomatoes*
2 large onions	*Sea salt*
Olive oil or vegetable oil—or a	*Freshly ground black pepper*
mixture	*Fresh parsley*
2 large cloves garlic	

Dice the zucchini and eggplant. Put the small cubes into a colander and sprinkle with salt. Place a plate with a weight on it on top and leave for at least a half hour for any bitter liquids to be drawn out of the eggplant and excess moisture out of the zucchini. Rinse the salt away and pat the vegetables dry.

Peel and slice the onions and sauté them in a little oil in a big saucepan until they're beginning to get soft; then add the garlic. Slice the peppers and remove the seeds; add the sliced pepper to the onions and garlic, together with the eggplant and zucchini. Cook gently, with a lid on the pan, for about 30 minutes. Add the tomatoes, skinned and chopped, and cook for another 30 minutes. Season with salt and pepper and sprinkle with chopped parsley.

RED CABBAGE AND CHESTNUT CASSEROLE

F R A N C E

Real warming winter food this, a rich burgundy-colored casserole of succulent red cabbage and sweet-tasting chestnuts cooked with butter, onions, and red wine. It's lovely served as a main dish with baked potatoes that have been split and filled with sour cream and chopped chives. Leftovers are very good as a cold salad. I rather lazily tend to use dried chestnuts but you could use fresh ones. You'll need about a pound (450 g) for this recipe. Prepare them in the way I've described on page 6, and add them to the casserole with the wine and seasoning. *Serves 3–4.*

¼ pound (115 g) dried chestnuts	*⅔ cup (160 ml) dry red wine*
1 large onion	*Sea salt*
4 tablespoons butter	*Freshly ground black pepper*
1½ pounds (675 g) red cabbage	*Sugar*

Cover the chestnuts with plenty of cold water and leave them to soak for several hours. Cook them gently until they're tender—this will take 1–1½ hours and you'll need to watch the level of the water and probably add some more so that they don't burn dry. Drain the chestnuts.

Preheat the oven to 300° F (150° C). Peel and chop the onion and sauté in the butter for 10 minutes; meanwhile, wash and shred the cabbage, add this to the onion, and turn the mixture so that everything is coated with the butter. Stir in the chestnuts, wine, and salt and pepper to taste. Bring the mixture to the boil, transfer it to an oven-proof casserole, cover, and bake slowly for 2–3 hours, until the cabbage is very tender. Check the seasoning—you'll probably need to add more salt and pepper and some sugar to bring out the flavor.

This dish can be made in advance and reheated—in fact I think this actually improves the flavor—and it can also be cooked at the bottom of a hotter oven if you want to bake potatoes at the same time.

RED KIDNEY BEAN STEW

BULGARIA

This stew is lovely with buttery brown rice, baked potatoes or creamy mashed potatoes, and a lightly cooked green vegetable. If you're pressed for time, you can use canned red kidney beans. *Serves 4.*

1 cup (250 ml) dried red kidney | Sea salt
  beans | Freshly ground black pepper
1 pound (450 g) onions | Sugar
4 tablespoons butter
2 cans (16 ounces/480 g each)
  tomatoes

Soak the kidney beans for 2–3 hours in plenty of cold water; drain and rinse them. Put the beans into a saucepan with a good covering of cold water and simmer them gently until they're tender. Drain the beans—you won't need the liquid for this recipe.

While the beans are cooking, peel and chop the onions and sauté them in the butter in a good-size saucepan for about 10 minutes, until they're soft but not browned. Add the tomatoes and beans to the onions with a good seasoning of salt, pepper, and a little sugar if desired. Let the mixture simmer gently for 10–15 minutes before serving.

RED PEPPERS WITH TOMATOES AND ONIONS

ITALY

This Italian dish, *peperonata*, is lovely served with rice, noodles, or potatoes; protein can be introduced in the appetizer, side dish, or dessert, if you wish. *Serves 4.*

1 pound (450 g) red peppers | 1 clove garlic, peeled and crushed
1 pound (450 g) onions | in a little salt (optional)
4 tablespoons oil | Sea salt
1 can (16 ounces/480 g) tomatoes | Freshly ground black pepper

Cut the peppers into even-size pieces, discarding seeds, stalk and core. Peel and slice the onions.

Heat the oil in a large saucepan and sauté the onions for about 5 minutes, or until they're beginning to soften; then add the peppers and cook for a few minutes more, stirring so that everything is coated with the oil. Mix in the tomatoes, garlic if you're using it, and some salt and pepper. Let the mixture simmer gently for about 20 minutes, stirring it from time to time, until all the vegetables are tender.

Some people let the vegetables cook to an almost purée-like consistency, but personally I prefer not to, as I think the flavor is fresher and sweeter and the texture more interesting when the dish is not overcooked.

CORN PUDDING

U S A

This is another of those dishes that's supposed to be served as an accompaniment to meat, but I think you'll agree it also makes a good main dish in its own right. I like to serve it with Brussels sprouts, roast potatoes, and cranberry sauce—rather a bizarre-sounding combination, I know, but it works. *Serves 3–4.*

1 cup (250 ml) milk
2 tablespoons butter
1 cup (250 ml) soft bread crumbs
1 can (17 ounces/510 g) whole
  kernel corn, drained
1 whole egg or 2 egg yolks

1 tablespoon chopped fresh
  parsley
½ teaspoon paprika
Sea salt
Freshly ground black pepper
Grated cheese, to taste

Preheat the oven to 375° F (190° C). Put the milk and butter into a saucepan and heat gently until the butter has melted. Remove from the heat and add the bread crumbs. Leave milk and bread to one side for a few minutes to allow the crumbs to soften; then stir in the corn, egg, parsley, paprika, and salt and pepper to taste. Spoon the mixture into a buttered ovenproof dish and sprinkle with grated cheese. Bake the corn pudding for 35–40 minutes, or until set and golden brown.

TIAN

FRANCE

This is a baked vegetable casserole, rather like a savory loaf except that it is served from the dish. It takes its name from the earthenware casserole dish in which it is cooked in Provence, and it can be made from any green vegetable, although spinach or Swiss chard are the most usual, with zucchini sometimes added too. It can be served hot or cold. If you're having it hot, try it with crunchy roast potatoes, tomato sauce, and a colorful vegetable such as carrots. Cold, it's nice with a garlic mayonnaise, tomato salad, and hot French bread. *Serves 4.*

1 cup (250 ml) brown rice
2 cups (500 ml) water
Sea salt
1 pound (450 g) fresh spinach
2 tablespoons olive oil
2–3 cloves garlic, peeled and
   crushed
1 tablespoon chopped fresh
   parsley

1 cup (250 ml) grated cheese
2 eggs
Freshly ground black pepper
2–3 tablespoons dry bread crumbs
2–3 tablespoons grated Parmesan
   cheese
2 tablespoons olive oil

Wash the rice and then put it into the saucepan with the water and a teaspoonful of salt; bring it to the boil, then turn the heat down and leave the rice to cook very slowly, covered, for 40–45 minutes, until it's tender and all the liquid has been absorbed. (If there's still some water left in the saucepan just leave it to stand off the heat but with the lid on for 10–15 minutes, after which you should find it has been absorbed.)

Preheat the oven to 400° F (200° C). Wash the spinach thoroughly in three changes of water, then chop it up—you can use the stalks too. Heat the olive oil in a large saucepan and put in the spinach, turning it in the hot oil for 2–3 minutes until it has softened slightly and looks glossy. Take it off the heat and add the rice, garlic, parsley, and grated cheese. Beat in the eggs and mix everything together, seasoning with salt and a good grinding of pepper. Spoon the mixture into a shallow ovenproof dish and sprinkle the crumbs, Parmesan, and olive oil on top. Bake uncovered for 30–40 minutes, or until it's puffed up and golden brown and crispy on top.

SPLIT PEA PURÉE WITH VEGETABLES

GERMANY

In Germany this would probably be served as an accompaniment to meat, much as the British serve their pease pudding, but I think it makes a good main dish with baked potatoes. *Serves 4.*

2 cups (500 ml) yellow split peas
4 cups (1 liter) water
3 onions, sliced
2 carrots, sliced
1 leek, sliced
2 celery stalks, sliced

½ teaspoon mint or marjoram
4 teaspoons lemon juice
Sea salt
Freshly ground black pepper
4 tablespoons butter

Soak the split peas in cold water for an hour or two or overnight; rinse them and put them into a pan with the water, half the sliced onion, and all the other vegetables and the herbs, and let everything simmer gently until the split peas are soft and the vegetables tender. This takes 30–40 minutes. Purée in your blender or food processor. Add the lemon juice. Season the mixture with salt and pepper and turn it into a shallow ovenproof dish. Preheat the oven to 350° F (180° C) or preheat the broiler, set fairly high. Sauté the remaining onion in the butter until it's beginning to soften, then pour over the top of the split pea purée, and put it into the oven for 20–30 minutes, or under the broiler until the top is slightly crusted and the onion crisp and brown.

STUFFED
VEGETABLES

Stuffed Eggplant in Béchamel Sauce
Eggplant Stuffed with Cheese
Stuffed Eggplant à la Duxelles
Stuffed Zucchini Bake
Zucchini Stuffed with Cheese and Onion
Stuffed Onions
Stuffed Peppers
Red Cabbage Stuffed with Chestnuts
Tomatoes Stuffed with Cheese
Stuffed Tomatoes à la Provençale
Tomatoes Stuffed with Rice
Stuffed Vine or Cabbage Leaves

I LOVE STUFFED VEGETABLE DISHES BECAUSE THEY always look festive and special, and I think they're ideal for entertaining. Some of them, particularly the eggplant *à la duxelles*, the stuffed eggplant in Béchamel sauce, the red cabbage stuffed with chestnuts, the stuffed zucchini bake, and the stuffed onions make good main courses. Others are more suitable for serving as a first course—I think the stuffed tomatoes and stuffed vine leaves are particularly good for this.

Some of these stuffed vegetables contain a fair amount of protein but others don't, so you may wish to take this into consideration and plan the meal accordingly. If you want to serve one of the low-protein stuffed vegetables, you can add nourishment to the meal very simply by serving the vegetables with a well-flavored cheese sauce or with the green salad with Gruyère cheese. Or of course you can have a protein-rich appetizer or dessert—*hummus* or the Middle Eastern bean dip is particularly good with the Greek recipes, with ground rice and rosewater pudding, yogurt tart, or honey cheesecake as suggestions for dessert; or, for the French recipes, *coeurs à la crème* or little coffee custards; and coffee ricotta or ice cream after the Italian ones.

With the exception of the red cabbage, which needs a good deep saucepan or flameproof dish big enough to hold the whole cabbage, the stuffed vegetables need to be cooked in a large, shallow ovenproof dish. I find one measuring about 11 × 7 inches (28 × 18 cm) is just right for recipes serving 4 people; when I'm doing recipes that serve 6 people, I use an oval Pyrex one measuring about 15½ × 10½ inches (39 × 27 cm). It looks vast and institutional when it's empty, but it's just right and looks super when it's filled with delicious vegetables bursting with tasty stuffings. I've also seen some lovely large shallow French ovenproof dishes in deep muted shades, and one of these would look even better.

STUFFED EGGPLANT IN BÉCHAMEL SAUCE

GREECE

Really, ground meat is traditionally used for this recipe, and you might feel that the lentils I've suggested are rather a corruption. But, as lentils are used so much in Middle Eastern cookery, I don't think they're too far-fetched, and they do make a tasty and satisfying dish. *Serves 6.*

3 medium-size eggplants—about
  1½ pounds (675 g) in all
Salt
3–4 tablespoons oil
2 medium-size onions, peeled and
  chopped
3 tablespoons tomato paste
3 cloves garlic, peeled and crushed
  in a little salt

1 cup (250 ml) lentils
1 cup (250 ml) water
2 tablespoons chopped fresh
  parsley
1½ cups (180 ml) grated cheese,
  divided
Sea salt
Freshly ground black pepper

FOR THE SAUCE:

4 tablespoons butter
4 tablespoons all-purpose flour
2 cups (500 ml) milk

1 egg
Nutmeg

Cut the eggplants in half lengthwise and then scoop out the centers to leave space for the stuffing; chop up the scooped-out flesh and sprinkle it and the inside of the skins with salt. Leave for half an hour, then squeeze out the bitter brown juice, rinse the eggplant flesh and skins with water, and pat dry. Heat 3 tablespoons of oil in a skillet and sauté the eggplant shells for about 5 minutes on each side to soften them; drain them and put into a shallow ovenproof dish. Preheat oven to 350° F (180° C). Sauté the onion in the same saucepan, adding a little more oil if necessary; when it is soft but not brown—about 10 minutes—add the eggplant flesh, tomato paste, garlic, lentils, and water and cook for 20–30 minutes, until the lentils are done. Remove from the heat, add the parsley and ¾ cup of the grated cheese, and season carefully with salt and pepper to taste. Divide the filling among the eggplant shells, piling it up well.

To make the Béchamel sauce, melt the butter in a saucepan and stir in the flour; then add a third of the milk and stir over a fairly high heat until the mixture is smooth and thick; repeat the process twice more using the rest of the milk. Remove from the heat and beat in the egg and grated nutmeg to taste. Pour the sauce over the stuffed eggplant, sprinkle with the remaining ½ cup of the grated cheese, and bake them in the oven for 35 minutes, or until they're tender and the sauce is bubbly and golden brown.

This dish is especially nice served with a crisp green salad with herbs or a cooked green vegetable.

EGGPLANT STUFFED WITH CHEESE

YUGOSLAVIA

This is a simple but delicious way of serving this versatile vegetable. I think a tomato sauce goes well with it, and also something crisp— triangles of toast, for instance, or crunchy roast potatoes. *Serves 4.*

4 medium-size eggplants—about 1½ pounds (675 g) in all	*1½ cups (375 ml) grated cheese*
Sea salt	*1 egg*
2 tablespoons butter	*1 tablespoon chopped fresh parsley*
1 onion, peeled and finely chopped	*Freshly ground black pepper*

Preheat oven to 400° F (200° C). Wash the eggplant and remove the stalk ends. Fill half a good-size saucepan with cold water, add a teaspoonful of salt, and bring to the boil. Cook the eggplant in the water for about 5 minutes, until they feel just barely tender when pierced with the point of a knife. Drain and cool them, split them in half lengthwise, and scoop the flesh out into a bowl, leaving the skins intact.

Arrange the skins in a lightly oiled, shallow ovenproof dish. Mash the eggplant flesh with a fork, then stir in the onion, grated cheese, egg, parsley, and salt and pepper to taste. Bake the eggplant for 30–40 minutes, until they're golden brown.

STUFFED EGGPLANT À LA DUXELLES

FRANCE

If you chop up very finely an onion and some mushrooms, and cook them slowly in a little butter until they make a thick, dry purée-like mixture, you have what the French call *duxelles*. It will keep in a screw-top jar, ready for flavoring soups and sauces, but in this recipe the whole amount is used to give the eggplant a rich mushroomy flavor.

This dish is nice served with a wine or tomato sauce, and new potatoes or *gratin dauphinois*. There isn't much protein in the egg-plant mixture itself, though, so you may want to serve a protein-rich first course, such as individual cheese soufflés, or round off the meal with nourishing *coeurs à la crème* or little coffee custards for dessert. *Serves 4.*

1 pound (450 g) fresh mushrooms	1 cup (250 ml) cottage cheese or
1 onion	low-fat ricotta
2 tablespoons butter	Freshly ground black pepper
2 medium-size eggplants	½ cup (125 ml) grated Parmesan
Sea salt	cheese
Oil	½ cup (125 ml) fine bread crumbs
2 tablespoons chopped fresh	
parsley	

To prepare the *duxelles*, wash the mushrooms, and then chop them finely; peel and finely chop the onion. Put the chopped mushrooms and onion into a cloth and squeeze firmly to extract excess liquid—this can be saved and added to a soup or a sauce. Melt the butter in a large saucepan, stir in the chopped mushroom and onion, and sauté, uncovered, until the mixture is thick, dry, and purée-like—15–20 minutes. Remove from the heat.

While the *duxelles* is cooking start preparing the eggplant: Cut them in half lengthwise and scoop out the centers to form cavities for stuffing. Sprinkle the scooped-out flesh and the insides of the shells with salt, and leave them to one side for about 30 minutes for the bitter juices to be extracted. Then squeeze the liquid out of the egg-plant, rinse it under cold water, and pat dry.

Preheat the oven to 350° F (180° C). Sauté the eggplant shells on both sides in hot oil, then drain them and put them into a shallow ovenproof dish, ready for stuffing. Sauté the scooped-out eggplant flesh in a couple of tablespoons of oil for about 5 minutes, then add the *duxelles*, chopped parsley, cottage cheese or ricotta, and most of the Parmesan. Taste the mixture and season as necessary, pile it into the prepared shells, and sprinkle the tops with the bread crumbs and remaining grated Parmesan. Cover the dish with foil and bake for about 40 minutes, removing the foil for the last 10 minutes so that the crumbs get crisp.

STUFFED ZUCCHINI BAKE

S P A I N

In this dish zucchini are filled with a mixture of tomatoes, onion, and garlic, then baked in a well-flavored cheese sauce. It's best to use fairly large zucchini, as these hold the filling well. *Serves 4.*

4 medium-size zucchini—about 1½ pounds (675 g) in all
2 large onions
4 tablespoons butter
1 pound (450 g) tomatoes, peeled,

or 1 can (16 ounces/480 g) tomatoes
2 cloves garlic
Sea salt
Freshly ground black pepper

FOR THE SAUCE:

4 tablespoons butter
4 tablespoons all-purpose flour
2½ cups (625 ml) milk

¾ cup (280 ml) grated Parmesan cheese

Preheat oven to 375° F (190° C). Peel the zucchini, cut them in half lengthwise, and scoop out the seeds with a teaspoon. Cook the zucchini in ½ inch (1 cm) boiling water for 5–10 minutes, or until they're just tender, but don't let them get soggy. Drain the cooked vegetable well and pat dry with paper toweling. Leave the zucchini to one side while you prepare the filling and make the sauce.

To make the filling, peel and chop the onions and sauté them in the butter in a medium-size saucepan for 10 minutes. Remove the seeds from the tomatoes and chop the flesh. If you're using canned tomatoes drain off the juice—you won't need it for this recipe. Peel the garlic and crush it in a little salt. Add the garlic to the onions, together with the tomatoes, and cook the mixture for a further 10–15 minutes, until it is fairly thick and will hold its shape. Season with salt and pepper.

While the tomato mixture is cooking, make the sauce: Melt the butter in a medium-size saucepan and stir in the flour; cook for a moment or two, and then pour in a third of the milk. Stir over a fairly high heat until the milk is incorporated and the mixture has become very thick and smooth; then repeat with the rest of the milk, adding it in two installments. When you have added all the milk and have a smooth sauce, take the saucepan off the heat and stir in the grated Parmesan cheese and salt and pepper to taste.

Pour half the sauce into a shallow ovenproof dish and arrange the zucchini halves on top. Spoon the tomato mixture into the cavities and pour the remaining sauce on top. Sprinkle with grated cheese and bake on the top rack of the oven for about 40–45 minutes, until the mixture is bubbly and golden brown on top. Serve at once. They're nice with buttery new potatoes, rice or noodles, and a green vegetable such as spinach, with fresh fruit for dessert.

◆——◆——◆

ZUCCHINI STUFFED WITH CHEESE AND ONION

CARIBBEAN

This is a simple dish combining tender zucchini and a delicious crisp cheese topping. It's a good recipe for dieters if you cook the onions in a minimum of butter in a non-stick saucepan and use Edam cheese. On the other hand, for a special occasion it's delicious with a couple of tablespoons of white wine added. *Serves 4.*

4 large zucchini—about 6 ounces (180 g) each	*1 clove garlic, peeled and crushed*
4 tablespoons butter	*2 cups (750 ml) grated cheese*
2 large onions, peeled and chopped	*½ teaspoon dried thyme*
	Sea salt
	Freshly ground black pepper

Preheat oven to 375° F (190° C). Wash the zucchini thoroughly, then cut them in half lengthwise. Heat ½ inch (1 cm) of water in a large saucepan. When it boils add the zucchini halves and simmer them gently for about 3 minutes, just to soften them a little, then drain them well. Using a teaspoon, scoop out the center of the zucchini to leave a cavity for stuffing. Chop up the scooped-out zucchini center.

Melt the butter in a medium-size saucepan and sauté the onion for 5 minutes; then add the garlic and chopped zucchini flesh, and cook for a further 4–5 minutes. Remove the saucepan from the heat and stir in the grated cheese. thyme, and salt and pepper to taste. Oil or butter a shallow oblong dish and arrange the zucchini halves in it. Divide the onion and cheese mixture among the zucchini shells. Bake in the pre-heated oven for 20–30 minutes, until the shells are tender and the filling is golden brown.

Serve with fresh tomato sauce. New potatoes and spinach or green beans complement this dish, too.

STUFFED ONIONS

ITALY

Onions, macaroons, cheese, and sultanas sound a very strange mixture, but the combination of sweet and savory really works well (like cheese and chutney or curry and banana). I especially like to use big Spanish onions when making this dish. *Serves 4.*

4 large Spanish onions	½ cup (125 ml) grated Parmesan
4 macaroons	cheese
2 cups (500 ml) soft whole-wheat	⅓ cup (80 ml) sultanas
bread crumbs	(golden raisins)
¼ teaspoon ground cinnamon	Sea salt
¼ teaspoon ground cloves	Freshly ground black pepper
¼ teaspoon grated nutmeg	1 tablespoon butter
2 eggs, beaten	

Rinse the onions but don't peel them. Put them into a large saucepan of water and simmer them for about 20 minutes, until they feel tender when pierced with the point of a knife. (They should not be com-pletely cooked through at this stage.) Drain the onions and let them get cool enough to handle, then remove the skins and root ends, and cut the onions in half horizontally. Scoop out the center of each half, making a nice cavity for the stuffing and leaving three or four layers of onion. Arrange the onion halves in an oiled or buttered shallow ovenproof dish.

Preheat oven to 350° F (180° C). Now make the stuffing. Chop the scooped-out onion fairly finely and put it into a bowl. Crush the macaroons—press them with a rolling pin or pop them into the blender for a moment or two; add them to the onions. Now stir in the bread crumbs, spices, eggs, cheese, and sultanas until everything is well mixed to a softish consistency. You might need to add a drop or two of milk but I usually find the natural juiciness of the onions, together with the eggs, sufficient. Season with salt and a good grinding of pepper, and spoon the mixture into the onion cavities. Put a piece of butter on top of each and bake them, uncovered, for 30 minutes.

STUFFED PEPPERS

S P A I N

In this recipe bell peppers are stuffed with rice, mushrooms, onions, and grated cheese and baked in a simple fresh tomato sauce. They're nice as a main course, served with buttery new potatoes. *Serves 4.*

½ cup (120 ml) brown rice	1 teaspoon dried thyme
1 cup (250 ml) water	½ teaspoon mustard powder
Sea salt	2 teaspoons lemon juice
2 medium-size green peppers	1 cup (250 ml) grated cheese
1 large onion, peeled and chopped	Freshly ground black pepper
1 clove garlic, peeled and crushed in a little salt	1 pound (450 g) tomatoes, peeled and chopped—or 1 can
4 tablespoons olive oil	(16 ounces/480 g) tomatoes
¼ pound (125 g) mushrooms, washed and finely sliced	

To cook the rice, put it into a heavy-bottomed saucepan with the water and a pinch of salt. Bring it to the boil and then turn the heat down and let it cook very gently, covered, for about 40 minutes, until the rice is tender and has absorbed all the liquid. (The rice can be cooked well in advance because it will keep for several days in the fridge.)

Preheat oven to 350° F (180° C). Halve the peppers, remove the center and seeds, and rinse them under the cold tap. Put the peppers into a saucepan half full of cold water and bring it to the boil. Take the peppers off the heat, drain them, and leave to one side.

Sauté the onion and garlic in the oil for 10 minutes. Mix half the onion and garlic with the cooked rice, and add the mushrooms, thyme, mustard, lemon juice, grated cheese, and a good seasoning of salt and pepper.

Mix the tomatoes with the remaining onion and garlic in the pan, and add salt and pepper to taste. Pour the tomato mixture into a shallow ovenproof dish and place the peppers on top. Spoon the rice mixture into the peppers, piling it up well. Bake the peppers, uncovered, for about 40 minutes, until the stuffing is golden brown and the peppers tender.

RED CABBAGE STUFFED WITH CHESTNUTS

FRANCE

The sweetness of chestnuts goes particularly well with red cabbage and, if you add butter and red wine too, you get a really rich-tasting, warming dish, just right for winter, when chestnuts and cabbage are in season. This dish is low in protein, however, so it's a good idea to follow it with a protein-rich dessert, such as *crème brûlée* or rice and almond pudding. *Serves 6.*

1½ pounds (675 g) fresh chestnuts
   or ½ pound (225 g) dried
   chestnuts
1 small/medium red cabbage,
   about 3 pounds (1¼ k)
8 tablespoons butter
2 large onions, peeled and
   chopped

1 tablespoon lemon juice
Sea salt
Freshly ground black pepper
2 carrots, peeled and sliced
1 tablespoon red currant jelly
1¼ cups (310 ml) dry red wine

First prepare the chestnuts. If you're using fresh ones, slash each one with a sharp knife and simmer them for about 10 minutes, or until the cuts open and you can remove the skins using a small, sharp knife. Keep the rest of the chestnuts in the hot water as you work because the skins get hard again as they cool. If you've decided to save time by using dried chestnuts, as I must admit I usually do, let them soak in some cold water for a while if possible—this isn't essential but it helps as they can be very hard sometimes. Then simmer them gently in plenty of water for at least an hour, until they're tender, and then drain them.

Now wash and trim the cabbage, removing any tough or damaged leaves and cutting the stalk end level. Slice a lid from the top of the cabbage and, using a small sharp knife and a spoon, scoop out as much of the inside of the cabbage as possible, leaving a neat, good-size cavity for stuffing. Chop the cabbage that you've scooped out fairly finely. Heat half the butter in a largish saucepan and sauté half the onion for about 5 minutes, without browning; then stir in the chopped-up cabbage and cook for 5 minutes, covered, stirring occasionally. Add the chestnuts and half the lemon juice and season with salt and pepper. Leave to one side. Put the whole cabbage into a large saucepan filled half way with cold water. Bring to the boil, then reduce heat and simmer for 2 minutes, covered. Drain and rinse the cabbage under cold water.

Melt the remaining butter in a saucepan that's large enough to hold the cabbage, and sauté the remaining onion and the carrots for 5 minutes. Mix the red currant jelly and the rest of the lemon juice with the onion and carrots, add some salt and pepper, and then place the cabbage on top and carefully fill the cavity with the chestnut mixture, piling it up high. Pour the wine around the sides of the cabbage, put the saucepan over a low heat, and cover. Leave it to cook very gently for about 3 hours, or until the cabbage feels beautifully tender when pierced with the point of a knife.

It's easiest to serve this straight from the cooking pot, hearty country-style, and is delicious with really light mashed potatoes.

TOMATOES STUFFED WITH CHEESE

PORTUGAL

These juicy tomatoes with their cheesy bread-crumb stuffing make a delicious hot first course or light supper dish for late summer when tomatoes are plentiful. *Serves 4.*

8 large tomatoes—about
   1½ pounds (675 g) in all
Sea salt
3 cups (750 ml) loosely packed,
   soft whole-wheat bread crumbs

2 cups (500 ml) grated cheese
1 clove garlic, peeled and crushed
Freshly ground black pepper
1 tablespoon olive oil

Preheat oven to 375° F (190° C). Halve the tomatoes and scoop out the centers. Sprinkle a little salt inside each tomato and put them upside down on a plate to drain off any excess liquid while you make the filling. Chop the tomato centers and mix them with the bread crumbs, grated cheese, and garlic. Season with salt and pepper to taste. Arrange the tomato halves in a shallow oiled dish. Pile the stuffing mixture into the tomato halves and sprinkle the olive oil on top. Bake the tomatoes for 20–30 minutes, until they're tender and the filling is golden brown.

   They're nice served with creamy mashed potatoes, buttered noodles, or brown rice, and a cooked green vegetable or crisp green salad.

STUFFED TOMATOES À LA PROVENÇALE

FRANCE

These tomatoes, with their herb and garlic flavored stuffing, make a very good first course, but if you serve them with some buttery noodles or rice and a sharp cheese sauce, they also make an excellent lunch or supper, with a crisp green salad to accompany them. *Serves 4.*

8 large tomatoes—about
   1½ pounds (675 g) in all
Sea salt
1 large onion
⅔ cup (160 ml) olive oil
4 cloves garlic, peeled and crushed

2 cups (500 ml) soft fine fresh
   whole-wheat bread crumbs
4 tablespoons chopped fresh
   parsley
½ teaspoon dried thyme
Freshly ground black pepper

Cut a thin slice off the top of each tomato and leave these slices to one side to use as lids later. Using a teaspoon, scoop out the tomato pulp to leave a cavity for stuffing (you won't need the pulp for this recipe, but it can be used to flavor sauces and soups). Sprinkle the inside of each tomato with a little salt and then turn them upside down on a large plate and leave them while you prepare the filling.

Peel and finely chop the onion. Heat the olive oil in a large skillet and sauté the onion until it's golden; then take it off the heat and add the garlic, bread crumbs, herbs, and a good seasoning of salt and pepper.

Preheat oven to 400° F (200° C). Place the tomatoes in a lightly oiled baking dish; fill each with some of the stuffing mixture and arrange the reserved lids on top.

Bake the stuffed tomatoes for 15–20 minutes, to heat them right through, and then serve them at once.

◆——◆——◆

TOMATOES STUFFED WITH RICE

GREECE

Like the stuffed tomatoes in the previous recipe, these can be served either as a first or main course. If you're making them your main dish, I think it's a good idea to start off with a first course like *hummus* and finish with the yogurt tart or special ground rice, all of which add protein to the meal and continue the Middle Eastern theme. *Serves 4.*

½ cup (120 ml) brown rice
1 cup (250 ml) water
Sea salt
8 large tomatoes—about
    1½ pounds (675 g) in all
2 tablespoons olive oil
1 medium-size onion, peeled and
    chopped
2 cloves garlic, peeled and
    crushed

6 tablespoons tomato paste
6 tablespoons chopped fresh
    parsley
2 tablespoons chopped fresh mint
Pinch of oregano
Freshly ground black pepper
⅔ cup (160 ml) stock—or dry red
    wine is delicious

Put the rice (washed or not, depending on the state in which you are able to buy it) into a heavy-bottomed saucepan with the water and a little salt; bring it to the boil and then turn the heat right down, putting a lid on the saucepan and cooking the rice very gently for about 40 minutes, until it's tender and all the water has been absorbed.

While the rice is cooking prepare the tomatoes. Cut a small piece off the top of each and hollow out the center, using a teaspoon; keep the sliced-off tomato tops to use as lids later. Sprinkle some salt inside each tomato and then leave them upside down to drain.

Preheat oven to 350° F (180° C). Next make the stuffing. Heat the oil in a fairly large saucepan and sauté the onion until it's beginning to soften—about 5 minutes. Then add the garlic, rice, scooped-out tomato pulp, half the tomato paste, the herbs, and seasoning. Cook over a high heat until the mixture is fairly dry. Arrange the tomatoes in an oiled ovenproof dish, fill them with the stuffing, and put the slices back as lids. Mix the remaining tomato paste with the stock or red wine and a little salt and pepper and pour it around the tomatoes. Bake them for about 20 minutes, or until they're tender.

A cheese sauce goes well with these, and a crisp green salad.

STUFFED VINE OR CABBAGE LEAVES

GREECE

These *dolmades,* or little leafy parcels of rosemary-flavored rice with nuts and raisins, can be served hot or cold. If you're serving them cold —as is frequently done in Greece—you can omit the sauce and just bake them in some seasoned tomato juice or a mixture of tomato paste and stock. This is really the more authentic preparation, but I'm giving my version too, which has a flour-thickened sauce because I've found this is the most popular. I also like to finish them off with a crunchy topping of crumbs and grated cheese, but this isn't very Greek either, so you might prefer just to sprinkle them with chopped parsley after cooking.

I think the *dolmades* are very much better served hot, with a crisp green salad and dry white wine to drink. The *dolmades* also make rather a nice, unusual hot appetizer if you bake them in individual ovenproof dishes. *Serves 3–4 as a main course, 4–6 as an appetizer.*

36 fresh or canned vine leaves; or
    about 18 cabbage leaves
1 large onion
2 tablespoons olive oil
2 cups (500 ml) cooked brown rice
1 teaspoon fresh rosemary,
    chopped, or ½ teaspoon dried
½ cup (125 ml) chopped mixed
    nuts

⅓ cup (80 ml) raisins
Sea salt
Freshly ground black pepper
1½ cups (375 ml) soft whole-
    wheat bread crumbs and
½ cup (125 ml) grated cheese; or
A little fresh parsley

FOR THE SAUCE:

4 tablespoons butter
4 tablespoons all-purpose
    flour

2½ cups (675 ml) water or
    vegetable stock
2 tablespoons tomato paste

If you're using fresh vine leaves or cabbage leaves, first of all fill a large saucepan halfway with water and bring it to the boil. Trim the leaves, removing the tough cabbage stalks with a 'V' shaped cut, and put them into the boiling water; cover and simmer for 2 minutes. Then drain them and run them under the cold tap to refresh them; drain well. With canned vine leaves, just drain them and rinse them well under the cold tap.

Preheat oven to 350°F (180°C). Make the filling by peeling and chopping the onion and sautéeing it in the olive oil for 10 minutes; don't let it brown; then stir in the rice, rosemary, nuts, raisins, and salt and pepper to taste. Mix well, then put a spoonful of this filling on each leaf, fold over the edges, and place the little bundles side by side in a shallow ovenproof dish.

To make the sauce, melt the butter in a saucepan and stir in the flour; cook it for a minute or two, then mix in a little of the water, stirring vigorously over a high heat until the mixture is thick and smooth. Then add a bit more water and continue in this manner until all the water has been used and you have a smooth, thick sauce. Then stir in the tomato paste and salt and pepper to taste. Pour this sauce over the stuffed leaves, making sure they are completely covered, then sprinkle them with the crumbs and grated cheese, and bake in the oven for 30 minutes. (If you haven't used the crumb topping, sprinkle the top of the dish with chopped parsley before serving.)

Note: Pine nuts are really the correct nut to use for this dish, but they are so expensive that I use this more economical mixture of chopped mixed nuts (which you can get at any supermarket) and pine-flavored rosemary.

GRAIN, RICE, AND CURRY DISHES

Biriani

Bulgur Wheat Pilaf

Cheese Curry

Couscous

Gnocchi alla Romana

Khitchari

Paella

Red Bean Rice

Fried Rice

Rice and Peas

Rice and Peas with Tomato Sauce

Risotto Bianco

Vegetable Curry

THESE DISHES ARE SATISFYING TO MAKE BECAUSE the grains provide a good basis to which you can add all sorts of colorful and tasty ingredients. The red bean rice from the Caribbean, the vegetarian *paella* from Spain, and the Indian *biriani* are all examples of this, and they're very good to eat.

I use brown rice for all these recipes and I find it perfectly satisfactory. I've found, however, that rice can vary in its ability to absorb water, sometimes needing 2 cups of water to 1 cup of rice and sometimes only 1¾ cups of water, so a little experimentation is probably advisable when you buy a new type. Generally you will be safe, though, if you follow the package directions for any good-quality brown rice.

The other grains used in this section are bulgur wheat, couscous, and semolina. Bulgur is a delightful grain to use. In the packet it looks rather like a very granular semolina, but when you soak it in boiling water for a few minutes it quickly absorbs the water and puffs up to become light and fluffy, and you then simply heat it through. As it's quick, I find it more useful for emergency meals than rice, and in fact it can take the place of boiled rice for serving with vegetable stews and casseroles.

Couscous is a form of coarse-grained semolina and rather like bulgur to look at. You have to sprinkle couscous with cold salted water and allow it time to absorb the water, then steam it for 20–30 minutes. It's nice for a change, served with a spicy sauce. If you can't get couscous, you could use bulgur wheat instead.

Semolina is used in one of the recipes, the tasty cheese *gnocchi* from Italy (and also in one of the dishes in the fritter section). I know people don't always like the idea of serving semolina as a savory dish, but *gnocchi* is cheap and tasty and well worth trying. If you can get whole-wheat semolina, that is ideal—you use it in exactly the same way as ordinary semolina and it isn't too dark-looking when it's cooked.

You will notice that I suggest using *ghee* (clarified butter) in the Indian recipes. This does give a lovely nutty flavor and makes the food taste that much more Indian, but if you haven't got any don't worry, just use butter or vegetable oil instead. If you like Indian food and make it a lot, though, you might like to make your own *ghee*, which is quite easy to do and keeps for 2 or 3 months at room temperature, and longer in the refrigerator.

To make the *ghee*, cut ½ pound (240 ml) unsalted butter into rough pieces and melt it very gently, in a heavy-bottomed saucepan.

Don't let the butter brown. When it has melted, stir it, then let it simmer, uncovered and over a very low heat, for about 45 minutes, or until the solids at the bottom of the melted butter turn golden brown and the butter on top becomes transparent. Strain the *ghee* through a sieve lined with 4 layers of damp muslin. If any of the solids come through, strain the *ghee* again; it must be perfectly clear to keep properly.

If you store the *ghee* in the refrigerator, it will solidify and before using it you will need either to stand the container in a warm place, or to melt the *ghee* in a saucepan, but it will taste just as good.

BIRIANI

I N D I A

This deliciously spicy Indian rice dish is popular in our family. I usually serve it with lots of little bowls of extras for people to add at the table, and the children love helping themselves to these. Favorites include chopped apple, mango chutney, diced cucumber, roasted peanuts, raisins, desiccated coconut, sliced onion, quarters of tomato, and chopped hard-boiled egg. *Serves 4.*

2 cups (500 ml) uncooked brown rice	*2 teaspoons ground coriander*
4 teaspoons turmeric	*2 teaspoons poppy seed*
2 teaspoons sea salt	*2 teaspoons mustard seed*
4 cups (1 liter) water	*½ teaspoon chili powder*
4 onions	*1 can (8 ounces/240 g) tomatoes*
3 tablespoons ghee or	*¼ pound (125 g) green beans or*
6 tablespoons butter	*okra*
2 teaspoons garam masala	*Freshly ground black pepper*

Put the rice, turmeric, sea salt, and water into a heavy-bottomed saucepan and bring to the boil; then turn down the heat, put a lid on the saucepan, and leave the rice to simmer gently for 40 minutes.

While the rice is cooking, peel and chop the onions and sauté them in the *ghee* or butter for 10 minutes, until they're soft and golden but not browned. Stir in the garam masala, coriander, poppy seed, mustard seed, and chili powder, and cook for 2 minutes. Add the tomatoes and cook gently for another 10 minutes. Preheat oven to 350°F (180°C).

When the rice has cooked sufficiently, add the tomato mixture to the saucepan and also the green beans or okra; mix lightly with a fork. Season with salt and pepper. Transfer the mixture to an ovenproof dish and bake the *biriani,* covered, for 20–30 minutes.

Biriani is nice served with curry sauce, a moist side salad and some crunchy golden *poppadums.* A cool, yogurt or some other milky dessert goes well with it and supplies some extra protein.

◆——◆——◆

BULGUR WHEAT PILAF

MIDDLE EAST

You can get bulgur wheat from health-food shops. It looks like a very large-grain semolina and is a pre-cooked cracked wheat. It makes a delicious pilaf and is quick and easy to use. I like it very much as a change from rice and you can make this pilaf the basis of a lovely Middle Eastern-style meal, starting with *hummus* or chilled cucumber soup and ending with the special ground rice pudding. *Serves 3–4.*

1½ cups (375 ml) bulgur wheat	*⅓ cup (80 ml) raisins*
2½ cups (675 ml) boiling water	*Sea salt*
2 large onions	*Freshly ground black pepper*
1–2 cloves garlic	*½–1 cup (125–250 ml) roasted*
1 red pepper	*cashew nuts, almonds, or*
4 tablespoons butter	*pine nuts*

Put the bulgur wheat into a large bowl and cover it with boiling water. Leave it to one side for 15–30 minutes; it will absorb most of the water and swell up.

While the bulgur is soaking, peel and chop the onions, peel and crush the garlic, and chop the pepper, discarding the seeds. Heat the butter in a large saucepan and sauté the onions for 5 minutes, without browning them; then put in the garlic and pepper and sauté gently for another 5 minutes. Drain the bulgur and add it to the onion mixture together with the raisins, stirring over the heat until the bulgur is well coated with butter. Season with salt and pepper to taste. Let the bulgur cook gently for 5–10 minutes, until it's hot.

You can serve the dish at this point, but I think it's even better if you put a lid on the saucepan and let the pilaf stand for another 10–15 minutes, gently cooking in its own heat. Serve it sprinkled with the nuts. You may also wish to stir in 1½–2 cups diced or grated Cheddar cheese; if so, you should add the cheese just before serving, when the dish is piping hot, and eliminate the nut topping if you wish. A green or tomato salad goes well with this dish.

Note: I find you can make the bulgur pilaf in advance and heat it through in a covered casserole in a moderate oven for about 30 minutes, but if you do this it's still best to add the nuts before serving so that they retain their crispness.

CHEESE CURRY

INDIA

In India the cheese for this curry would probably be made at home from yogurt. As this is rather a laborious process, I use white Lancashire or Cheddar cheese instead. You may feel my method is cheating a bit, but I think you'll agree the spicy sauce and melting, creamy cheese make a delicious combination. *Serves 3–4.*

1 large onion	1 bay leaf
2 tablespoons oil, butter or ghee	1¼ cups (310 ml) water
1–2 cloves garlic, peeled and crushed	1 package (10 ounces/300 g) frozen green peas
1 can (8 ounces/240 g) tomatoes	Sea salt
½ teaspoon ground ginger	Freshly ground black pepper
1 teaspoon ground cumin	1½–2 cups (375–500 ml) diced
2 teaspoons ground coriander	Lancashire or Cheddar cheese

Peel or chop the onion and then sauté it in the butter, oil, or *ghee* in a large saucepan for 10 minutes, until it's tender but not browned. Add the garlic, tomatoes, spices, and bay leaf to the onions, mixing everything together thoroughly. Pour in the water and bring to the boil, then turn the heat down, partially cover the saucepan, and leave the mixture to simmer for about 20 minutes. Add the peas and cook for another 3–4 minutes, just to heat them through. Season with salt and pepper. Stir the cheese into the curry just as you are about to serve it. Don't add it too soon or it will melt too much and spoil the curry. Serve with hot cooked rice and mango chutney.

◆———◆———◆

COUSCOUS

MOROCCO

Couscous looks rather like tiny grains of rice, but it's actually made from semolina formed into little pellets. You sprinkle the pellets with salted water and then steam them and serve them with a spicy vegetable stew. In Morocco couscous is cooked in a *couscousier,* but you don't really need any special equipment—I cook mine in a steamer with the vegetable stew cooking in the saucepan below. You could equally well put the couscous into a metal colander, put it on top of the saucepan of vegetables, and cover with a lid or some foil. *Serves 3–4.*

1⅓ cups (300 g) precooked
   couscous
½ teaspoon sea salt dissolved
   in a cupful of warm water

A little butter or olive oil

FOR THE VEGETABLE STEW:

1 large or 2 medium-size onions
3 tablespoons oil
2 large carrots
2 tomatoes, peeled and chopped
⅔ cup (160 ml) chick peas,
   soaked, cooked until tender,
   and drained
1 teaspoon cinnamon
1 teaspoon ground cumin

1 teaspoon ground coriander
2 tablespoons tomato paste
½ cup (125 ml) raisins
2 cups (500 ml) water
1 tablespoon chopped parsley
2 teaspoons lemon juice
Sea salt
Freshly ground black pepper

First of all start preparing the couscous: If you have bought it unpackaged spread the couscous out on a large plate and sprinkle it with about a third of the salted water; rub the grains gently between your fingers —rather like rubbing fat into flour for pastry—to help separate the grains. Leave the couscous for 10 minutes and then repeat the process twice more, using the rest of the water. (If you are using packaged couscous, follow the directions on the package.)

While you're waiting for the couscous, you can begin the stew. Peel and chop the onions and sauté them in the oil in a large saucepan for 10 minutes, or until they're tender. Peel and dice the carrots and add them to the onions together with the tomatoes, chick peas, spices, tomato paste, raisins, and water. Bring the mixture to the boil.

Line a steamer or metal colander with a piece of clean muslin or a double layer of cheese cloth and put in the couscous. Set the steamer over the saucepan containing the vegetable mixture and cover with a lid or a piece of foil. Let it simmer gently for about 30 minutes, until the vegetables are cooked and the couscous is tender. Add some more water to the vegetable mixture if it is too thick, and stir in the parsley, lemon juice, and salt and pepper to taste.

Stir the couscous gently with a fork to make sure the grains are separated and fluffy, and mix in a little butter or olive oil to add flavor and make the couscous look shiny and appetizing.

To serve, spoon the couscous onto a large, warmed dish and pour the stew in the center. Couscous makes a pleasant change from curry and rice. It shouldn't be too hot-tasting, just warmly and fragrantly spiced.

◆———◆———◆

GNOCCHI ALLA ROMANA

ITALY

When this is brought from the oven, sizzling and golden brown, people find it difficult to believe it's made from semolina, which they often associate with dull puddings. It's delicious and, though you've got to allow time for the semolina mixture to cool completely, it's not a difficult dish to make: It can be done in stages and prepared in advance. It also freezes well.

Gnocchi should really be made with Parmesan cheese, which of course gives it a lovely flavor, but when I'm making it for the family I use Cheddar spiced up with plenty of dry mustard and a pinch of cayenne pepper. For more flavor you can also add some crushed garlic and/or grated onion to the basic mixture.

This dish is lovely baked in little individual dishes and served as a first course. Or I like to serve it as a main dish with a tasty tomato sauce and either a lightly cooked green vegetable or a green salad. Another variation, which is totally un-Italian, is gnocchi with french fries and parsley sauce!

Many people add semolina to milk by sprinkling it over the top of the boiling milk and stirring. I find it's all too easy to get lumps this way, so as you will see I use a different method, which I find works well. *Serves 4 as a main dish, 6–8 as a first course.*

¾ cup (180 ml) semolina—you
    can buy the whole-wheat
    variety from health-food shops
1½ teaspoons sea salt
A good grinding of black
    pepper and nutmeg
3¾ cups (930 ml) milk

¾ cup (180 ml) grated cheese—
    including some Parmesan
    or Cheddar with 1½
    teaspoons dry mustard and
    a pinch of cayenne
2 eggs
Oil

Put the semolina into a large bowl with the salt, pepper, and nutmeg and mix it to a cream with some of the milk. Bring the rest of the milk to the boil, then pour it into the semolina mixture, stirring all the time. Tip the semolina and milk mixture back into the saucepan and stir over a fairly high heat until it thickens. Then, stirring from time to time, let the mixture simmer gently until it's very thick and has lost its very granular appearance. In Italy they say that the mixture is ready when a spoon will stand up in it unsupported. In practice I find you can only achieve this if you've happened to use a small, deep saucepan, and that 10 minutes of simmering is about right. Remove the saucepan from the heat and stir in two-thirds of the cheese (and the mustard and cayenne if you're using them) and the two eggs, which will cook in the heat of the mixture (so stir constantly and gently to prevent the eggs from scrambling). Taste and add more seasoning if necessary. Lightly oil a large plate, tray, or other suitable flat surface and turn out the semolina mixture onto this, spreading it to a thickness of about ¼ inch (6 mm). Leave it completely—overnight if possible.

When the mixture is cold it should be firm enough to cut into shapes. Traditionally it should be cut into circles with a pastry cutter, which makes the finished dish look very attractive and doesn't really take long, but squares will do if you're in a hurry. Brush a large flat ovenproof dish with oil—I use one of those big white pizza plates—and arrange the *gnocchi* in slightly overlapping circles, like roof tiles. Brush the top of the *gnocchi* with some oil and sprinkle with the remaining grated cheese, then either bake for about 15 minutes in a fairly hot oven—400° F (200° C)—or put the whole dish under a hot broiler for about 20 minutes, if you have a broiler that is big enough. When the *gnocchi* are really crisp and golden, serve them at once.

◆——————◆——————◆

KHITCHARI

This is the dish from which the English kedgeree is derived. Although modern kedgeree is usually a fish dish, the original *khitchari* was a spicy mixture of rice and lentils, ideal for vegetarians.

The usual way of making this, and the method I used to use, is to cook the lentils and rice together. But it's difficult to judge the amount of water and the timing, and recently I've been cooking them separately, then mixing them together, and find that this gives a better result—light and slightly dry. I like *khitchari* with a juicy tomato salad and some mango chutney or lime pickle, but some people like to have curry sauce with it. *Serves 4.*

8 ounces (240 g) dried lentils	2 tablespoons butter or ghee
3 cups (750 ml) water	1 clove garlic, peeled and
1 bay leaf	crushed
Sea salt	2 teaspoons curry powder
1 cup (250 ml) brown rice	1 teaspoon cumin seed (optional)
2 cups (500 ml) water	Freshly ground black pepper
2 large onions	1–2 teaspoons lemon juice

Put the lentils into a saucepan with the water and bay leaf and simmer them gently until the lentils are tender and have absorbed most of the water making a thickish purée. Take out the bay leaf. Keep the lentils warm.

While the lentils are cooking, boil the rice in the water until just tender—this will take 40–45 minutes—then drain and rinse it.

Peel and chop the onion and sauté it in the butter or *ghee* in a small saucepan for 5 minutes. Stir in the garlic, curry powder, and cumin seeds, and cook for another 5 minutes, until the onion is softened but not browned.

To assemble the dish, gently mix together the rice and lentils—use a fork for this to avoid damaging the grains of rice—and gently stir in the onion mixture. Season with salt and pepper and add a little lemon juice to taste.

You can vary *khitchari* in a number of ways. It's good with sliced tomatoes, chopped hard-boiled eggs, or fried mushrooms or green pepper stirred in just before serving.

PAELLA

Paella usually consists of saffron-flavored rice with onions, tomatoes, fish, and sausages, but the composition varies enormously depending on the whim of the cook and the contents of his or her cupboard, so I hope you won't think my vegetarian version too far-fetched. Anyway, people seem to enjoy this mixture of pale yellow saffron rice, tomatoes, and green peas with its crunchy topping of golden brown slivered almonds. We like it with a fresh-tasting tomato sauce and a Spanish green salad. A chilled protein-rich dessert goes well with it—*crème brûlée* or little coffee custards—or chocolate and orange mousse if you want to continue the Spanish theme. *Serves 4.*

2 large onions
6 tablespoons olive oil
1½ cups (375 ml) brown rice
3¾ cups (930 ml) water
1 packet of saffron—2 packets
   give a more intense color and
   flavor for a special occasion
2 teaspoons sea salt
Freshly ground black pepper

2 large cloves garlic, crushed
4 large carrots
1 large red pepper
4 tomatoes, peeled
1 cup (250 ml) frozen green peas
1 cup (250 ml) slivered almonds
   toasted on a dry baking sheet
   in a moderate oven for 10–15
   minutes

Peel and slice the onions. Heat the oil in a large saucepan and sauté the onions for 10 minutes, until they're soft but not browned. Wash the rice and add it to the onion together with the water, saffron, salt, a good grinding of pepper and the garlic. Bring the water to the boil and then turn the heat down; put a lid on the saucepan and leave the rice to cook very gently for 40 minutes. While the rice is cooking, scrape the carrots and cut them into chunky pieces. Cut the pepper into rings, discarding the seeds, and quarter the tomatoes. After the rice has been cooking for 20 minutes, add the carrots—just put them in on top of the rice, and put the lid back on the saucepan.

Ten minutes later add the pepper in the same way. When the rice has cooked for its 40 minutes, put the tomatoes and peas into the saucepan, too. Put the lid back on and leave the rice, off the heat, for another 15 minutes, to finish cooking slowly in its own heat. Then gently reheat the mixture, stirring with a fork to mix the rice with all the other vegetables. Sprinkle the nuts on top of the paella just before you serve it, so that they keep nice and crisp.

RED BEAN RICE

This rice dish is a lovely medley of reds: tomato-colored rice, with pieces of bright red pepper and deep crimson kidney beans—warming fare indeed and with a spicy taste to match! Serve it with pumpkin soup as a first course, a well-dressed green salad as an accompaniment, and an exotic fruit salad for dessert for a delicious Carribbean meal. *Serves 4.*

¾ cup (180 ml) red kidney beans, soaked then drained, rinsed and simmered for 1 hour or so until tender
2 large onions, peeled and chopped
3 tablespoons vegetable oil
2 large cloves garlic, peeled and crushed
2 large red peppers, seeded and sliced

1 can (16 ounces/480 g) tomatoes
1 cup (250 ml) water or vegetable stock
1 cup (250 ml) brown rice
Sea salt
3 teaspoons ground coriander
½–1 teaspoon chili powder
Freshly ground black pepper

Drain the kidney beans; leave to one side. Peel and chop the onions and sauté them for 10 minutes until they're tender. Stir in the garlic and red pepper and sauté for another minute or two, stirring so that everything gets coated with the oil. Add the can of tomatoes and the water or stock. Rinse the rice in cold water, then put this into a saucepan together with a teaspoonful of salt, the spices, and a grinding of pepper. Bring the mixture to the boil and then turn the heat right down and leave it to cook very gently for 40–45 minutes, until the rice is tender. Take the saucepan off the heat and leave it to stand, with the lid still on, for 10–15 minutes. Add the kidney beans, mixing them in gently with a fork. Check the seasoning then reheat.

◆——◆——◆

FRIED RICE

This is a basic recipe for a spicy rice to eat with curry dishes. It comes out a pretty bright yellow because of the turmeric. You can vary it by stirring in some nuts, sesame seeds, or poppy seeds at the end to make it more crunchy and nutritious; or you can add raisins or currants for sweetness, or chopped red or green peppers for extra color. *Serves 4.*

1¼ cups (310 ml) brown rice	*3 cloves*
1 tablespoon butter	*1 bay leaf*
2½ cups (625 ml) boiling water	*Salt and pepper*
1 teaspoon turmeric	

Wash the rice thoroughly, then drain it and, if possible, leave it for half an hour or so to dry off a little.

Melt the butter in a heavy-bottomed saucepan and add the drained rice. Stir-fry the rice over a gentle heat until it has become opaque—this will take about 5 minutes and it's best to stir the rice all the time so that it doesn't brown—then put in the boiling water, turmeric, cloves, and bay leaf and a seasoning of salt and pepper. When the mixture is boiling vigorously, turn down the heat and put a lid on the saucepan. Leave the rice to cook very gently for about 45 minutes, after which it should be tender and have absorbed all the liquid. Take out the cloves and bay leaf before serving the rice. (If there is still a little water left in the saucepan let the rice stand, still covered, for another 10–15 minutes; or simply remove the lid and let simmer for a few minutes so that the extra liquid evaporates.)

RICE AND PEAS

This Italian dish, *risi e bisi*, is really halfway between a risotto and a soup, and has a lovely creamy consistency. It's easy to make and good served with a tomato salad and triangles of crisp toast. *Serves 6.*

2 large onions
2 tablespoons butter
2 cups (500 ml) brown rice
5 cups (1.2 liters) water
Sea salt
3 cups (750 ml) frozen green peas

1½ cups (375 ml) finely grated
cheese
1 teaspoon dry mustard
Freshly ground black pepper
Grated nutmeg

Peel and chop the onions. Melt the butter in a large saucepan and add the onions; sauté them gently for about 10 minutes, until they're soft and buttery but not browned. Wash the rice and put it into the saucepan with the onion; stir in the water and a rounded teaspoonful of salt. Bring the mixture to the boil, cover, turn the heat down, and leave the rice to cook gently for 40 minutes.

If the peas are very icy, put them into a strainer and rinse them under hot water; then put them into the saucepan on top of the rice 5 minutes before it's cooked. At the end of the cooking time take the rice off the heat and leave it, covered, for 10 minutes, to finish cooking in its own heat. After this you should find that the rice and peas are both cooked but that there is still some liquid left in the saucepan.

Stir the mixture with a fork, mixing in the cheese, dry mustard, salt, pepper, and nutmeg to taste. Reheat very gently, and then serve at once.

RICE AND PEAS WITH TOMATO SAUCE

GERMANY

This German dish, *Schoten*, is made from ingredients similar to those used for the Italian *risi e bisi,* but the result is different: The rice and pea mixture is drier, more like a pilaf, and it's served with a tomato sauce, which provides moisture and color. *Serves 4.*

1½ cups (375 ml) brown rice
3¾ cups (930 ml) water
Sea salt
3 cups (750 ml) frozen peas

4 tablespoons butter
1 onion, peeled and chopped
1 can (16 ounces/480g) tomatoes
Freshly ground black pepper

Wash the rice and put it into a heavy-bottomed saucepan with the water and a rounded teaspoonful of salt. Bring it to the boil and then turn the heat down, cover, and let the rice cook very gently for 40 minutes. If the peas are very frozen, tip them into a strainer, put them under the hot tap for a minute, and then put them on top of the rice 5 minutes before it's ready.

When the rice is cooked, take it off the heat and leave it, covered, for 10 minutes, to finish steaming in its own heat. Meanwhile, make the sauce. Melt half the butter in a medium-size saucepan and sauté the onion for 10 minutes until it's tender. Stir in the tomatoes and cook for 2–3 minutes; then purée the mixture in your blender. Season with salt and pepper and reheat gently.

To finish the dish add the remaining butter to the peas and rice and stir gently with a fork. Season carefully and serve with the tomato sauce.

RISOTTO BIANCO

I T A L Y

The proper way to make *risotto* is to add the liquid a little at a time, as each batch is absorbed. This means that you have to stand over the saucepan and, with brown rice, which takes a long time to cook, it's very time-consuming. So I make *risotto* by cooking the rice slowly with a lid on the saucepan in the usual way, then beating it to make it creamy. You could leave out the sautéed mushrooms or red pepper if you want to, but I think they make the dish more interesting.

You might think that the quantity of rice I've given is rather large, but as you won't be serving potatoes and will probably just have a salad with the *risotto,* I think this is the right quantity. But if there's any left over it makes lovely little croquettes, rolled in crumbs and fried until crisp and golden. *Serves 4–6.*

2 large onions
6 tablespoons butter
2¼ cups (560 ml) brown rice, washed
6 cups (1.5 liters) water, vegetable stock or, for special occasions, replace ⅔ cup (160 ml) of the liquid with dry white wine
Sea salt

1 cup (250 ml) grated Parmesan cheese
½ pound (225 g) fresh mushrooms, lightly sautéed in a little butter; or 1 red pepper, chopped and sautéed in butter; (optional)
Freshly ground black pepper

Peel and chop the onions. Melt the butter in a heavy-bottomed sauce-pan and sauté the onions for 5 minutes, but don't let them brown. Add the rice and stir for a minute or two until it is well mixed with the buttery onion. Pour in the liquid and add a pinch of salt. Bring the mixture to the boil, then put a lid on the saucepan, turn the heat right down, and leave the rice to cook gently for 45 minutes. There will still be a little liquid left in the saucepan after the rice is done. Now beat the mixture with a wooden spoon to break up the grains of rice a bit and create a creamy texture.

Just before you serve the rice stir in the grated cheese (and mush-rooms or red peppers if you're using them). Check the seasoning and then take the rice to the table while it's still beautifully hot and the melting cheese all soft and creamy. *Risotto* is delicious with a tomato salad or a well-dressed green salad.

◆——◆——◆

VEGETABLE CURRY

INDIA

This vegetable curry is spicy but not hot. If you wish, you can make it spicier by increasing the amount of chili powder. It's lovely with plain boiled rice or the spicy fried rice on page 143, some mango chutney, and crunchy golden *poppadums* or *chapatis*. I usually serve it with a juicy side salad, too, which is cooling and refreshing. *Serves 4.*

4 tablespoons ghee or butter	1 can (16 ounces/240 g) tomatoes
1 large onion, peeled and chopped	1 teaspoon sea salt
2 cloves garlic, peeled and crushed	Freshly ground black pepper
	2½ cups (625 ml) water
1 bay leaf	2 cups (500 ml) carrots, scraped and sliced
3 teaspoons ground coriander	
3 teaspoons ground cumin	2 cups (500 ml) potatoes, peeled and diced
1 teaspoon ground ginger	
¼ teaspoon chili powder	1 cup (250 ml) frozen green peas

Heat the *ghee* or butter in a large saucepan and sauté the onion for 7–8 minutes; then add the garlic, bay leaf, and spices and stir over the heat for 2–3 minutes. Mix in the tomatoes, salt, a grinding of pepper, and the water. Simmer for 5–10 minutes while you prepare the vegetables. Add the potatoes and carrots to the tomato mixture and simmer gently for 15–25 minutes, until the vegetables are almost tender; then put in the peas and simmer for another 5 minutes. Check the seasoning before serving.

CHEESE AND
EGG DISHES

Baked Stuffed Eggs
Bread and Cheese Pudding
Cheese Fondue
Curried Stuffed Eggs
Gougère with Mushrooms, Onions, and Red Wine Sauce
Cold Gougère with Cream Cheese Filling
Omelette
Pipérade
Cheese Soufflé
Leek Soufflé
Mushroom Soufflé
Potato and Watercress Soufflé
Welsh Rabbit

THIS SECTION CONTAINS PERHAPS THE MOST CLASSIC recipes of the vegetarian repertoire, with its omelettes and soufflés from France and cheese fondue from Switzerland, all delicious and surprisingly easy to make. There are also a couple of quick bread-and-cheese dishes, two interesting stuffed egg recipes, and two beautiful savory choux pastry rings, which make an impressive centerpiece to a special meal.

Although I know it's a straightforward chemical process that makes a soufflé rise in the oven, I still feel a thrill of pride and delight when I open the oven and see a puffed-up golden soufflé! And, despite its simplicity, a soufflé always seems to impress people and convince them you're a wonderful cook—but really if you've got the proportions right in the mixture all you need are punctual guests, good nerves and the right-size dish. Actually, regarding the first two requirements, although a soufflé really is best if you eat it as soon as it's done, I have found that as long as it is fairly well cooked it will stay risen in the oven for a few extra minutes if I turn off the heat. As far as the serving dish is concerned, you need one of the correct capacity, which I've given in the recipes, and as long as the dish is big enough it doesn't really matter, from the point of view of flavor, what shape it is. But if you want to produce a flamboyant, well-risen soufflé, you need a narrow, fairly deep dish, and the mixture should come about ½ inch below the rim. Don't pile it up any higher, as I rather foolishly did once, or you will find half your soufflé on the floor of the oven. If you would feel safer attaching a paper collar to your soufflé dish, do so by all means but be sure to butter the inside of it so that the cooked soufflé doesn't cling to it.

Of course all the dishes in this section are rich in protein. When I'm serving eggs or cheese for the main course, I try to plan for a low-fat or non-dairy appetizer and dessert: perhaps a vegetable purée soup or mushrooms *à la Grecque;* and a simple fruit to end the meal.

BAKED STUFFED EGGS

RUSSIA

Usually stuffed eggs are served cold as a first course or part of a salad, so this hot version from Russia is a pleasant variation. They're good as a first course baked in individual dishes and served with hot toast; or as a main course, with fluffy boiled rice and perhaps a buttery spinach purée. *Serves 4 as a main course, 8 as an appetizer.*

8 hard-boiled eggs
2 large onions
4 tablespoons butter
1 tablespoon chopped fresh
    parsley

Sea salt
Freshly ground black pepper

Preheat oven to 350°F (180°C). Cut the hard-boiled eggs in half and take out the yolks; put the whites to one side. Peel and finely chop the onions. Melt the butter in a medium-size saucepan and use some of it to brush a shallow oblong ovenproof dish that is big enough to hold all the cooked egg whites in a single layer. Add the onion to the rest of the butter in the saucepan and sauté it gently for 10 minutes, without letting it brown. Take the saucepan off the heat and add the egg yolks, mashing them into the onions until they're fairly creamy and smooth; then stir in the parsley, salt and pepper. Spoon the mixture into the egg white cavities, piling it up neatly, and put the egg whites into the greased dish. Cover the dish with foil and bake in the oven for about 30 minutes, until the eggs are heated through.

These are also good with ½–1 teaspoon dried dill, fennel, or caraway seeds added to the mixture, if you like the taste.

◆———◆———◆

BREAD AND CHEESE PUDDING

WALES

This is rather like a Welsh rabbit baked in the oven in one dish. It's useful if you want to make a toasted cheese dish that you can prepare in advance but cook later. You could use hard cider or beer instead of the milk for a more heady result, rather like a baked fondue. *Serves 4.*

8–10 slices of whole-wheat bread
Butter
¾ pound (350 g) grated double
    Gloucester or Cheddar cheese

1¼ cups (310 ml) milk

You need enough slices of bread to line the base of a shallow ovenproof dish, and the same again to make a bread topping for the cheese. Butter the dish lightly. Toast all the bread, and butter it on one side. Lay half the toast in the dish, unbuttered side down; then put most of the cheese and the remaining toast on top, buttered side down. Sprinkle with the last of the grated cheese. Pour the milk over the pudding and leave it to soak for about 30 minutes—or longer if you want. Put a few little pieces of butter over the top of the pudding.

When you're ready to cook the pudding, preheat the oven to 375°F (190°C) and bake for about 40 minutes, until the pudding is crusty and brown on top. This is quite rich, so it's nice served fairly simply, with a tomato or watercress salad, for example.

CHEESE FONDUE

SWITZERLAND

Although fondue is very quick and easy to prepare, I always think there's something rather festive and special about it—perhaps it's because everyone is dipping their bread into the communal pot of bubbling golden cheese.

Fondue is at its best when made with dry white wine, Gruyère and Emmentaler cheeses, and kirsch, but I've found you can make an excellent, much cheaper version with Edam cheese and dry hard cider, where available, or dry vermouth. *Serves 4–6.*

1 clove garlic
1¼ cups (310 ml) dry white wine,
  hard cider, or dry vermouth
½ pound (225 g) Gruyère cheese
  and ½ pound (225 g)
  Emmentaler cheese, grated; or
  use 1 pound (450 g) grated
  Edam cheese
1 tablespoon cornstarch

1–2 tablespoons kirsch (optional)
Sea salt
Freshly ground black pepper
Grated nutmeg
1 large French bread or crusty
  whole-wheat bread—or half of
  each—cut into bite-size pieces
  and warmed in the oven

Halve the garlic and rub the cut surfaces over the inside of a medium-size saucepan (or special fondue pan). Put the wine or cider (or vermouth) and cheese into the saucepan and heat gently, stirring all the time until the cheese has melted. Mix the cornstarch to a paste with the kirsch if you're using it, or use a drop more wine; pour this paste into the cheese mixture, stirring constantly until you have a lovely smooth creamy consistency. Occasionally the cheese goes all lumpy and stringy at this point. Don't despair; if you beat it vigorously for a moment or two with a rotary whisk all will be well. Season the fondue, place the pot or pan over the lighted burner, and let everyone start dipping their bread into the delicious mixture.

Fondue is rich so the menu planning needs some care. If you have a first course, keep it light; follow the fondue with something refreshing and non-creamy, like fresh peaches or pineapple sherbet.

CURRIED STUFFED EGGS

INDIA

This is a tasty dish: hard-boiled eggs stuffed with a curry mixture and baked in a spicy sauce. They're wonderful served with hot boiled rice, some mango chutney, and crisp *pappadums,* a waferlike Indian bread. *Serves 4.*

8 hard-boiled eggs	1 teaspoon ground coriander
1 large onion	1 teaspoon ground ginger
3 tablespoons ghee, oil, or butter	½ teaspoon turmeric
1 clove garlic	1¼ cups (310 ml) water
1 can (8 ounces/240 g) tomatoes	Sea salt
1 teaspoon ground cumin	Freshly ground black pepper

Halve the eggs; take out the yolks and put them into a bowl. Leave the whites to one side for the moment. Peel and finely chop the onion and sauté it gently in the *ghee* for 10 minutes. Peel and crush the garlic and add it to the onion, together with the tomatoes, spices, water, and some salt and pepper. Let the mixture simmer, with a lid on the saucepan, for 20 minutes; then strain or purée this sauce. Check the seasoning. Preheat oven to 350°F (180°C). Mash the egg yolks and stir in 2 or 3 tablespoons of sauce, enough to make a soft but not sloppy mixture.

Spoon the yolk mixture into the egg whites. Pour the curry sauce into a shallow ovenproof dish that's big enough to hold all the eggs in one layer, and then put the eggs in on top of the sauce. Cover with foil and bake for 30 minutes just to heat the eggs through.

GOUGÈRE WITH MUSHROOMS, ONIONS, AND RED WINE SAUCE

FRANCE

This is an impressive and delicious dish, a big puffed-up ring of golden choux pastry, the center filled with mushrooms and onions in red wine sauce. It's lovely served with baby Brussels sprouts and creamy mashed potatoes. *Gougère* is not difficult to make but it's best eaten as soon as it's ready, so you need to be able to get everyone to the table on time. Don't be put off by the long list of ingredients for the sauce; it's really quite easy to make. *Serves 6.*

FOR THE GOUGÈRE:

8 tablespoons butter or margarine
1¼ cups (310 ml) water
1¼ cups (310 ml) whole-wheat flour—or half whole-wheat and half unbleached white flour

1 teaspoon sea salt
4 eggs, each beaten separately
1½ cups (375 ml) grated Gruyère or Swiss cheese
A good pinch of cayenne pepper

FOR THE FILLING:

3 onions, peeled and sliced
1 tablespoon butter

½ pound (225 g) mushrooms, washed and left whole

FOR THE SAUCE:

2 cups (500 ml) stock—or water and a good teaspoon of vegetarian stock powder
2 cups (500 ml) red wine
1 bay leaf
1 small onion, peeled
1 clove garlic, peeled and sliced
A good pinch of thyme
½ teaspoon black peppercorns

1–2 parsley stalks
1 tablespoon red currant jelly
Sea salt
Freshly ground black pepper
Sugar
3 tablespoons soft butter
3 tablespoons unbleached all-purpose flour

You can do most of the preparation for the various parts of this dish in advance if that is most convenient for you. To make the *gougère,* put the butter or margarine and water into a medium-size saucepan and heat gently until the butter has melted; then turn up the heat and bring the mixture to the boil. Mix the flour with the salt and quickly pour into the saucepan all at once. Stir over the heat with a wooden spoon for 1 minute, by which time the mixture will have formed a glossy ball of dough; then take the saucepan off the heat and tip the dough into a clean bowl.

Add one beaten egg and beat vigorously with a wooden spoon until the dough has absorbed the egg and become smooth and glossy again; then add another egg and beat again. Repeat until all the egg has been used. I sometimes find when I'm using all whole-wheat flour that the mixture will only take three of the eggs; by then it is quite soft enough, and any more would make it too sticky—it must hold its shape softly. If this happens to you don't worry; just use the extra egg to glaze the top before sprinkling on the cheese and baking. Stir in about two-thirds of the grated cheese, and the cayenne pepper. You can cover the mixture with a plate and leave it at this point for several hours if you wish.

To make the filling, sauté the onions in the 1 tablespoon butter for 10 minutes until they're soft, and then add the mushrooms and sauté for another 3–4 minutes, or until they too are tender. Season with salt and pepper and leave to one side. If the mushrooms produce a great deal of liquid, drain it off and use it as part of the stock for the sauce.

For the sauce, put the stock and red wine into a good-size saucepan with the bay leaf, onion, garlic, thyme, peppercorns, and parsley stalks if you've got them, and bring to the boil. Let the mixture bubble away furiously without a lid for 10–15 minutes until it has reduced by half. Strain this liquid into a clean saucepan and stir in the red currant jelly, salt, pepper, and sugar to taste. Make a *beurre manié* by putting half the butter on a plate with the flour and mashing them together with the back of a spoon to make a paste. Add this *beurre manié* to the wine mixture in several pieces, beating well after each, and then put the sauce back on the heat and stir it for a minute or two until it's slightly thickened. After the sauce has simmered for 4–5 minutes to cook the flour, take the saucepan off the heat and dot the remaining butter over the surface of the sauce to prevent a skin's forming. Leave to one side until you're ready to serve the *gougère.*

To finish the *gougère,* preheat the oven to 400° F (200° C). Oil a a large ovenproof dish—one of those big white pizza plates is ideal if you have one but any large shallow ovenproof dish will do—and fill with the gougère mixture, pushing it out to the edge, heaping it up into as neat a ring as possible but leaving the center free. Sprinkle the top of the ring with the rest of the grated cheese and then bake the *gougère* for 40 minutes until it is puffed up and golden brown. When the *gougère* is nearly done, reheat the onions and mushrooms gently; also the sauce.

Take the *gougère* out of the oven, spoon the mushroom mixture into the center, and pour a little sauce over the mushrooms and onions; serve the rest of the sauce separately in a jug. Serve the *gougère* immediately, while it's hot and puffed.

You can, by the way, put other things into the center of the *gougère*; it's nice filled with a buttery purée of spinach and a cheese sauce on top.

COLD GOUGÈRE WITH CREAM CHEESE FILLING

FRANCE

If you make a *gougère* as in the previous recipe and bake it longer so that it's really firm, you can split it through the middle and serve it cold, with a layer of soft white cheese, and its center filled with crisp lettuce, tomato, watercress, and scallions. It makes an attractive buffet dish. *Serves 8–12.*

FOR THE GOUGERE:

See previous recipe

FOR THE FILLING:

3 packages (8 ounces/240 g each)	*Sea salt*
cream cheese	*Freshly ground black pepper*

TO GARNISH:

1 crisp lettuce	*4 tomatoes, sliced*
½ bunch watercress	*6 scallions, trimmed*

Make the *gougère* as described in the preceding recipe but bake it for a good full hour, until it is well risen and very firm—all "sizzling" should have ceased in the pastry. If it's not really firm it will collapse and be soggy inside.

Take the *gougère* out of the oven, slit it horizontally with a sharp knife, and leave it on the dish to cool completely.

It's best not to fill the *gougère* until just before you're going to serve it so that it stays as crisp as possible. Put the cheese into a bowl and mash it with a fork to break it up; then beat it until it's soft and light. Season the cheese with salt and pepper—a touch of garlic is nice too, if you like it. Carefully remove the top half of the *gougère* and spread the cheese over the bottom layer; then replace the top half. Arrange the salad in the middle of the circle. An alternative is to put the salad on top of the cheese inside the *gougère*.

OMELETTE

FRANCE

I think a well made omelette, light and golden on the outside, creamy and moist within, is still one of the best and quickest convenience foods of all. It's versatile, too, because you can serve it with all sorts of different fillings. The important thing is to have the filling all ready to pop into the omelette, and everyone sitting at the table, before you start to cook the omelette itself because it's speed that's the essence of success. *Serves 1.*

FOR THE FILLING:

(any of the following)
½ cup (125 ml) finely grated cheese
½ cup (125 ml) mushrooms, sliced and lightly sautéed
½ cup (125 ml) asparagus, heated in its own liquid and drained just before using

3 canned artichoke hearts, sliced, heated and drained just before using
1 tablespoon chopped fresh green herbs—parsley, chives, chervil, tarragon—whatever is available

FOR THE OMELETTE:

2 eggs
2 teaspoons cold water
Sea salt

Freshly ground black pepper
1 teaspoon oil
1 tablespoon butter

Beat the eggs in a bowl with the water, a pinch of salt, and a grinding of pepper. Put the skillet or omelette pan, if you have one (6–7 inches, or 15–18 cm), over a high heat for about 1 minute. Turn the heat down and put in first the oil and then the butter. When the butter has melted turn up the heat again and put in the beaten eggs. Using a flat wooden palette knife, immediately start gently lifting the edges of the omelette toward the center, tipping the pan as you do so as to make the liquid egg in the middle run to the edges and in the space you've created in lifting them. Keep the heat up high. All this happens very quickly—the omelette should be done in under a minute. Loosen the edges of the omelette quickly with the palette knife, spoon the filling on top, on one side, and then tip the pan away from you so that the omelette folds over itself. Gently slide it onto a warmed plate. Serve immediately.

◆——————◆——————◆

PIPÉRADE

FRANCE

This tasty mixture of tomatoes, peppers, and onions in creamy, lightly set scrambled egg makes a good quick supper dish. It's lovely served with warm crisp French bread or whole-wheat rolls. *Serves 4.*

2 onions	4 tablespoons butter
2 cloves garlic	6 eggs
1 green pepper	Sea salt
1 red pepper	Freshly ground black pepper
4 tomatoes	Chopped fresh parsley

Peel and chop the onions; peel and crush the garlic; wash, seed, and chop the peppers; peel and chop the tomatoes. Melt the butter in a large saucepan and sauté the onion in it for about 5 minutes without letting it brown. Mix in the garlic, peppers, and tomatoes and cook for another 5 minutes over a low heat and with the lid on the saucepan.

Meanwhile beat the eggs in a small bowl with some salt and pepper. When the vegetables are tender pour the eggs into the saucepan and stir gently over a low heat until they are lightly scrambled, but don't let them get too dry—it's best to keep the heat low the entire time and take *pipérade* off the stove while it's still runny. Check the seasoning and then serve at once, sprinkled with chopped parsley and accompanied by the warm bread. Follow with fresh fruit or some other fruit-based dessert.

CHEESE SOUFFLÉ

FRANCE

I think this is perhaps the best soufflé of all with its satisfying savory flavor and lovely golden color. The classic cheese to use is Gruyère but I find Cheddar is fine for everyday cooking whilst a cheese such as Leicestershire or double Gloucester makes the soufflé a beautiful rich golden color, which looks very appetizing. *Serves 4.*

3 tablespoons butter	*1 teaspoon dry mustard*
3 tablespoons flour	*Sea salt*
1 cup (250 ml) milk	*Freshly ground black pepper*
1 cup (250 ml) grated cheese	*5 egg whites*
4 egg yolks	

Grease a 3 pint (1¾ litre) soufflé dish with a little butter or oil. Melt the butter in a large saucepan and stir in the flour; cook for a few seconds and then add the milk, little by little, stirring constantly, until the mixture is thick and smooth. Take the saucepan off the heat and pour the mixture into a large bowl to cool slightly. Mix in the grated cheese, egg yolks, dry mustard, and a good seasoning of salt and pepper. (You can cover the mixture and leave it for several hours at this stage if necessary.)

Preheat oven to 375° F (190° C). If you have a baking sheet, place this on the top shelf of the oven—it will get hot and, when you put your soufflé dish on it, later, there will be a nice blast of heat from the base to get things off to a good start. Beat the egg whites. They should be stiff enough for you to be able to tip the bowl without their coming out, but not so stiff that you could almost slice them with a knife, so stop in time. Mix a rounded tablespoonful of the beaten egg whites into the cheese mixture to soften it. Add the rest of the egg whites on top of the mixture and, using the side of a flattish spoon or a spatula, cut and fold the egg whites into the cheese mixture until the whites have all been incorporated and you have a very airy mixture. Pour the soufflé gently into the prepared dish—ideally the mixture should come up nearly but not quite level with the rim; don't pile it up above the rim. Bake the soufflé for 30–35 minutes until it looks firm and golden—you can test it if you like with a fine skewer, which should come out clean.

Cheese soufflé is lovely with a green salad or simply cooked vegetables, such as new potatoes and green beans; it also makes an excellent first course, followed by a vegetable-based main course such as ratatouille and garlic bread or stuffed tomatoes à la Provençale and zucchini, with a fruit dessert afterward.

INDIVIDUAL SOUFFLÉS

If you prefer to make individual cheese soufflés, adjust your ingredients as follows, and bake for only 15–20 minutes. *Makes 3 individual soufflés.*

2 tablespoons butter or margarine	1 cup (250 ml) grated cheese
4 tablespoons all-purpose flour	2 eggs, separated
2/3 cup (160 ml) milk	
Pinch each of dry mustard and cayenne pepper	

These quantities will double satisfactorily to make 6 individual soufflés.

LEEK SOUFFLÉ

FRANCE

The chunky pieces of leek in this soufflé give it a lovely delicate flavor and interesting texture. Try to find really thin leeks if you can; then they can be sliced into nice neat pieces which will stay firm when they're cooked. *Serves 4.*

3–4 leeks	4 egg yolks
Sea salt	Freshly ground black pepper
3 tablespoons butter	Nutmeg
3 tablespoons all-purpose flour	5 egg whites
1¼ cups (310 ml) milk	

First of all butter a 2-quart (2-liter) soufflé dish generously. Then cut off the roots and leafy green tips of the leeks. Slit the leeks down one side and wash them carefully under running water; then cut them into 1-inch (2.5 cm) lengths. Cook the leeks in ½ inch (1 cm) boiling salted water until they're just tender—about 7–10 minutes. Drain the leeks well and put them to one side.

Melt the butter in a medium-size saucepan and add the flour; cook for a few moments until a paste is formed and then very gradually add the milk, stirring constantly, until the mixture is smooth and thick. Transfer the mixture to a large bowl—this cools it slightly, making it ready for adding the egg yolks and more convenient later when you want to fold in the egg white. Beat in the egg yolks one by one and gently stir in the leeks. Season the mixture with salt, pepper, and nutmeg—be fairly generous because the egg whites will "dilute" the mixture. Now you can leave this mixture to one side until just before you want to cook the soufflé; I have kept it (covered) for several hours in the fridge and it has been perfect.

When you're ready to cook the soufflé, place a baking sheet on the middle rack of the oven. Preheat oven to 375° F (190° C). Beat the egg whites until they're thick and standing in soft peaks but don't let them get hard and dry. Stir a generous heaped tablespoonful of egg whites into the leek sauce mixture to loosen it and then tip all the egg whites on top of them and gently fold in with a spoon or spatula. When it has all been incorporated, pour the mixture gently into your prepared dish—it should come up to just below the rim.

Put the soufflé on the baking sheet and bake for 30–35 minutes, until it looks firm and a skewer pushed gently down into the soufflé comes out clean. If it's done before you're quite ready, turn off the oven and the soufflé will keep for 4–5 minutes longer although it won't be quite so puffy. I think this soufflé is nicest served with just one well-cooked vegetable, such as butter baby carrots, Brussels sprouts, or green peas.

MUSHROOM SOUFFLÉ

FRANCE

This is a delicious soufflé—when you cut it open the chunks of mushroom look most appetizing. It's nicest made with those firm white button mushrooms. *Serves 4.*

⅓ pound (150 g) fresh mushrooms	1¼ cups (310 ml) milk
4 tablespoons butter	4 egg yolks
1 clove garlic, peeled and crushed	Sea salt
3 tablespoons all-purpose flour	Freshly ground black pepper
	5 egg whites

Butter a 2-quart (2-liter) soufflé dish. Wash and dry the mushrooms, and then cut them into halves or quarters so that the pieces are all roughly the same size. Melt 1 tablespoon of the butter in a medium-size saucepan and add the mushrooms. Cook them gently, uncovered, for about 5 minutes. Stir in the garlic.

Melt the rest of the butter in another medium-size saucepan and stir in the flour, making a paste, or roux. Gradually add the milk, stirring constantly, until the mixture is thick and smooth. Transfer to a large bowl. Once it has cooled a bit, mix in the mushrooms (draining off any excess liquid first), egg yolks, and seasoning to taste. Leave to one side (for several hours or overnight in the fridge if necessary) until you're ready to cook the soufflé.

Put a baking sheet on the top rack of your oven and preheat to 375° F (190° C). Beat the egg whites until they're stiff but not dry and fold them carefully into the mushroom mixture. Spoon the soufflé into the prepared dish—ideally it should come to a half inch or so below the rim but no higher—and bake it for 30–35 minutes, until it's golden brown, well risen, and firm. A skewer inserted should come out clean. Serve at once. This soufflé is nice served with green beans, baked tomatoes, and creamy mashed potatoes.

POTATO AND WATERCRESS SOUFFLÉ

HOLLAND

I have to admit that I've taken a bit of license here because the addition of the watercress is my own idea, and you could omit it if you want to be more authentic. But I found the plain potato soufflé rather dull, and so I added the watercress to give the soufflé a more interesting flavor and color. It makes a good light main dish and it's nice served as a protein-rich vegetable side dish. *Serves 4–6.*

1½ pounds (675 g) potatoes
Sea salt
4 tablespoons butter
⅔ cup (160 ml) milk or light
  cream

2 bunches watercress
4 egg yolks
Freshly ground black pepper
5 egg whites

Peel the potatoes, cut them into even-size pieces, and cook them in boiling water until they're tender; then drain and mash them with the butter and milk or cream. Wash the watercress carefully, remove the coarse stems, chop the leaves fairly finely, and stir them into the potato mixture together with the egg yolks and plenty of salt and pepper to taste.

You can prepare the soufflé up to this point in advance. When you're ready to cook it, preheat the oven to 375° F (190° C). Butter a 2-quart (2-liter) soufflé dish. Beat the egg whites until they're very stiff but not dry, and then fold them into the potato mixture. Spoon the soufflé into the dish and bake for 45 minutes, until it's puffed up and golden and looks firm when you move the dish slightly. Serve the soufflé at once—or within 5 minutes at the most. It's nice with home-made tomato sauce and a lightly cooked colorful vegetable, such as carrots.

WELSH RABBIT

WALES

Some people say that this dish derives its name from the fact that it was served instead of rabbit when times were hard; anyway, it's one of our favorite quick supper dishes. *Serves 2–4.*

4 large slices whole-wheat bread
2 cups (500 ml) grated Cheddar
  cheese

3 tablespoons milk or beer
Pinch of cayenne pepper
Freshly ground black pepper

Toast the bread; arrange the slices in a broiler pan or on a baking sheet that will fit under the broiler. Put the grated cheese and milk or beer into a saucepan and heat them together, stirring all the while, until the cheese has melted. Remove from the heat and add the cayenne pepper and a grating of black pepper. Pour the cheese mixture over the toast and pop it under a moderately hot broiler for about 5 minutes, until the cheese is bubbly and lightly browned. Serve immediately.

This goes well with a tomato and onion salad or a nice crisp green salad with fresh green herbs in it; or you may wish to serve the Welsh rabbit on its own and follow with some fresh fruit.

FRITTERS AND
RISSOLES

Glamorgan Sausages
Fried Gnocchi
Gnocchi in Mushroom Sauce
Ricotta Gnocchi
Spinach Gnocchi
Swiss Fried Potato Cake
Potato Pancakes
Rice Croquettes
Spicy Fritters
Corn Fritters
Fried Wheat Protein with Sweet and Sour Sauce

IT'S SURPRISING WHAT A VARIETY OF DISHES AP-
pears in this section. There are delicious, crisp little cheesy fritters—
the fried *gnocchi* and rice croquettes from Italy and the Glamorgan
sausage from Wales; there are spicy lentil fritters from the Middle
East and, from China, fritters made from wheat protein. From
Germany and Switzerland there are potato fritters that are crisp and
delicious but need to be served with some extra protein; and corn
fritters from the USA.

Perhaps the most unusual recipes are the *gnocchi*; which are a
kind of savory dumpling. They don't sound at all exciting but when
they're served all hot and puffed up and oozing with melted butter
and cheese they're delicious, excellent as either a first course or a main
course.

Some of the fritters need to be dipped in crisp crumbs. I make these
by cutting up a whole-wheat loaf and baking the slices in a low oven
until they're really dry and crisp, then crushing them with a rolling
pin or popping them into a blender or food processor. They keep
very well in an airtight jar. When it comes to coating the fritters with
the crumbs, which I think is a horrid, messy job, I find the task of
clearing up is greatly eased if you put the dry crumbs on a large piece
of waxed paper and work on this. Afterwards you can simply roll up
the paper with any left over crumbs and sticky eggy bits and pieces
and throw it away. (You may also wish to put the crumbs in a paper
or plastic bag, and toss your fritters in this.)

GLAMORGAN SAUSAGES

WALES

These little cheesy sausages are delicious and an excellent source of
protein. They're good with salad and some chutney, or with a parsley
or tomato sauce and cooked vegetables. If you make the sausages tiny,
they're lovely as a nibble with drinks. *Serves 4.*

¾ *pound (350 g) Cheddar cheese,*	*Freshly ground black pepper*
grated	*A little flour*
3 cups (750 ml) soft whole-wheat	*1 egg, beaten with 1 tablespoonful*
bread crumbs	*of cold water*
1 teaspoon dry mustard	*Dry bread crumbs for cooking*
6 tablespoons cold water	*Oil for frying*

Mix together the cheese, soft bread crumbs, mustard, cold water, and some pepper to taste. Gather the mixture into a ball, divide it into 8 pieces and roll each into a sausage shape on a floured board. Dip each little sausage into the beaten egg and then into dried crumbs. Heat a little oil in a skillet and sauté the sausages quickly until they're crisp, then drain them and serve immediately.

I've found that you can also make a delicious nut version of this recipe that I'm sure a Welshman wouldn't own but we prefer. Use 2 cups (500 ml) grated cheese and 1 cup (250 ml) grated cashew nuts or hazel nuts with the bread crumbs and water as above. It's particularly nice when flavored with a little chopped rosemary.

Both this mixture and the authentic version are good baked instead of sautéed. Press the mixture into a greased ovenproof dish and bake it at 400° F (200° C) for about 45 minutes. The result is a rather crisp savory cake that can be cut up and served with a parsley or tomato sauce; it's also nice cold with chutney and salad.

FRIED GNOCCHI

ITALY

This is my version of the fried *gnocchi*, or *bombolini*, sold in the market in Verona. *Serves 4.*

½ *cup (125 g) semolina—*	*1 cup (250 ml) grated Cheddar*
ordinary semolina or the	*cheese*
whole-wheat variety from	*1 teaspoon sea salt*
health-food shops	*A good grinding of black pepper*
2½ *cups (675 ml) milk*	*1 egg, beaten with a tablespoonful*
1 bay leaf	*of water*
1 small onion, peeled	*Dry bread crumbs*
1½ *teaspoons dry mustard*	*Oil for deep or shallow frying*

Put the semolina into a medium-size bowl and mix to a paste with a little of the milk. Heat the remaining milk with the bay leaf and onion; bring just to the boil and then cover the saucepan and leave it to one side, off the heat, for 10 minutes or so for the flavors to infuse the milk. Remove the bay leaf and onion, and reheat the milk. As soon as it boils, pour it over the semolina cream in the bowl; return the mixture to the saucepan and bring to the boil, stirring all the time. Let the mixture cook for a few minutes, until it's thick and has lost its granular appearance—about 10 minutes. Take the saucepan off the heat and stir in the mustard, grated cheese, salt and pepper. Taste the mixture and add more seasoning, if necessary, to give a tangy savory flavor.

Turn the mixture onto a lightly oiled plate, spread it out to a thickness of about ½ inch (1 cm), and leave it to cool completely. As it cools it will firm up and you will be able to cut it into small squares or other shapes. Dip the shapes first into the beaten egg, then into the dry crumbs, and deep- or shallow-fry them until they're golden brown and crisp. Drain the *gnocchi* on paper towels.

These are very popular with my children, who like them best with french fries, lemon slices, and parsley sauce. They freeze very well; I freeze them after coating them with egg and bread crumbs, then store them in a plastic bag. They can be shallow-fried straight from the freezer.

◆——◆——◆

GNOCCHI IN MUSHROOM SAUCE

AUSTRIA

Although in Italy *gnocchi* are usually served with grated cheese on top, in France and Austria it's more common to find them covered in a sauce, as in this version. *Serves 4.*

¾ cup (180 ml) flour—
   whole-wheat is fine
4 tablespoons butter
1 cup (250 ml) grated Cheddar
   cheese

½ teaspoon sea salt
½ teaspoon dry mustard
2 eggs
Dry bread crumbs
A little grated cheese

4 tablespoons butter	*¼ pound (115 g) mushrooms,*
4 tablespoons all-purpose flour	*washed, dried, and chopped*
1 bay leaf	*Freshly ground black pepper*
2 cups (500 ml) milk	*Grated nutmeg*

To make the *gnocchi*, mix together the flour, butter, cheese, salt, and mustard; break in the eggs one by one and blend well with a fork to make a dough. Form the dough into walnut-size balls on a lightly floured board. Heat half a saucepanful of salted water; when the water boils, drop in the little *gnocchi* and let them simmer gently for about 7 minutes, until they puff up, rise to the surface of the water, and look firm. (Cut one in half to see if it's cooked and firm inside.) Take the *gnocchi* out of the water with a slotted spoon and put them into a lightly greased shallow ovenproof dish.

For the sauce, melt the butter in a large saucepan and add the flour and bay leaf; stir for a moment or two and then add about ½ cup (125 ml) of the milk, stirring all the time over a high heat until the mixture is smooth. Continue adding the milk a little at a time and stirring, until all the milk has been added and you have a smooth sauce. Take the saucepan off the heat and mix in the mushrooms and salt, pepper, and nutmeg to taste. Pour the sauce over the *gnocchi* and sprinkle with the dry bread crumbs and a little grated cheese.

When you're ready to finish the *gnocchi*, set the oven to 375° F (190° C) and bake them for 30–40 minutes, until they're heated through and the topping is crisp and golden.

This is good served with either a salad or a cooked green vegetable. It also makes an excellent first course if you bake small portions in individual ovenproof dishes.

RICOTTA GNOCCHI

ITALY

These little savory dumplings are quick and easy to do and make a delicious light meal or first course with their golden cheesy topping. If it's more convenient you can make them in advance and just put them into a fairly hot oven for about 20 minutes to heat them through and brown the topping before you serve them. A green salad with a tasty dressing goes best with them I think. *Serves 4 as a main course, 6 as a first course.*

¾ cup (180 ml) flour,
  whole-wheat or unbleached
  all-purpose
4 tablespoons butter
1 cup (250 ml) grated Cheddar
  cheese—if you can include a
  little Parmesan, it gives a
  lovely flavor

½ cup (125 ml) ricotta or cottage
  cheese
½ teaspoon sea salt
½ teaspoon dry mustard
2 eggs

TO FINISH:

A little extra flour
2 tablespoons butter
1 clove garlic, peeled and crushed
  in a little salt

¾ cup (180 ml) grated cheese

Put the flour into a bowl and mix in the butter, Cheddar cheese, *ricotta* cheese, salt, and dry mustard; then break in the eggs, one by one, and mix well with a fork until everything is blended to form a dough. Put walnut-size pieces of the dough onto a lightly floured board and, with your fingers, mold them into smooth balls, using more flour to coat them as necessary.

Fill a large saucepan halfway with water, add a teaspoon of salt, and bring to the boil. Drop the *gnocchi* into the gently boiling water— you'll probably have to do them in 2 batches—and let them simmer gently for about 7 minutes. They will swell and rise to the surface of the water as they cook. When I think they're done I find it best to test one by cutting it in half to make sure it's cooked inside. Take the *gnocchi* out of the water with a slotted spoon and put them into a lightly greased shallow ovenproof dish. When all the *gnocchi* are done, melt the butter and mix it with the garlic; pour this over the *gnocchi* and sprinkle the grated cheese on top.

When you're ready to bake the *gnocchi*, set the oven to 400° F (200° C). Put the *gnocchi* in the oven for about 20 minutes, until they're golden brown on top, and then serve at once.

A variation of this recipe, which I sometimes make, is to sauté some chopped walnuts or slivered almonds in the butter and pour them, instead of the grated cheese, over the *gnocchi*.

◆——◆——◆

SPINACH GNOCCHI

ITALY

Spinach *gnocchi* are light and tender and, when served with a topping of melted butter and cheese, they're one of the most delicious dishes imaginable. The secret of success when making them is to let the spinach cool completely before mixing everything together. *Serves 4.*

1 pound (450 g) fresh spinach or	*2 eggs*
(10 ounces/300 g) frozen	*½ teaspoon sea salt*
chopped spinach	*½ teaspoon dry mustard*
¾ cup (180 ml) whole-wheat flour	*Grated nutmeg*
4 tablespoons butter	*Freshly ground black pepper*
1 cup (250 ml) grated cheese	

TO FINISH:

2 tablespoons melted butter	*Grated cheese*

Wash the spinach thoroughly and cook it in a large saucepan over a low heat and without any additional water until it's tender—about 10 minutes. Drain, cool, and chop the spinach. If you're using frozen spinach just let it thaw, then put it into a strainer and press out as much liquid as possible.

Mix the cold spinach with the flour, butter, cheese, eggs, and seasonings—it's easier to use a fork. Form the mixture into about 20 walnut-size balls and roll them in flour. Bring half a saucepan of salted water to the boil and drop in the *gnocchi*—you will probably have to do them in more than one batch. Let them simmer for 7–8 minutes. They will puff up and rise to the surface of the water; I think the best way to tell if they're done is to cut one in half and taste some of the middle to make sure it's not undercooked. Put the *gnocchi* into a lightly greased ovenproof dish, dot with butter, and sprinkle with grated cheese. Before you serve the *gnocchi*, heat them through in a moderate oven—350° F (180° C) for 25–30 minutes, or until they're piping hot and bathed in a buttery cheesy glaze.

Like the other *gnocchi*, they make an excellent first course or supper dish. If you're serving them for supper, a tomato salad and some crusty garlic bread will go well with them (bake the garlic bread in the oven with the *gnocchi*.)

SWISS FRIED POTATO CAKE

SWITZERLAND

Swiss potato cake, *rösti*, is different from German potato pancakes in that it's made with cooked potatoes and forms one large cake that fills the whole skillet. This makes a good base for a hot supper; protein can be introduced into the meal by serving a protein-rich salad or by having something like yogurt, cheesecake, or wafers and cheese for dessert. *Serves 4.*

2 pounds (900 g) cooked potatoes   4 tablespoons vegetable oil
Sea salt

Grate the potatoes coarsely—this is easiest to do if you chill them beforehand for a while in the fridge. Season them with salt. Heat half the oil in a large skillet and put in all the potato, pressing it down gently with the back of a spoon. Cook the potato over a moderate heat until the underside is golden brown; then turn the cake over and cook the other side, adding the remaining oil if necessary. You may be able to turn the cake with a spatula; otherwise you can turn it out onto a plate and then tip it back into the skillet again, crispy side uppermost. When the second side is cooked, turn the potato cake out onto a hot plate and serve it in big chunky wedges.

You can vary this basic recipe in a number of ways: It's nice with chopped herbs or scallions mixed in; sunflower seeds, sesame seeds, and chopped hazelnuts are also good.

POTATO PANCAKES

GERMANY

These crispy little pancakes make a good quick supper dish or children's meal. It's typically German—and I think delicious—to serve them with a sharp-tasting apple or cranberry sauce, but children usually prefer them with tomato ketchup. *Serves 4.*

1 pound (450 g) potatoes,
   scrubbed
1 onion, peeled
Sea salt
Freshly ground black pepper

2 eggs
3 tablespoons flour
Oil for shallow frying
Cranberry or applesauce

Grate the potatoes coarsely, peeled or unpeeled according to preference.
Grate the onion. Mix potatoes and onion with salt and pepper, eggs,
and flour, and stir to make a batter. Heat a little oil in a skillet and
fry tablespoonfuls of the mixture until golden and crispy, turning
them over so that both sides are cooked. Drain on paper towels and
serve immediately with the sauce and a crunchy salad.

RICE CROQUETTES

ITALY

These crisp croquettes are good for a first course if you serve them on
small plates with a tomato or mushroom sauce; or, with vegetables and
potato, they make a tasty supper. They're an excellent way of using
up leftover risotto and I sometimes make an extra large batch specially
with this in mind—you simply form the risotto into little rounds and
coat them in beaten egg and dried crumbs. But if you're making the
croquettes from scratch, this is the way to do them. *Serves 4.*

1¼ cups (310 ml) brown rice
1 teaspoon sea salt
2 cups (500 ml) water
1 large onion, peeled and finely
   chopped

2 tablespoons butter
1 cup (250 ml) grated cheese
½–1 teaspoon dry mustard
1 egg
Freshly ground black pepper

TO FINISH:

1 egg, beaten with 1 tablespoon
   of cold water

Dry bread crumbs
Oil for deep or shallow frying

Wash the rice and put it into a saucepan with the salt and water.
Bring to the boil, then turn the heat down low, put a lid on the
saucepan, and leave it to simmer for 40 minutes, or until the rice is

cooked. Then take it off the heat and leave it to stand, with the lid still on the saucepan, for another 10 minutes.

While the rice is cooking, sauté the onion gently in butter for 10 minutes, until it's golden and soft. Stir the onion into the cooked rice together with the grated cheese, dry mustard, and egg. Mix well and season to taste with salt and plenty of pepper. It's easier to shape the mixture into croquettes if it's cool, and better still if there's time to chill it in the fridge. Dip tablespoonfuls of the mixture first into the beaten egg, then into the dried crumbs, shaping them into rounds with your hands. Fry the croquettes in deep or shallow oil until they're crisp all over. Drain them on paper towels and serve them as soon as possible.

SPICY FRITTERS

MIDDLE EAST

This is a cheating recipe for these spicy chick pea fritters, or *felafel*, as they're called. This red lentil recipe is just as tasty but much quicker and easier to do. *Serves 4.*

1½ cups (375 ml) lentils	1 tablespoon chopped fresh
3 cups (750 ml) water	parsley
2 tablespoons butter or margarine	1 egg
1 medium-size onion, peeled and	Sea salt
grated	Freshly ground black pepper
1½ teaspoons ground cumin	A little whole-wheat flour
1½ teaspoons ground coriander	Oil for shallow frying

Put the lentils and water in a medium-size saucepan and bring to the boil. Let the lentils simmer gently until they are soft and golden and all the water has been absorbed. Mash the lentils with the butter or margarine and mix in the onion, cumin, coriander, parsley, and egg. Season the mixture with salt and pepper to taste.

Chill the lentil mixture in the refrigerator for 1 hour. When thoroughly chilled, form the lentil mixture into small flat cakes on a lightly floured board. Fry the little cakes in hot shallow oil and drain them well.

Served with pita bread and a salad of lettuce, tomatoes, cucumber, and scallions tossed in vinaigrette, these little fritters make a tasty and filling lunch. They're also nice with garlic mayonnaise, chilled yogurt, or mango chutney; or, with gravy, potatoes, and a cooked vegetable, they make a simple cooked meal that usually appeals to children.

CORN FRITTERS

U S A

Although these fritters are usually served as an accompaniment to meat, they are quite filling and make a good supper or lunch dish, with tomato sauce, a soup, and a green vegetable. They also make an interesting first course. *Serves 3.*

1 can (12 ounces/360 g) whole kernel corn	*Sea salt*
1 egg, separated	*Freshly ground black pepper*
2 tablespoons whole-wheat flour	*Oil for shallow frying*

Drain the corn and put it into a bowl with the egg yolk, flour, and some salt and pepper, and mix well. Beat the egg white until it's standing in soft peaks, then gently fold it into the corn mixture. Heat a little oil in a skillet and fry the corn mixture, a tablespoonful at a time, on both sides, until crisp. (Stand back as you do so because the corn tends to "pop.") As soon as they're ready, drain the fritters on paper towels. Keep the first ones warm while you fry the remainder, and then serve them straight away.

FRIED WHEAT PROTEIN WITH SWEET AND SOUR SAUCE

C H I N A

We talk about "knitted soya steaks" and textured vegetable proteins as though they were something very new and unusual, but the inventive Chinese have been using wheat protein, or wheat gluten, for centuries and it's an entirely natural product that you can make from strong flour in your own home if you want to. You just make a dough with flour, a little salt, and water; soak it in a bowl of cold water for 1 hour; then pummel and knead it under cold running water. As you do this the white starch washes away and you're left with a firm, pliable piece of dough that you can then simmer in well-flavored stock and use in stews and casseroles—or in this recipe. It's quite easy to do but a bit labor-intensive, so I usually buy it in a can: You can get it at Chinese-food shops or from health-food shops where it's sometimes called meatless savory cuts. The wheat contains good protein, and I think it's delicious fried like this and served in a sweet and sour sauce. The ingredients and proportions for the sauce are those recommended by the distinguished Chinese cook and author, Kenneth Lo. *Serves 4.*

FOR THE SAUCE:

4 teaspoons brown sugar
2 tablespoons red wine vinegar
4 teaspoons corn starch
4 teaspoons tomato paste or
  tomato ketchup

4 teaspoons soy sauce
1 tablespoon dry sherry
1 tablespoon orange juice
4 tablespoons cold water

FOR THE FRIED WHEAT PROTEIN:

1 can (15 ounces/450 g) and
  1 can (8 ounces/240 g) wheat
  protein
1 clove garlic
Sea salt
1 egg, beaten
1 piece of fresh gingerroot, about
  1 inch (2.5 cm) long; or

½ teaspoon ordinary ground
  ginger
Dry bread crumbs
Oil for shallow frying—sesame
  oil if possible

First prepare the sauce. Put all the ingredients into a small saucepan and mix to a smooth paste. Leave to one side while you prepare the wheat protein.

If the wheat protein has been prepared with liquid, drain this off and keep it to one side. Cut the wheat protein into chunky bite-size pieces. Peel the garlic, crush it with a knife, and then mix it to a creamy paste with a little salt and put it into a smallish bowl with the beaten egg. Peel the ginger root and grate it finely into the bowl with the garlic and egg, or add the ground ginger. Mix it all together. Dip the pieces of wheat protein into the egg mixture and then coat them with the dry bread crumbs. Fry the little fritters in hot shallow oil, turning them so that they're crisp all over. Drain them well on paper towels and keep them warm.

Now quickly finish the sauce by putting the small saucepan over a moderate heat and stirring the mixture for a couple of minutes, until it has thickened. If you think it's too thick, thin it down with a little extra orange juice, water, or the liquid from the canned wheat protein. Pour the sauce over the hot fritters and serve at once.

This is nice served with hot cooked rice and some Chinese vegetables. Chinese cabbage or *chop suey* go well with it and so does Chinese plum sauce, which you can get at Chinese-food shops—or you can use ordinary chutney.

PASTA AND
CREPES

Blini

Chick Peas and Vermicelli

Lasagne with Spinach and Cheese

Macaroni and Cheese

Asparagus-Filled Crêpes

Cheese-Filled Crêpes in Spicy Tomato Sauce

Crêpes Stuffed with Mushrooms and Artichoke Hearts

Tortillas Filled with Spicy Red Kidney Beans

Pasta and Beans

Pasta with Cream Cheese and Walnuts

Pasta with Lentils

Spaghetti with Pesto Sauce

P ASTA AND CRÊPE DISHES ARE WARMING AND FILL-
ing, and some of them are also very quick and easy to make. They
are also perfect served with just a simple salad, which helps to cut
down on preparation time.

For all the pasta recipes, I use whole-wheat pasta. It's very easy to
get these days and, although it looks rather dauntingly dark in the
package, it cooks up much lighter and is just as quick to use as
ordinary egg pasta. One of the secrets of cooking whole-wheat pasta
successfully is to use a big saucepan and plenty of water so that the
pasta can move around as it cooks. It's also helpful to add a couple of
tablespoons of cooking oil to the water, as this prevents the pasta from
sticking together and the water from frothing up and boiling over.
When the pasta is cooked so that it's just tender, I find it best to drain
it and then put it back into the still hot saucepan with a knob of butter
or a little olive oil. There's no need to rinse the pasta in either hot or
cold water.

Although stuffed crêpes, which I've also included in this section,
are not particularly quick to make, I do think they're quite convenient
when you're busy, because each part—the crêpes, the filling, and the
sauce—can be quickly made on its own when you can fit it in, and
then the whole dish can be assembled at the last minute. Actually
stuffed crêpes are one of my favorite dishes for entertaining; I can
make everything the week before and freeze it. Then I just thaw the
entire meal the day I want to serve it. Also stuffed crêpes don't spoil
if they're kept covered with foil in a moderate oven (about 300° F/
150° C) for quite a long time, which gives me a chance to relax and
enjoy myself without worrying about what's going on in the oven. I
take the foil off the top of the dish and turn the oven up when we
start the meal to brown the top of the crêpes.

You can make excellent nutty-tasting crêpes with whole-wheat
flour. If you want them very light, use half whole-wheat flour and
half unbleached all-purpose; if these are successful you might like to
try them with all whole-wheat, which is fine as long as you take care
to make the crêpes really thin.

When you're making crêpes, the important thing is to have the
right-size crêpe pan or skillet. I have a small non-stick pan measuring
6–7 inches (17–18 cm), and it's ideal because the crêpes turn out just
the right size, and, because the pan is non-stick, I only have to add
a minimum of butter or oil to cook the crêpes, which makes them
easier to control in the pan and of course less fattening when they're
finished.

A large shallow ovenproof dish is best for baking the stuffed crêpes in because they are nicest if you can arrange them in one layer. I put them in the same big Pyrex dish that I use for stuffed vegetables—it measures about 10 × 15 inches (25 × 38 cm). A similar-size porcelain or earthenware dish would be even better.

BLINI

RUSSIA

These buckwheat yeast crêpes from Russia have a character all their own. They come out light and delectable; the buckwheat gives them a dark, nutty flavor. I think they're nicest served hot from the pan with melted butter or sour cream, accompanied by a big bowl of crunchy salad; hearty chunks of lettuce, celery, scallions, tomatoes, and carrot sticks. *Serves 4.*

2 cups (500 ml) milk	*½ teaspoon salt*
1 teaspoon sugar	*2 tablespoons sour cream*
1 package active dry yeast	*3 eggs, separated*
2 cups (500 ml) all-purpose flour	*Oil for shallow frying*
¾ cup (180 ml) buckwheat flour	*Sour cream or melted butter to*
2 tablespoons butter	*serve*

Heat two-thirds of the milk to lukewarm; add the sugar and yeast and leave in a warm place for 5 minutes to prove. Put the all-purpose flour and half the buckwheat flour into a bowl and add the yeast mixture. Knead hard until smooth, then cover and put in a warm place until doubled in bulk—about 1½ hours. Add the rest of the buckwheat flour and beat the mixture again. Put back into a warm place for another 2 hours.

Melt the butter in a small pan and add the remaining milk; heat the mixture to lukewarm. Add this to the flour mixture together with the salt, sour cream, and egg yolks. Beat well. Beat the egg whites until they're standing in peaks, then fold them gently into the mixture with a rubber spatula. Cover the bowl and leave for another 30 minutes.

Heat a little oil in a skillet; put 2 tablespoonfuls of the *blini* mixture into the hot oil and leave until crisp on one side; flip the little crêpe over with a metal or heatproof plastic spatula and cook the other side.

These crêpes can also be served as a dessert, with sour cream and/or jam, syrup, or sugar.

◆———◆———◆

CHICK PEAS AND VERMICELLI

ITALY

At first glance this seems a strange mixture but it works well, the firm golden chick peas contrasting with the soft creamy-colored vermicelli, and both shiny with olive oil and pungent with garlic and Parmesan cheese. Incidentally, if you use canned chick peas for this recipe, it then falls into the quick-to-make emergency meal category. *Serves 4.*

8 ounces (240 g) dried chick peas
Sea salt
6 tablespoons olive oil
8 ounces (240 g) vermicelli or fine
   whole-wheat spaghetti

1–2 cloves garlic, peeled and
   crushed
Freshly ground black pepper
¼–½ cup (60–125 ml) grated
   Parmesan cheese

Cover the chick peas with cold water and leave them to soak for several hours; then drain and rinse them, put them into a saucepan with plenty of fresh water, and simmer them gently until they're tender. Keep them hot. Fill half a large saucepan with cold water; add a teaspoon of salt and 2 tablespoons of the olive oil and bring to the boil. Cook the pasta in the water until it's just tender. Drain the pasta and return it to the hot saucepan with the rest of the olive oil, the garlic, and salt and pepper. Drain the hot chickpeas and add them to the pasta, turning the mixture gently so that everything gets coated with the oil. Serve immediately, sprinkled with grated Parmesan cheese.

This dish is rich in protein and is lovely served with a simple tomato or green salad.

◆———◆———◆

LASAGNE WITH SPINACH AND CHEESE

ITALY

This is an easy-to-make dish that's very tasty and filling. The exact amount of lasagne needed will depend on the brand you're using and the shape of your dish. I think it's best to try to fit the pieces of lasagne in the dish before you cook them: Arrange the strips in a shallow square or oblong ovenproof dish so that they make a complete layer but don't overlap, and then allow the same amount again so that you will have 2 layers in the finished dish. This will probably be about 4 ounces (125 g) of lasagne—if the dish you're planning to use calls for very much more than this you'll probably have to double all the other ingredients, and you will then be able to feed 6 or 8 people.

This lasagne is lovely served with a juicy tomato salad. *Serves 3–4.*

About 4 ounces (120 g) lasagne
1 pound (450 g) spinach or
   10 ounces (300 g) chopped
   frozen spinach
Sea salt
Freshly ground black pepper
1 pound (450 g) ricotta or low-fat
   cottage cheese

¼ cup (60 ml) grated Parmesan
   cheese
2 eggs
1½ cups (310 ml) grated Edam
   cheese

Preheat oven to 400° F (200° C). Fill half a large saucepan with salted water. When the water is boiling put in the strips of lasagne—stand them in the water and, as the ends soften, gradually ease the rest of the lasagne down until it's all submerged. Simmer the lasagne gently for about 15 minutes, until it's tender, and then drain it in a colander.

While the lasagne is cooking, wash and pick over the spinach and then put it into a large saucepan; don't add water, as the moisture still clinging to the spinach should be sufficient. Put a lid on the saucepan and cook the spinach for about 7–10 minutes, until it's tender. Drain the spinach, then chop it in the saucepan. Season with salt and pepper. Mix the *ricotta* or cottage cheese with the Parmesan, eggs, and salt and pepper.

Lightly grease your ovenproof dish and put half the spinach in the bottom of it, followed by half the cheese mixture. Spread a layer of lasagne evenly over the top, then repeat these 3 layers. Sprinkle the grated cheese on top, and bake for 45 minutes, until it's golden brown on top, hot and bubbly within. Serve at once.

MACARONI AND CHEESE

ENGLAND

People usually laugh when I tell them I like macaroni and cheese, but I think it's delicious if it's well made, quite as good as some of the Italian pasta dishes people rave about. I think the secret with macaroni and cheese is to make the sauce quite thin so that you get a light, moist result. It's lovely with a juicy tomato salad or a crisp green salad. You can cook macaroni and cheese in the oven or under the broiler, whichever is more convenient. *Serves 4.*

2 cups (500 ml) whole-wheat short macaroni
Sea salt
3 tablespoons butter
3 tablespoons unbleached all-purpose flour
3 cups (750 ml) milk

1½ cups (375 ml) grated cheese, preferably double Gloucester, which gives a lovely color
1 teaspoon dry mustard
Freshly ground black pepper
Dry bread crumbs
A little extra grated cheese

If you're going to bake the macaroni and cheese, preheat the oven to 400° F (200° C). Fill half a large saucepan with water and add a teaspoonful of salt. Bring the water to the boil; put in the macaroni and let it simmer until it's just tender—this will be in about 10 minutes (the time given on the package will be a guide but keep your eye on it and bite a piece when you think it's nearly done to check it). Drain the macaroni.

While the macaroni is cooking, make the sauce. Melt the butter in a large saucepan and stir in the flour; let it cook over the heat for a few moments, then mix in about a fourth of the milk. Keep the heat up high and stir vigorously until the mixture is smooth, then add some more milk as before and repeat until it's all been added and you have a smooth, rather thin sauce. (You may think it's *too* thin, but don't worry; it will be all right.) Take the saucepan off the heat and mix in the grated cheese, dry mustard, and salt and pepper to taste.

Stir the macaroni into the sauce and then pour the mixture into a lightly greased shallow ovenproof dish. Cover the top all over with the dried crumbs and a little grated cheese. Bake the macaroni and cheese in the oven for about 40 minutes or put it under a hot broiler for about 15–20 minutes, until it's bubbling and golden and crisp on top.

ASPARAGUS-FILLED CRÊPES

FRANCE

I'm afraid this is rather an extravagant dish, using an awful lot of asparagus, but for a special occasion it really makes a lovely main course that's no more expensive than good meat or fish would be. *Serves 6.*

FOR THE CRÊPES:

1 cup (250 ml) unbleached all-purpose flour—I use whole-wheat but you could also use a mixture of whole-wheat and white

A pinch of sea salt
2 eggs
2 tablespoons vegetable oil
1 cup (250 ml) milk
Extra oil for frying

FOR THE FILLING:

4 cans (10½ ounces/319 g each) cut asparagus

2 tablespoons chopped parsley

FOR THE SAUCE:

6 tablespoons butter
¾ cup (180 ml) unbleached all-purpose flour
3¾ cups (930 ml) milk
1 bay leaf

1–1½ teaspoons dry mustard
1½ cups (375 ml) grated cheese, preferably double Gloucester
Sea salt
Freshly ground black pepper

TO FINISH:

½ cup (125 ml) grated cheese

First make the crêpe batter; the easiest way to do this is to put all the ingredients into the blender and purée until you have a smooth creamy mixture. If you do this, I have found that it doesn't matter if you don't let the batter stand for 30 minutes, as in the traditional method. If you haven't a blender, put the flour and salt into a bowl, break in the eggs and beat, then gradually mix in the oil and milk until you've got a creamy mixture. Beat well, then leave the batter to stand for 30 minutes and beat again.

To make the crêpes brush a small crêpe pan or skillet with oil and set it over a moderate heat. When it is hot, pour in enough batter to coat the base of the pan thinly. Tip and swirl the pan so that the mixture runs all over the bottom. Then put the pan over the heat for 20–30 seconds, until the top of the crêpe is set and the underside is flecked golden brown. Flip the crêpe over using a small palette knife and your fingers if necessary. Cook the other side, and then lift it out onto a plate. Brush the pan with more oil if necessary (I find with a non-sticking pan I only have to do this after about every 3 crêpes) and make another crêpe in the same way, putting it on top of the first one when it's done. Continue until you've finished the mixture and have a nice pile of 12 to 15 crêpes. (You can do all this well in advance if you want to.)

To make the filling, drain the asparagus and mix with the chopped parsley. This may seem a rather simple filling but it's delicious in combination with the crêpes and sauce.

For the sauce, melt the butter in a large saucepan and stir in the flour; cook for a moment or two and then add about a fourth of the milk and the bay leaf, and stir over a good heat until the mixture is smooth and very thick. Then add another portion of milk and repeat the process until all the milk has been incorporated and you've got a smooth sauce. Take the saucepan off the heat, stir in the dry mustard and grated cheese, and season the sauce carefully. If you're having white wine with the meal, a couple of tablespoons of it will make a delicious addition.

To assemble the dish, put a heaped tablespoonful of asparagus on each crêpe, roll the crêpe neatly, and place it in a large shallow greased casserole. These crêpes look best arranged in a single layer, but you will need a big dish to accommodate them. When the crêpes are all in the dish, pour the sauce evenly over them, removing the bay leaf. Sprinkle the grated cheese over the top and cover the dish with a piece of foil.

When you're ready to bake the crêpes, preheat the oven to 350° F (180° C). Bake them for about 20 minutes, removing the foil about 5 minutes before the end of the cooking time to brown the cheese on top.

These pancakes are good served with *gratin dauphinois* and either a green salad or a cooked green or yellow vegetable.

CHEESE-FILLED CRÊPES IN
SPICY TOMATO SAUCE

MEXICO

When you put a spoon into this dish, the creamy white filling oozes out and looks very appetizing against the golden crêpes and tomato sauce. The "crêpes" are actually tortillas, which are very easy to make; they're not as light as crêpes but very good and very filling. You can of course use ordinary whole-wheat crêpes instead if you prefer. *Serves 6–8.*

FOR THE TORTILLAS:

See recipe, page 283

FOR THE FILLING:

3 cups (750 ml) cottage or ricotta
   cheese
3 cups (750 ml) grated cheese
1½ teaspoons dry mustard

2 cloves garlic, peeled and crushed
Sea salt
Freshly ground black pepper

FOR THE SAUCE:

1 large onion, peeled and chopped
1 tablespoon oil
1 clove garlic, peeled and crushed

1 can (28 ounces/840 g) tomatoes
½–1 teaspoon chili powder

TO FINISH:

1 cup (250 ml) grated cheese

Make the filling by mixing together the cottage or *ricotta* cheese, the grated cheese, dry mustard and garlic; add salt and pepper to taste.

Sauté the onion in the oil for 10 minutes, then stir in the garlic, tomatoes, chili powder, and salt and pepper to taste. Strain or purée the sauce.

Heat the oven to 375° F (190° C). Grease a large shallow oven-proof dish. Spoon the filling onto the tortillas, rolling them neatly round and dividing the mixture evenly among them. Place the plump rolls side by side in the dish and pour the tomato sauce over them. Sprinkle the grated cheese on top.

Cover the dish with foil and bake the crêpes, or *enchiladas*, as they're called in Mexico, for 45 minutes; then take off the foil and leave them in the oven for another 15 minutes or so to brown the top.

They're lovely with just a lightly cooked green vegetable such as Brussels sprouts, or with a green salad.

◆———◆———◆

CRÊPES STUFFED WITH MUSHROOMS AND ARTICHOKE HEARTS

FRANCE

I think full, fresh mushrooms are the best to use for this recipe because they have a lovely rich flavor when they're cooked. Like the crêpes filled with asparagus, this dish is a bit extravagant, but it's a delicious mixture of tender crêpes, a tasty filling, and a light cheesy sauce. *Serves 4.*

FOR THE CRÊPES:

1 cup (250 ml) flour—all
 whole-wheat or half
 whole-wheat and half white
Pinch of sea salt

2 eggs
2 tablespoons vegetable oil
1 cup (250 ml) milk

FOR THE FILLING:

1 onion, peeled and finely
 chopped
4 tablespoons butter
1½ pounds (675 g) mushrooms
2 large cloves garlic, peeled and
 crushed

1 can (14 ounces/420 g) artichoke
 hearts, drained and sliced
2 tablespoons chopped parsley
4 tablespoons cream
2–3 teaspoons lemon juice
Freshly ground black pepper

FOR THE SAUCE:

6 tablespoons butter
6 tablespoons flour
1 bay leaf
3¾ cups (930 ml) milk

1½ cups (375 ml) grated cheese,
 preferably double Gloucester
1–1½ teaspoons dry mustard

TO FINISH:

½ cup (125 ml) grated cheese

Prepare the crêpe batter as directed in the recipe on pages 188–89. This should make 12 or 15 small thin crêpes. This can be done several days in advance, if convenient.

For the filling, sauté the onion in the butter for 10 minutes but don't let it brown. Wash the mushrooms and pat them dry in a cloth, then halve or quarter them and add them to the butter; let them cook for 5 minutes, or until they're tender. If the mushrooms produce much water, let them boil vigorously until the mixture is fairly dry. Take the saucepan off the heat and stir in the garlic, artichoke hearts, parsley, and cream. Sharpen the mixture with a little lemon juice and add salt and pepper to taste.

To make the sauce, melt the butter in a largish saucepan and add the flour. Cook for a moment or two, then add the bay leaf and about a fourth of the milk and stir vigorously over a high heat until you have a smooth, very thick mixture. Repeat, stirring in another fourth of the milk and continue in this way until all the milk has been added and you have a smooth sauce. Take the saucepan off the heat and mix in the grated cheese, salt and pepper, and enough dry mustard to give the mixture a nice tang. This, like the crêpes and the filling, can be made in advance.

When you're ready to assemble the dish, divide the filling among the crêpes, rolling them up neatly and placing them side by side in a shallow ovenproof dish. Take the bay leaf out of the cheese sauce and pour the sauce evenly over the crêpes; sprinkle with the grated cheese. Cover the dish with foil and bake the crêpes at 350° F (180° C) for about 20 minutes, taking the foil off for about the last 5 minutes to brown the top of the dish.

The crêpes are equally good served with a cooked vegetable or a green salad.

TORTILLAS FILLED WITH SPICY RED KIDNEY BEANS

MEXICO

If you don't like making ordinary crêpes you might like to try this recipe, which (as in the recipe on page 190) uses tortillas instead. The tortillas are very easy to make from a combination of whole-wheat flour and corn meal (or just whole-wheat flour). *Serves 6–8.*

See recipe, page 283

FOR THE FILLING:

1 large onion, peeled and chopped
1 tablespoon oil
2 cloves garlic, peeled and crushed
1 can (28 ounces/840 g) tomatoes
8 ounces (240 g) dried red kidney

beans, soaked, cooked and
  drained
½–1 teaspoon chili powder
Sea salt
Freshly ground black pepper

FOR THE SAUCE:

6 tablespoons butter
6 tablespoons flour
3¾ cups (930 ml) milk

1½ cups (375 ml) grated cheese
1½ teaspoons dry mustard

TO FINISH:

1 cup (250 ml) grated cheese

First make the filling. Sauté the onion in the oil in a large saucepan for
10 minutes, until it's soft but not browned, and then stir in the garlic,
tomatoes, red beans, and enough chili powder, salt and pepper to give
a good flavor. Mash the beans and tomatoes a bit with a spoon to break
them up.

Next make the sauce. Melt the butter in a medium-size saucepan
and stir in the flour. Cook for a moment or two and then pour in about
a fourth of the milk. Stir over a high heat until you have a smooth,
very thick mixture; add another portion of milk and continue in this
way until all the milk has been added and you have a smooth sauce.
Take the saucepan off the heat and mix in the grated cheese, dry
mustard, and a good seasoning of salt and pepper.

When you're ready to assemble the dish, preheat the oven to 375° F
(190° C). Grease a large shallow ovenproof dish. Put some of the
bean mixture onto each tortilla and roll the tortilla up neatly. Place
the tortillas side by side in the dish and cover them evenly with the
sauce. Sprinkle the grated cheese over the top and cover the dish with
a piece of foil. Bake for 45 minutes, then remove the foil and leave the
tortillas in the oven for another 15 minutes or so to brown the top.
Serve with crisp green salad or cooked green vegetable.

PASTA AND BEANS

ITALY

You can serve this mixture as soon as it's ready or you can spoon it into a shallow ovenproof dish, sprinkle the top with bread crumbs and grated cheese, and bake until it's crisp and golden. Whichever you do, I think you'll agree it's a tasty, satisfying, and economical dish. *Serves 3–4.*

¾ cup (180 ml) dried red kidney
   beans
½ cup (125 ml) split red lentils
1 large onion, peeled and chopped
2 tablespoons olive oil
1 clove garlic, crushed
2 tomatoes, peeled
4 cups (1 liter) water

1 cup (250 ml) whole-wheat
   macaroni
1 tablespoon tomato ketchup
2 tablespoons chopped parsley
1 teaspoon ground cinnamon
1 teaspoon lemon juice
Sea salt
Freshly ground black pepper

OPTIONAL TOPPING:

Dry bread crumbs

½ cup (125 ml) grated cheese

Put the beans and lentils into a big bowl, cover with plenty of cold water, and leave for several hours if possible, then drain and rinse them. In a large saucepan sauté the onion in the oil for 10 minutes. Add the garlic, tomatoes, beans, lentils, and the water. Bring to the boil, put a lid on the saucepan, and leave it to simmer for 1–1¼ hours, until the beans are tender. At this stage the mixture will look more like soup than anything else, but don't worry. Add the macaroni, tomato ketchup, and parsley to the saucepan and let the mixture simmer for about 10 minutes, until the macaroni is tender. The mixture should still be quite moist—add a little liquid if necessary (red wine if you've got any). Then stir in the cinnamon, lemon juice, and salt and pepper to taste. Serve immediately; or spoon the mixture into a lightly greased shallow casserole, sprinkle with the crumbs and grated cheese, and bake in a moderate oven for 20–30 minutes, or until golden brown.

    This is lovely served with a fresh juicy salad with a good dressing.

PASTA WITH CREAM CHEESE
AND WALNUTS

ITALY

Although it's quick and easy to do, this dish is rich and luxurious. I think it's nicest made with whole-wheat pasta rings, but you could use other types of pasta. Hazelnuts can be used instead of walnuts— bake them first for about 20 minutes in a moderate oven until the skins rub off easily and the nuts underneath are golden brown. *Serves 4.*

Sea salt
1 tablespoon oil
2 cups (500 ml) whole-wheat
   pasta rings
1 tablespoon butter
1½ cups (375 ml) low-fat cottage
   cheese—or 4 packages

(3 ounces/90 g each) cream
cheese, but I think this makes
   the dish rather too rich
1 clove garlic, crushed
Freshly ground black pepper
1–1½ cups (250–375 ml) walnuts,
   roughly chopped

Fill half a large saucepan with water; add a teaspoon of salt and the oil. Bring to the boil, then put in the pasta rings and simmer them gently until they're just tender.

While the pasta rings are cooking, make the cheese sauce. Melt the butter in a medium-size saucepan over a gentle heat and then add the cottage cheese or cream cheese and garlic. Stir constantly, over the heat, until the cheese is very smooth and creamy. Season with salt and pepper to taste.

Spoon the pasta into a hot serving dish, pour the sauce over the top, and sprinkle with the chopped nuts. Serve with a green salad but don't put too much dressing on it, as the pasta dish is rather rich.

PASTA WITH LENTILS

MIDDLE EAST

In the Middle East this would probably be made with noodles, but I generally use fine whole-wheat spaghetti instead. *Serves 4.*

FOR THE LENTILS:

8 ounces (240 g) split red lentils

1 large onion, peeled and chopped

2 tablespoons oil

2 cloves garlic

1 small green pepper or ¼ pound
(115 g) fresh mushrooms

2½ cups (625 ml) water

1 tablespoon tomato ketchup

1 tablespoon chopped parsley

½ teaspoon ground cinnamon

Sea salt

Freshly ground black pepper

FOR THE PASTA:

8 ounces (240 g) noodles or
whole-wheat spaghetti

2 tablespoons oil

Wash the lentils. Sauté the onion in the oil in a large saucepan for 5 minutes. Meanwhile, peel and crush the garlic and wash, seed, and chop the pepper (or wash and chop the mushrooms). Add the garlic and pepper (or mushrooms) to the saucepan and cook for another 2–3 minutes; then add the lentils and stir them so that they are coated with the oil. Mix in the water, tomato ketchup, parsley, and cinnamon; bring to the boil and then cover the saucepan and leave the mixture to simmer gently until the lentils are cooked—from 30 minutes to an hour. Season with salt and pepper.

When the lentils are nearly done, cook the noodles or spaghetti in plenty of boiling salted water for about 10 minutes. Drain the pasta and toss it in the oil. Serve the pasta with the lentils. A green salad goes well with this.

SPAGHETTI WITH PESTO SAUCE

ITALY

Pesto looks a curious thick green mixture when it's first made, but when it's added to the hot, cooked spaghetti it really transforms the pasta into something special with a delicious, rich flavor. You should really use fresh basil for this recipe, but if it's not easy to get I find that a bunch of fresh parsley plus a good seasoning of dried basil makes a fairly good alternative. *Serves 4.*

FOR THE PASTA:

8 ounces (240 g) whole-wheat
spaghetti

Sea salt

2 tablespoons vegetable oil

2 cloves garlic, peeled and crushed   *⅓ cup (80 ml) pine nuts*
1 large bunch of fresh basil—or   *⅓ cup (80 ml) grated Parmesan*
   a large bunch of fresh parsley   *cheese*
   and 2–3 teaspoons dried basil   *½ cup (125 ml) olive oil*

Fill half a large saucepan with water and add a teaspoon of salt and the vegetable oil. Bring to the boil and then gently ease in the spaghetti, pushing it down into the water as it softens. Let the spaghetti simmer gently until it's just tender—about 10 minutes. Drain the spaghetti and return it to the hot saucepan.

While the spaghetti is cooking make the *pesto*. Take the stalks off the fresh basil or parsley and put the leaves into your blender jar, together with the dried basil, if you're using it, the garlic, pine nuts, Parmesan, and olive oil. Blend at medium speed until you have a thick purée the consistency of softly whipped cream.

Put the pasta onto a hot serving dish and spoon the *pesto* on top; or serve the *pesto* separately and let everyone help themselves.

You'll perhaps want to serve a protein appetizer or dessert with this for a balanced meal—or you could offer a protein-rich salad.

SAVORY
PASTRIES, PIZZAS,
AND QUICHES

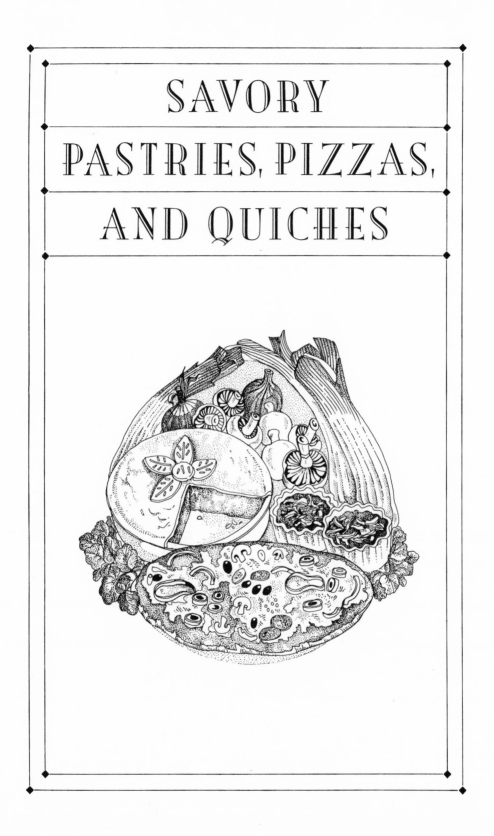

Individual Asparagus Tarts
Cheese Pie
Cheese Tartlets
Cheese and Onion Quiche
Leek Quiche
Leek Pie
Mushroom Quiche
Onion Quiche
Pizza
Quick Non-Yeast Pizza
Samosas
Spinach Pie

Savory PASTRIES ARE ALWAYS POPULAR AND
there are some lovely vegetarian ones: light and delicious quiches
from France, flaky golden pies from the Middle East, and cheesy pizzas
from Italy, all of which fill the kitchen with their warm fragrance as
they cook and make your mouth water.

These are useful dishes for the cook because they're so adaptable.
Most of them can be served either hot or cold, with salad or with
cooked vegetables, for lunch or for supper. They make good first as
well as main courses and are also splendid picnic food.

The quiches and flans in this section are made from three basic
types of pastry. For the quiches there's a light, crumbly shortcrust
pastry made from whole-wheat flour, and a quick flaky pastry that uses
half whole-wheat and half white flour; and for the flans I use a whole-
wheat shortcrust that cooks up crisp.

One of the main problems when making these savory pastry dishes
is to get the pastry crisp while keeping the filling light and moist. Over
the years I've tried all sorts of different methods: You may wish to use
a technique discovered by a friend, a super cook, who very kindly told
me her secret. All you do is brush the pastry with a little very hot oil
as soon as you take it out of the oven. Or you may prefer to partially
cook the crust, weighting it down with dried beans, uncooked rice, or
aluminum pastry pellets spread on waxed paper or buttered aluminum
foil that is set down on the raw crust when it first goes in the oven,
and then removed.

It also helps if you use a metal tart pan with removable bottom,
although the methods I've described work well even with a porcelain
dish. I do think it helps, too, if you put a baking sheet on the oven rack
and heat it up with the oven, then stand the tart pan or quiche dish on
this to get things off to a good start.

These are filling dishes and most of them contain a good amount
of protein, so a vegetable appetizer and a fruity dessert go well with
them.

INDIVIDUAL ASPARAGUS TARTS

FRANCE

These light, creamy little tarts make a very good first course for a dinner party; they're also nice with salad for lunch. They would be lovely made in individual quiche dishes if you've got them. Otherwise use tart pans or any small ovenproof containers. *Serves 6.*

FOR THE PASTRY:

*2 cups (500 ml) whole-wheat
    flour
Pinch of salt*

*6 tablespoons butter
5–6 teaspoons cold water
2 tablespoons oil (optional)*

FOR THE FILLING:

*1 onion, peeled and finely
    chopped
1 small clove garlic, peeled and
    crushed
2 tablespoons butter
4 egg yolks or 2 whole eggs
1¼ cups (310 ml) milk or light
    cream*

*Sea salt
Freshly ground black pepper
Grated nutmeg
1 can (10½ ounces/315 g) cut
    asparagus, drained*

Place a baking sheet in the center of the oven and preheat oven to 400° F (200° C). To make the pastry, measure the flour, baking powder, and salt into a bowl. Rub in the butter with your fingertips until the mixture looks like bread crumbs; then stir in enough water to make a dough. Roll out the pastry on a lightly floured board and use it to line 6 individual tart pans. Prick the pastry with a fork and place the tart pans on the baking sheet in the oven. (If you prefer to weight down your crust as you partially bake it, no need to prick the pastry, the purpose of which is to prevent the dough's puffing up while cooking.) Bake for 10–15 minutes, until crisp and golden brown. If you use the very hot oil, brush this over the pastry as soon as you take the tart crusts out of the oven. Turn the oven setting down to 350° F (180° C).

Sauté the onion and garlic in the butter over a gentle heat for 10 minutes, but don't let them brown. Take the saucepan off the heat. Beat together the eggs and milk or cream and then add these to the onion and garlic and cook very gently, stirring all the time, until the mixture thickens. Season with salt and pepper and add some grated nutmeg to taste. Arrange the asparagus in the pastry shells and then pour in the egg mixture, dividing it equally among them.

Bake the savory tarts in the preheated oven for 20–30 minutes, until the filling is set. Serve them hot or warm.

CHEESE PIE

GREECE

This is a beautiful flaky, golden pie with a creamy mild-tasting cheese filling. In Greece the crust would be made from phyllo dough and the filling from feta and *mitzithra* cheeses. I make it with a quick flaky pastry, and a filling of cottage cheese or *ricotta* and Lancashire cheese if I can't find feta. I also sometimes add some lightly sautéed onion, which gives extra flavor. You might think all this is taking too many liberties with the original recipe, but it still makes a lovely pie! It's nice as a hot appetizer or as a main meal with a cooked vegetable, such as cauliflower in tomato sauce. If you want to try making the pie with phyllo dough, see page 216. *Serves 6.*

FOR THE PASTRY:

2¼ cups (560 ml) flour—I use   *1 cup (250 ml) cold butter*
  half whole-wheat and half   *Cold water to mix*
  white flour

FOR THE FILLING:

1½ pounds (675 g) cottage cheese   *⅔ cup (160 ml) plain yogurt*
  or ricotta   *3 eggs*
2 cups (500 ml) feta or   *Sea salt*
  Lancashire cheese, grated   *Freshly ground black pepper*
½ cup (125 ml) flour

First make the pastry—you need to do this an hour or so in advance to give it a chance to chill before you use it. Sift the flours into a bowl, adding any residue of bran from the whole-wheat flour left in the sieve; then grate in the hard butter using a coarse grater. Very lightly mix the butter with the flour, using a fork or wire pastry blender and making sure that there are no large lumps of butter clinging together. The consistency of the dough mixture should, at this point, be crumbly; the butter having formed small pellets as it's been cut into the flour. Stir in enough cold water to make a soft, manageable dough. Wrap the dough in a piece of waxed paper and put it into the refrigerator to chill for at least an hour.

Meanwhile you can make the filling for the pie. Put the cottage cheese or *ricotta* into a large bowl and stir in all the other ingredients, beating them together until you've got a nice creamy mixture. Season with salt and pepper. (If you want to add some onion to the pie, chop 1 or 2 onions, sauté them in a little butter, and add them to the mixture when they're tender.)

Preheat oven to 400° F (200° C). Roll out two-thirds of the pastry and use it to line a 9-inch pie dish. Dampen the edges with cold water. Fill with the cheese mixture and then roll out the remaining pastry and put that on top, pressing the edges together. Trim and decorate the pie, making two or three holes in the top to allow the steam to escape. Bake the pie for 35 minutes, until it's golden brown. Serve it while it's all hot and light and flaky.

If you want to freeze this pie, I think it's best to do so *after* cooking it. To serve, let the pie defrost for about 3 hours. Heat the pie through before serving it.

CHEESE TARTLETS

RUSSIA

In Russia these little tartlets, *vatrushki*, are usually served either on their own as a first course or as an accompaniment to *borsch*. I think they make a lovely first course if you serve them hot from the oven and pass 'round a bowl of sour cream and chopped dill for people to spoon over the tartlets. They are also very good with the *borsch*, of course, but such an unusual combination is best saved for those with adventurous palates! *Serves 4 for lunch or supper, 4–6 as an appetizer.*

FOR THE FILLING:

1 cup (250 ml) cottage cheese or
   ricotta
1 egg

Sea salt
Freshly ground black pepper

FOR THE PASTRY:

2 cups (500 ml) whole-wheat
   flour
2 teaspoons baking powder

8 tablespoons butter or margarine
   and shortening, mixed
2 tablespoons cold water

FOR THE GLAZE:

1 egg beaten with ½ teaspoon salt

Preheat oven to 425° F (220° C). Make the filling by mixing the cottage cheese or *ricotta* with the egg, and seasoning with salt and pepper.

Measure the flour, baking powder, and a pinch of salt into a bowl and rub in the fat until the mixture resembles fine bread crumbs; then add the water and mix to form a dough. Roll the pastry out fairly thinly on a lightly floured board and cut into 16 or 18 3-inch (7.5 cm) rounds. Put a heaping teaspoonful of the cheese mixture on each round. Press the edges of the rounds up toward the center to make a rim. Brush the tartlets with the beaten-egg glaze and then bake them for about 20 minutes, until set, puffed up, and golden brown. They're nicest served immediately.

◆——◆——◆

CHEESE AND ONION QUICHE

SWITZERLAND

This is a good tart and the layer of little cubes of cheese seems to help keep the pastry nice and crisp. The proper cheeses, Gruyère and Emmentaler, are expensive and I generally use Edam instead—it gives a very similar result. *Serves 4–5.*

FOR THE PASTRY:

2 cups (500 ml) whole-wheat
   flour—or a combination of
   whole-wheat and white flour
Pinch of salt

4 tablespoons butter
1 tablespoon cold water
1 tablespoon oil

1 *medium onion, peeled and
chopped*
2 *tablespoons butter*
¼ *pound (115 g) Gruyère cheese
and ¼ pound (115 g)
Emmenthal cheese; or use
½ pound Edam cheese*

2 *eggs*
⅔ *cup (160 ml) light cream or
milk*
Sea salt
Freshly ground black pepper
Grated nutmeg

Put a baking sheet in the center of the oven and then preheat oven to 400° F (200° C). Sift the flour and salt into a bowl; rub in the butter until the mixture resembles fine bread crumbs, then add the cold water and mix to form a dough. On a lightly floured board, roll the pastry out to fit a 9-inch (23 cm) quiche dish or pan. Press the pastry gently into place, trim the edges and prick the shell. Cook it on the baking sheet in the preheated oven for 15 minutes, until it's crisp, and then remove from oven. (You may wish to brush the shell all over with hot oil—this will help to keep the pastry crisp.) If you prefer weighting the shell down to pricking it, bake the shell (filled with a lining of waxed paper and then the dried beans etc.) for 10 minutes; then remove the weight and bake another 5 minutes.

While the shell is cooking, make the filling. Sauté the onion gently in the butter for 10 minutes, until it's soft but not browned. Dice the cheese into ¼-inch (6 mm) chunks. In a small bowl beat the eggs and cream together and season them with salt, pepper, and nutmeg. Scatter half the cheese over the cooked shell, put the onions on top and then the rest of the cheese; finally gently pour in the egg mixture. Bake the quiche for 30–35 minutes, until it's puffed up and golden. Serve hot.

This makes a good lunch with a juicy tomato salad and fresh fruit as dessert.

LEEK QUICHE

FRANCE

Leeks make a delicious quiche, delicate in flavor and color, and there are many versions of this dish. I like to use sour cream or yogurt because I think their sharp creaminess contrasts well with the slight sweetness of the leeks. *Serves 4.*

FOR THE PASTRY:

1½ cups (375 ml) whole-wheat
   flour
Pinch of salt

6 tablespoons butter
1 tablespoon cold water
1 tablespoon oil

FOR THE FILLING:

2 pounds (900 g) leeks
2 tablespoons butter
⅔ cups (160 ml) sour cream or
   plain yogurt

4 egg yolks or 2 whole eggs
Sea salt
Freshly ground black pepper

Put a baking sheet in the center of the oven and preheat oven to 400° F (200° C). Measure the flour and salt into a bowl and rub in the butter until the mixture looks like bread crumbs. Then add the water and mix to form a dough. Roll out the pastry on a lightly floured board and use it to line a 9-inch (23 cm) lightly greased quiche dish or tart pan. Prick the shell with a fork, place it on the baking sheet in the oven, and bake it for about 15 minutes, until set and golden. Just before the pastry is ready, heat the tablespoon of oil in a small saucepan and when the shell is out of the oven, immediately brush the surface with the oil. Reduce the oven temperature to 350° F (180° C).

To make the filling, cut the roots and most of the green leaves off the leeks; then slit them down the side and open up the layers under cold running water to wash away the grit. Slice the leeks fairly finely. Melt the butter in a large saucepan and put in the leeks; let them cook over a gentle heat for 10–15 minutes, with a lid on the saucepan, until they're tender. Stir them often and don't let them brown or this will spoil the flavor.

When the leeks are ready, take them off the heat and stir in the sour cream. Beat the eggs and add them to the creamy leek mixture, together with seasoning to taste. Pour the mixture into the pastry shell and bake in the preheated oven for about 30 minutes, until the filling is set.

Serve the quiche hot or warm with cooked vegetables such as baby carrots, string beans, and perhaps a good homemade tomato sauce, or serve it with a juicy tomato salad. It's also nice cold, but I think it's at its best when warm.

LEEK PIE

ENGLAND

This pie from Cornwall is rather similar to the French *flamiche*. Both these pies usually contain small quantities of crumbled bacon, but you can also make a very good vegetarian version, rich and creamy. You could use a little of the bacon-flavored soya protein, "Bacon Bits," with the leeks if you like, or sprinkle them with Parmesan cheese to add extra flavor.

Like many savory pies, this one has no bottom pastry shell, only a top crust. My method of making the pie differs a little from the traditional one. Instead of baking the leeks under the pie crust, then carefully removing the crust and pouring in the cream, which is very tricky if the pastry is light and crumbly, I find it best to boil the leeks first, then mix them with the cream, cover with the pastry, and bake for about 20–25 minutes, until the pastry is golden and the filling set. *Serves 4.*

FOR THE FILLING:

2¼ pounds (1 kg) leeks
¼ cup (60 ml) grated Parmesan
    cheese
⅔ cup (160 ml) heavy cream or
    low-fat ricotta *if you want a less
    rich, healthier dish*

2 eggs, beaten
Sea salt
Freshly ground black pepper

FOR THE PASTRY:

1½ cups (375 ml) whole-wheat
    flour
1½ teaspoons baking powder
½ cup (125 ml) shortening and
    margarine, mixed

1 tablespoon cold water
A little beaten egg (optional)

Wash the leeks and cut them into 1-inch (2.5 cm) pieces. Put them into a large saucepan, cover them with cold water, and bring to the boil. Simmer the leeks gently for 10–15 minutes, until they're tender, then drain them very well in a colander, using a spoon to press out all the water.

While the leeks are cooking, make the pastry. Measure the flour and baking powder into a bowl. Rub in the fat until the mixture resembles fine bread crumbs; then add the water and form the mixture into a dough. On a lightly floured board roll the pastry out big enough to fit your 8- or 9-inch (20–23 cm) pie dish. Preheat the oven to 400° F (200° C).

Mix the leeks with the Parmesan cheese, cream or low-fat *ricotta*, eggs, and salt and pepper to taste. Put the mixture into the pie dish and cover with the pastry, trimming it to fit and decorating it as you please. Brush it with a little beaten egg if you want a shiny finish. Bake the pie for 20–25 minutes, until the pastry is golden brown. Serve it immediately with cooked vegetables. The cream makes this a rich dish so I think it's best to serve a fresh salad or simple vegetable soup as a first course, with fruit for dessert.

◆——◆——◆

MUSHROOM QUICHE

FRANCE

Creamy, light, and delicately flavored, I think this is my favorite quiche. It is delicious for a special lunch or supper. As it is rich I try to plan the rest of the meal accordingly: a simple cooked vegetable or salad to accompany the quiche and a fresh-tasting fruity dessert to follow it. *Serves 4–6.*

FOR THE PASTRY:

1½ cups (375 ml) whole-wheat
  flour
Pinch of salt

6 tablespoons butter
1 tablespoon cold water
1 tablespoon oil

FOR THE FILLING:

1 onion
1 clove garlic
4 tablespoons butter
½ pound (225 g) fresh
  mushrooms
1 heaping tablespoon chopped
  parsley

4 egg yolks or 2 whole eggs
⅔ cup (160 ml) light cream or
  milk
Sea salt
Freshly ground black pepper
Grated nutmeg

Place a baking sheet in the center of the oven and preheat oven to 400° F (200° C). To make the pastry, measure the flour and salt into a bowl and rub the butter into the dry ingredients until the mixture looks like bread crumbs; then add the water and mix to form a dough. Roll out the pastry and use to line a 9-inch (23 cm) quiche dish. Prick the pastry shell and place in the oven on the baking sheet and bake for about 15 minutes, until it's cooked and golden. Heat the oil in a saucepan and immediately brush the cooked shell with it. Reduce the oven temperature to 350° F (180° C).

To make the filling, peel and chop the onion, peel and crush the garlic, and cook them together in the butter for 10 minutes, until the onion is soft but not browned. Meanwhile wash and slice the mushrooms; add these to the onion and garlic and sauté for another 3 minutes or so, without a lid on the saucepan; then stir in the chopped parsley. Put the egg yolks into a medium-size bowl and beat them with the cream or milk. Add this to the mushroom mixture and season with salt and pepper to taste. Heat the mixture gently, stirring all the time, until it begins to thicken. This will happen quickly but don't worry even if it gets really very thick because it will be all right once it's baked.

Pour the mushroom mixture into the cooked pastry shell—it doesn't matter if the pastry is still hot—and bake in the oven for about 30 minutes, until the creamy mixture is set. Serve hot or warm.

◆——◆——◆

ONION QUICHE

FRANCE

This is a good quiche with a creamy onion filling and crisp pastry base. I usually make it with milk, but of course for special occasions it's lovely made with light cream instead—or a mixture. *Serves 4–6.*

FOR THE PASTRY:

1½ cups (375 ml) whole-wheat flour	*6 tablespoons butter*
Pinch of salt	*1 tablespoon cold water*
	1 tablespoon oil

FOR THE FILLING:

1 pound (450 g) yellow onions,
  peeled and thinly sliced
2 tablespoons butter
4 egg yolks or 2 whole eggs
⅔ cup (160 ml) milk or light
  cream
½ cup (125 ml) grated Swiss or
  Gruyère cheese

½ teaspoon dry mustard
Sea salt
Freshly ground black pepper
1 tomato, sliced, to decorate the
  top

Put a baking sheet in the center of the oven and preheat oven to 400° F (200° C). Measure the flour and salt into a bowl, cut the butter into small pieces, and rub these into the flour with your fingertips so that the mixture looks like fine bread crumbs; then mix in the water. Press the mixture lightly together to make a dough. Roll the pastry out on a lightly floured board and use it to line a 9-inch (23 cm) quiche dish. Trim the edges neatly and prick the bottom. Put the shell on the baking sheet in the oven and bake it for 15 minutes, until it's crisp and golden brown. Just before you take the flan out of the oven heat the oil until it's smoking hot, then brush the cooked shell all over with oil as soon as you take it out of the oven. If you prefer not to use the hot oil, you may wish to eliminate pricking the uncooked shell and to weight the pastry down with rice or beans during cooking. Turn the empty oven down to 350° F (180° C).

To make the filling, sauté the onions lightly in the butter in a saucepan until they're soft and golden—about 10 minutes. Beat the eggs or egg yolks and the milk or cream together and then add these to the onions in the saucepan and stir over a gentle heat until the mixture thickens. Take the saucepan off the heat and mix in the grated cheese, dry mustard, and salt and pepper to taste. Pour this mixture into the pastry shell. Arrange the tomato slices on top. Put the quiche into the oven on the baking sheet and bake for about 30 minutes, until the filling is set.

This quiche is delicious served hot with some tender green beans or zucchini or a crisp salad. It also makes a good protein-rich first course before a vegetable-based main course.

◆——◆——◆

PIZZA

Pizza makes a very good vegetarian meal. It's filling and tasty and looks and smells so appetizing with its topping of red tomatoes, golden cheese, and black olives, and with its mouth-watering aroma of homemade bread. Although it sounds complicated, pizza isn't really too difficult or time-consuming to make and only needs a crunchy green salad to accompany it.

The quantity given here is enough to make two large 11-inch pizzas (or 4 8-inch) and feeds 4–8 people depending on how hungry they are. Mozzarella cheese is the authentic one and is available in both whole-milk and skim-milk versions. *Serves 4–8.*

FOR THE DOUGH:

½ teaspoon sugar
1 package active dry yeast
½ cup (125 ml) warm water
2½ cups (675 ml) whole-wheat or unbleached all-purpose flour

Pinch of salt
3 tablespoons soft butter or margarine
1 egg

FOR THE TOPPING:

2 large onions
2 tablespoons oil
1 can (28 ounces/840 g) tomatoes, chopped
2 cups (500 ml) mozzarella or Lancashire cheese

Sea salt
Freshly ground black pepper
8–12 ripe olives, pitted and halved
A little olive oil

To make the dough, first put the sugar, yeast and warm water into a small bowl and mix them gently. Leave to one side for about 10 minutes for the yeast to ferment. While this is happening put the flour and salt into a bowl and rub in the butter or margarine. Add the yeast to the flour, also the egg, mixing them with your hands to make a dough. It should be soft enough to knead without effort, but firm and pliable. Add a tiny bit more flour or water if necessary to adjust the consistency, then turn the dough onto a clean floured board or working surface and knead for about 5 minutes. Put the kneaded dough into a greased bowl, cover with a clean damp cloth, and leave in a warm place to double in size—this takes 45–60 minutes.

While you're waiting for the dough to rise, make the topping. Peel and slice the onions and sauté them gently in the oil for about 10 minutes, until they're soft but not browned. Drain and chop the tomatoes, reserving the juice; shred or grate the cheese into thin slices.

When the dough has doubled in size, punch it down and turn it out onto a lightly floured board again. Knead the dough briefly, then divide it into two or four pieces (depending on your preference) and roll each out to fit your pizza tray(s). Butter the tray(s) and lay the dough on them, pressing it down and tucking in the edges to fit. Cover the top of the dough with the chopped tomatoes, adding a little of the juice as necessary to moisten the mixture, then arrange the fried onions and sliced cheese on top and garnish with the olives. Sprinkle a little oil over the top of the pizza and brush some over the edges of the dough.

Preheat the oven to 400° F (200° C). Put the pizzas (uncovered) to one side to prove for 15 minutes while the oven is heating up. I stand mine on top of the stove so that they get the benefit of the heat from the oven as it warms up, but this isn't essential. Bake the pizzas for 15–20 minutes until the crust is puffed up and the cheesy topping all golden brown and delicious-looking.

Pizza freezes very well. If you want to prepare them in advance, place the uncooked pizza in the freezer and open-freeze until firm, then wrap it in foil or plastic wrap. When you want to have the pizza, remove the coverings, leave for 15–30 minutes to defrost while the oven heats up, and then bake as usual.

MUSHROOM PIZZA

Make this as above, but omit the olives. Instead, arrange on top of the pizza ¼ pound (125 g) washed and finely sliced fresh mushrooms, brushed lightly with olive oil.

HERB PIZZA

Sprinkle the top of the pizza with plenty of dried oregano or marjoram; drip a little extra olive oil over the top to moisten the herbs.

GREEN PEPPER PIZZA

Wash and seed a large green or red pepper. Cut the pepper into strips and sauté these with the onions, adding them to the saucepan after 5 minutes. Arrange the slices on top of the pizza with the onions—you can make a very pretty pizza with a lattice of pepper strips on top.

ARTICHOKE PIZZA

Finely slice 3 or 4 canned artichoke hearts; arrange the slices on top of the tomato mixture. Omit the olives.

QUICK NON-YEAST PIZZA

ITALY

This pizza, *pizza al tegame*, is made from a flour-and-baking-powder dough cooked in a skillet in a little hot oil, then finished off under the broiler or in the oven. It's very useful for those emergencies when you find yourself having to rustle up food unexpectedly, because it's quick to make and uses basic ingredients. It's a dish I often make when we're on vacation with more limited cooking facilities than usual, but with heartier appetites! *Serves 4.*

FOR THE PIZZA DOUGH:

2 cups (500 ml) whole-wheat flour
2 teaspoons baking powder

½ teaspoon salt
2 tablespoons oil
6–8 tablespoons cold water

FOR THE TOPPING:

1 large onion
2 tablespoons oil
1 clove garlic, peeled and crushed
2 cans (16 ounces/450 g each) tomatoes
1 teaspoon marjoram

Sea salt
Freshly ground black pepper
1 cup (250 ml) grated Parmesan cheese
Oil for shallow frying

Measure the flour, baking powder, and salt into a bowl. Mix in the oil and enough water to make a soft but not sticky dough. Knead the dough lightly on a floured board; then leave it to rest for a minute or two while you make the pizza topping.

Peel and chop the onion and sauté it in the oil in a large saucepan for 10 minutes, until it's soft but not browned; then stir in the garlic. Drain the juice from the tomatoes—you won't need it for this recipe but it's useful for soups, sauces, and for the non-cream version of the potato dish on page 86. Add the tomatoes to the onion and garlic, breaking them up a bit with a spoon. Stir in the marjoram and salt and pepper to taste; then keep this mixture warm while you finish making the crust.

Divide the dough and roll each piece into a circle to fit your skillet—probably about 8-inches (20 cm). Heat a little oil in the skillet and cook the first pizza over a moderate heat. When the underside is cooked, turn it over and cook the other side; then carefully remove the pizza and put it on to a dish or ovenproof plate that will fit under the broiler. Spread half the tomato mixture over the pizza, then arrange half the cheese on top. Put the pizza under the broiler for a few minutes, just to heat up the topping and melt the cheese. Keep it warm while you make the other pizza in the same way.

A watercress salad or a cabbage and apple salad goes well with this and can be prepared while you're waiting for the pizzas to cook.

SAMOSAS

INDIA

These little Indian pastries with their spicy vegetable filling are delicious for a main meal with Indian curry sauce and perhaps a curried vegetable or side salad. They are also nice cold with yogurt or mayonnaise to dip them into, and a crisp salad. *Serves 6.*

FOR THE FILLING:

1 *large onion*
1 *large clove garlic*
2 *tablespoons* ghee or butter
1 *teaspoon dry mustard*
1 *teaspoon ground ginger*
1 *teaspoon ground cumin*
1 *teaspoon ground coriander*

2 *pounds (900 g) cooked mixed*
   vegetables: potatoes, carrots,
   and frozen peas, or whatever is
   available
Sea salt
Freshly ground black pepper

FOR THE PASTRY:

2 cups (500 ml) whole-wheat flour	4 tablespoons ghee or butter
½ teaspoon sea salt	6–7 tablespoons cold water
½ teaspoon baking powder	Oil for deep or shallow frying

First make the filling. Peel and chop the onion, peel and crush the garlic, and sauté them gently in the fat for 10 minutes, stirring in the spices. Mix well, then add the cooked vegetables and toss these gently with a spoon so that they all are coated with the spicy onion and oil. Season with salt and pepper and then let the mixture cool.

To make the pastry, measure the flour and salt into a bowl and rub in the butter or *ghee* and enough water to make a soft but not sticky dough. Knead the dough for 5 minutes, then divide it into 16 pieces. Roll each piece into a ball and then use a rolling pin to roll each into a circle about 6 inches (15 cm) in diameter. Cut the circles in half to get 32 half-circles. Put a heaping teaspoonful of the filling onto each half-circle of pastry; dampen the edges with a pastry brush dipped in cold water and fold the corners over to make a little tri-angular-shape packet, pressing the edges together. When all the *samosas* are ready, deep or shallow fry them a few at a time until they are golden and crisp. Drain them well and serve them hot or cold.

SPINACH PIE

MIDDLE EAST

This combination of crisp golden pastry, buttery spinach, and soft white cheese is very delicious. Like the cheese pie from Greece, this should really be made with phyllo dough, which you can sometimes get in delicatessens and shops specializing in foreign foods. It's not always easy to obtain but if you do get some you'll need about ½ pound (225 g) for the pie. Brush a 9-inch (23 cm) pie dish with melted butter and lay a piece of the pastry in it; then brush this with more butter and put another piece on top. Repeat this until you have used half the pastry and then put in your filling. Cover the filling with more layers of pastry and melted butter as before. Trim the pie and brush more melted butter over the top. Bake the pie as for the flaky pastry version given below. You need to work fairly fast with phyllo dough, as it hardens as the air gets to it—it's a good idea to keep the pieces you're not actually using in a plastic bag until required.

If you're using the flaky pastry version below, you need to get organized in advance to allow time for the pastry to chill and rest. *Serves 4 as a main course, 6 as a first course.*

FOR THE PASTRY:

2¼ cups (560 ml) flour—I use
   half whole-wheat, half white
   for this pastry

Pinch of salt
1 cup (250 ml) cold butter
Cold water to mix

FOR THE FILLING:

2 pounds (900 g) fresh spinach, or
   2 packages (10 ounces/310 g
   each) frozen chopped spinach
1 large onion
Olive oil
1 clove garlic
Chopped mixed fresh herbs, such
   as parsley, chives, thyme

1½ cups (375 ml) crumbled feta
   cheese
Sea salt
Freshly ground black pepper
A little beaten egg (optional)

First make the pastry. Sift the flour and salt into a large bowl and cut in the butter. Add enough cold water to make a manageable dough— it should be pliable but not sticky. Roll the dough into a ball, wrap it in waxed paper, and put it in the refrigerator for 2 hours.

Next make the filling—this too can be done in advance. If you're using fresh spinach, wash it thoroughly and cook it in a dry saucepan until it's tender, then drain and chop it. If you're using frozen spinach, put it into a colander and leave it to defrost, then drain off the excess water; press the spinach with a spoon to squeeze out as much water as possible. Peel and chop the onion and sauté it in a little oil in a fairly large saucepan for about 10 minutes until it is tender. Take the saucepan off the heat and stir in the garlic, spinach, herbs, cheese, and salt and pepper to taste. Leave the mixture to cool.

When you're ready to finish and cook the pie, preheat the oven to 450° F (230° C). Roll out two-thirds of the pastry on a lightly floured board and gently lay the pastry in a deep 9-inch (23 cm) pie dish. Spoon the filling into the pastry-lined dish. Roll out the remaining piece of pastry and use this to cover the top of the pie. Trim the pastry and crimp or fork the edge. Brush the top of the pie with some beaten egg if you want a shiny finish. Bake the pie for 20 minutes, then turn the heat down to 400° F (200° C) and cook for another 20 minutes.

This pie makes a delicious main course if you serve it with creamy mashed potatoes and a brightly colored vegetable, such as carrots. Or serve it on its own as a warming and welcoming first course before one of the lighter main dishes.

The pie can be frozen; I think it's best to freeze it before glazing and cooking. When you want to serve the pie, thaw for 2–3 hours and then glaze it with the beaten egg, if you want to, and cook as usual.

DESSERTS

Apple Snow
Apricot and Almond Pudding
Banana Fritters with Lime
Chocolate and Orange Mousse
Coeurs à la Crème
Little Coffee Custards
Coffee Ricotta Pudding
Crème Brûlée
Crêpes Suzette
Dried Fruit Compote
Exotic Fruit Salad
Fresh Fruit Salad
Fruity Muesli
Gooseberry Fool
Rice Flour and Rosewater Pudding
Lemon Whip
Mont Blanc
Fresh Orange Salad
Pashka
Fresh Peach Salad
Stuffed Peaches
Pears Baked in Wine
Pineapple Sherbet
Prune Delight
Pumpkin in Orange Syrup
Red Fruit Pudding
Rhubarb Compote
Rice and Almond Pudding
Trifle
Vanilla Ice Cream
Yogurt

MOST PEOPLE LIKE TO FINISH A MEAL WITH A sweet dish—and most adults probably feel slightly guilty about eating them! For this reason I have included a number of light, fruity desserts that round things off nicely without being either too rich or fattening.

One nice thing about vegetarian cooking is that it gives you the opportunity to plan a meal to take full advantage of the dessert course. You can have a simple first course, such as a puréed vegetable soup; followed by a plain but tasty main course based on rice or vegetables, such as paella or tomatoes à la Provençale with noodles and French beans; then finish the meal with a flourish by serving something like a real trifle, luscious homemade ice cream with meringues, or gorgeous crêpes suzette. Or you could offer one of the tarts from the next section of this book if you want a more substantial dessert.

Some of these desserts are rich in protein, a point worth exploiting when you're planning a meal. Remember, protein is just as good if you eat it for dessert as it is in the main course; serving a nutritious dessert after a high-protein main course means you're probably eating more protein than you need and the excess is just used for energy, as is true of carbohydrates, which is wasteful. Vegetarian cookery gives you the flexibility to utilize protein economically if you wish.

◆———◆———◆

APPLE SNOW

FINLAND

This is a perfect dessert to serve after a filling meal because it's light and refreshing, but it's also nourishing because of the egg whites. *Serves 4.*

1 pound (450 g) cooking apples	*2 egg whites*
½ cup (125 ml) sugar	*A little grated lemon rind*

Peel, core, and slice the apples, then put them into a heavy-bottomed saucepan with the sugar and cook them over a gentle heat, with a lid on the saucepan, until they're soft and puréelike. If the apples have produced a great deal of liquid, take the lid off the saucepan and cook them for a few minutes more to thicken them up, but watch them carefully and stir them often so that they don't burn. Cool the apples and then strain or purée them.

Beat the egg whites until they're stiff but not dry and then fold them into the apple purée. Grate enough lemon rind into the mixture to give a refreshing tang. Divide the mixture between four individual bowls and serve chilled. It's nice with some crisp cookies—macaroons are ideal.

◆——————◆——————◆

APRICOT AND ALMOND PUDDING

SWEDEN

This easy-to-make dish from Sweden is actually halfway between a pudding and a cake—a light, gooey, almond-flavored sponge with apricots baked into the middle. It's best eaten warm, with cream if you like; or cold, when it can be decorated with piped whipped cream and toasted almonds, if you want to make it extra special. You can use either canned apricots or soaked dried apricots. If you're using the latter, I think it's worth getting the best quality whole (pitted) ones if possible. It's best to use a springform pan if you have one; otherwise use an ordinary deep cake pan or soufflé dish lined with buttered foil. *Serves 4.*

½ cup (125 ml) soft vegetable
    margarine
½ cup (125 ml) superfine or
    firmly packed brown sugar
2 eggs
2 cups (500 ml) whole-wheat
    flour

1 cup (250 ml) ground almonds
¾ cup (180 ml) dried apricots,
    soaked and cooked until tender,
    or use 1 can (16 ounces/480 g)
    apricot halves
A few slivered almonds

Lightly butter and flour an 8-inch (20 cm) springform pan. Preheat the oven to 325° F (160° C). Put the margarine and sugar into a bowl and cream them until they're light; then add the eggs and beat again. Add the flour and ground almonds and beat the mixture until it's very light and fluffy. Put half the mixture into the springform pan. Drain the apricots and arrange them on top of the almond mixture, then spread the remaining mixture on top and scatter with the almonds.

Bake the pudding for 60–70 minutes, until it is set and golden brown. Cool in the pan, then slip a knife 'round the edges, ease the pudding out, and serve.

BANANA FRITTERS WITH LIME

CARIBBEAN

The recipe for these puffy banana fritters was given to me by a friend in the Caribbean, and they make an interesting and unusual dessert. The only snag is they really need to be fried just before you serve them, so it means getting up from the table to do them, but they don't take long if you have everything ready in advance. I've found you can even shallow fry them if you prefer and they're still puffy and good. *Serves 4.*

2 cups (500 ml) whole-wheat
   flour
½ *teaspoon baking powder*
Pinch of salt
3 *firm, ripe bananas*
½ *teaspoon Angostura bitters*

4 *teaspoons milk*
1 *egg white*
Oil for deep or shallow frying
Slices of lime or lemon
Soft brown sugar

Measure the flour, baking powder, and salt into a bowl. Peel the bananas and mash them with a fork, then add them to the flour, together with the Angostura bitters and milk. (You can do all this in advance.)

When you're ready to finish the fritters, beat the egg whites until they're standing in soft peaks, and fold them into the banana mixture. Drop tablespoonfuls of the mixture into hot deep or shallow oil and fry them until they're browned on one side; then turn them over to cook the other side. Take the fritters out with a perforated spoon and drain them on paper towels; then transfer them to a hot dish and serve them at once, garnished with the lime or lemon slices. Serve the soft brown sugar separately for people to help themselves to.

CHOCOLATE AND ORANGE MOUSSE

This is a wickedly delicious dessert: smooth dark chocolate flavored with the sharp freshness of orange. It's also very easy to make. *Serves 6.*

8 squares (8 ounces/240 g)
   semi-sweet chocolate
2 tablespoons orange juice
Grated rind of 1 orange
1 tablespoon orange liqueur
   such as Curaçao or Grand
   Marnier—or use brandy

4 eggs, separated
A little whipped cream
A few toasted almonds or
   chocolate curls

Break up the chocolate and put it into a bowl. Set the bowl over a saucepan of boiling water, or pop it into a moderate oven for about 10 minutes, until the chocolate has melted. Stir the orange juice and rind into the melted chocolate, then the liqueur or brandy and the egg yolks. Beat the egg whites until they're standing in soft peaks; then, using a cutting and folding motion, gently fold them into the chocolate mixture. Spoon the mixture into six little dishes—it looks very nice in those little white individual soufflé dishes. Put the mousse into the refrigerator for at least 2 hours to chill and set. You can leave it overnight if this is convenient.

This mousse lovely served just as it is, or you can garnish it with some whipped cream and toasted slivered almonds or chocolate curls. To make the chocolate curls, just run a potato peeler down the flat side of a bar of chocolate.

Chocolate mousse is good after Spanish vegetable rice or any grain- or vegetable-based dish.

COEURS À LA CRÈME

Hearts of creamy white cheese surrounded by shiny red strawberries make a beautiful summer dessert that's rich in protein and ideal for serving after something like ratatouille and rice. You need to start making the hearts the night before you want to serve them. The quantities I've given are right for five of those white heart-shaped china dishes you can get with little holes in the base. Otherwise you can make holes in the cream, yogurt, or small cottage cheese cartons and use these; I've also used a colander successfully. Use cheesecloth to line the molds. *Serves 5.*

2 cups (500 ml) cottage cheese, strained

½ cup (125 ml) heavy cream

2 tablespoons superfine sugar

1 pint (about 450 g) fresh strawberries

A little extra superfine sugar

Put the cheese into a large bowl, mix it with the cream and sugar, and beat with a wooden spoon until the mixture thickens and holds its shape. Line your white china dishes, yogurt, cream, or cottage cheese pots, or colander, with cheesecloth; then spoon in the creamy mixture and smooth the surface. Stand the containers or the colander on a plate or rimmed soup bowl(s) to catch the liquid that will drain off, and place them in the refrigerator overnight.

Next day wash and hull the strawberries, halving or quartering any larger ones as necessary. Then sprinkle them lightly with sugar and leave to one side.

To serve, turn the creamy cheese mixture out onto a large plate or bowl and carefully peel off the cheesecloth. Arrange the strawberries round the cheese or cheeses.

Don't assemble this dish until just before you need it; the juice from the strawberries can spoil the look of it. This is, by the way, a good way of making a few strawberries go further when they're expensive.

If you're dieting, I've found you can make this dish equally well using plain yogurt instead of cream. The result is very similar though not so creamy-tasting, and I find if I use 2 cups (500 ml) low-fat *ricotta* or cottage cheese, ½ cup (125 ml) plain yogurt, and 3–4 tablespoons superfine sugar, the mixture fills four white china hearts, not five as it does when made with heavy cream. The yogurt version also gives off a little more liquid as it drains and settles in the refrigerator.

◆——◆——◆

LITTLE COFFEE CUSTARDS

F R A N C E

These little dishes of velvety, chilled coffee custard make a lovely dessert: simple, quick to make, yet luxurious. They are splendid for serving when you want to increase the protein content of a meal. I've given a rather economical version of this dessert; for a special occasion it's superb with light cream replacing some or all of the milk. You can top the custards with a whirl of whipped cream or toasted nuts, which give a pleasant crispness. *Serves 4.*

4 eggs	*1¼ cups (310 ml) milk*
1 tablespoon instant coffee	*¼ cup (60 ml) superfine sugar*
A little whipped cream or	
toasted nuts (optional)	

Preheat the oven to 300° F (150° C). Break the eggs into a medium-size bowl and beat them until they're frothy. Put the instant coffee, milk, and sugar into a small saucepan and heat almost to boiling point. Remove the saucepan from the heat and gradually add the milk to the beaten eggs, stirring all the time. Strain the mixture into a jug, then pour it into four little ovenproof dishes—little white ramekins are ideal. Cover each dish with a piece of foil. Stand the dishes in a baking pan filled with 1 inch (2.5 cm) very hot water. Place the pan in the oven and bake the custards for 45–50 minutes, or until they are firmly set and a knife put into the center comes out clean. Cool the custards, keeping the foil over them, which prevents a hard skin from forming; then put them into the refrigerator. Serve the little custards straight from the refrigerator so that they're beautifully cold and refreshing; garnish them with whipped cream or toasted nuts.

COFFEE RICOTTA PUDDING

I T A L Y

This very easy-to-make, protein-rich pudding is lovely served after one of the vegetable casseroles or grain-based main dishes, or after a low-protein pasta dish. *Serves 4.*

2 teaspoons best quality instant
  coffee, continental type
1 tablespoon water, rum, or
  Tia Maria
	2 cups (500 ml) ricotta cheese or
	  small-curd cottage cheese
	¼ cup (60 ml) superfine sugar

Dissolve the coffee by mixing it with the water, rum, or Tia Maria. If the cheese is very lumpy it might be best to push it through a strainer; otherwise put it straight into a bowl. Add the coffee mixture and sugar to the cheese, stirring until everything is combined. Spoon into small dishes; serve chilled. It's nice with macaroons or other small crunchy cookies or wafers.

CRÈME BRÛLÉE

ENGLAND

Although this dessert sounds French, it is in fact English and originated at Trinity College, Cambridge. It's a useful dessert to serve when you want to add protein to the meal. At its richest and most luxurious, it's made entirely with light cream, but you can also make a less extravagant version using a mixture of light cream and milk, or even just milk. You can also use two whole eggs instead of the egg yolks, but the mixture is not as smooth-tasting. *Serves 6.*

2 cups (500 ml) milk ½ cup (125 ml) light cream 3 tablespoons sugar 4 egg yolks or 2 whole eggs	A vanilla bean or a few drops of vanilla extract A little confectioners sugar

Put the milk and cream into a suacepan and bring to the boil, then take off the heat. In a medium-size bowl beat together the sugar and egg yolks or eggs and then add the milk, stirring. Strain the mixture back into the saucepan or into the top of a double boiler and add the vanilla bean or a few drops of vanilla extract. Stir the mixture over a gentle heat for a few minutes, until it thickens; then take it off the heat, remove the vanilla bean (this can of course be washed, dried, and used again and again) and pour the custard into little individual oven-proof dishes. Let the custard cool completely. Two or three hours before you want to serve them, sift a little confectioners sugar over the top of each custard so that they are covered completely but not too thickly. Place the custard under a hot broiler for about 5 minutes to melt and lightly brown the sugar. Cool, then chill the desserts in the refrigerator, and serve them nice and cold.

CRÊPES SUZETTE

FRANCE

Crêpes suzette sound so complicated and people are always quite impressed by them, but they're really not at all difficult to make, and you can do all the main preparation well in advance. *Serves 4–6.*

FOR THE CRÊPES:

1 cup (250 ml) all-purpose flour—
   I use all whole-wheat or half
   whole-wheat, half white
Pinch of salt

2 tablespoons sweet butter,
   melted and cooled
2 eggs
1 cup (250 ml) milk

FOR THE ORANGE SAUCE:

8 tablespoons sweet butter
⅔ cup (160 ml) superfine sugar
Grated rind and juice of 3
   medium-size oranges
Grated rind and juice of 1 lemon

2 tablespoons orange liqueur
   such as Curaçao or Grand
   Marnier
4 tablespoons brandy

First of all make the crêpes. If you want to you can do this a day or two in advance, keeping the crêpes in the refrigerator or freezer. To make the batter, either put all the ingredients into your blender jar and blend until smooth and creamy; or sift the flour and salt into a bowl, make a well in the middle, put in the butter and eggs, and gradually beat in the milk until everything is well mixed. If you've made the batter by hand, let it stand for 30 minutes; then beat it again before you use it.

To cook the crêpes set a small skillet or crêpe pan over a moderate heat and brush the base with a thin film of butter. Pour a little batter into the hot pan, tilting and turning it so that the batter runs quickly all over the bottom and coats it thinly. When the underside of the crêpe is golden brown and the top is just set—about 20–30 seconds—

turn it over using a small spatula and your fingers, and cook the second side; this only takes a few seconds. Take the crêpe out and put it onto a plate. Brush the pan with a little more butter (unless you're using a non-stick pan, which only needs greasing after about every 3 or 4 crêpes) and make another crêpe in the same way. Continue until all the batter is used and you have a pile of about 14 thin crêpes. Cover them, separating them with waxed paper if you wish, and keep them in a cool place until needed.

You can assemble the dish an hour or so in advance. Put the butter, sugar, grated rinds, juices, and the orange liqueur if you're using it, into a large skillet or shallow flameproof dish that you can take to the table, and heat gently to melt the butter and sugar. Turn off the heat, then dip the crêpes in this mixture, one by one, coating each side and then folding each one in half, and in half again, so that a triangle shape is formed. As each crêpe is done, push it to the side of the pan. When all the crêpes have been dipped, leave them in the pan or your serving dish until you're almost ready to eat them; then put the pan back over the heat to warm through the sauce and the crêpes. When they're ready, turn up the heat high for about 1 minute to make the sauce very hot, quickly pour in the brandy, and set it alight with a lit match. You can take everything to the table at this point, while the flame continues. The flame will die out in a few seconds. Serve immediately.

This is a protein-rich dessert that's delicious after a light main course.

◆——◆——◆

DRIED FRUIT COMPOTE

GERMANY

A dried-fruit compote has an intense, intriguing flavor that comes from the slow simmering of the fruits, and which I think is delicious. You can buy 8 ounces (240 g) packages of mixed dried fruits. If you prefer to make up your own selection, you can buy dried apricots, apple rings, peaches, pears, and prunes separately and mix them as you wish. Leave out the ginger in the recipe if you don't like it; I don't think it's authentically German but it makes this recipe taste specially good. *Serves 4.*

2 packages (8 ounces/240 g each)
mixed dried fruit
2 or 3 thin strips of lemon rind
1 or 2 tablespoons of ginger
preserves

4 tablespoons ginger syrup (from
the jar of preserves)
A little softly whipped cream
Crisp shortbread or almond
cookies

Wash the dried fruit and put it into a bowl; cover generously with boiling water and leave to soak for a few hours. Transfer fruit and liquid to a large saucepan and add the lemon rind and a little extra water if necessary to bring the level of the liquid just up to the fruit. Bring to the boil, then leave it to simmer very gently for 30 minutes with a lid on the saucepan. The fruit should be very tender and the liquid reduced to a glossy-looking syrup. Remove the lemon rind and add the ginger and ginger syrup. Leave to cool, then chill the mixture. Serve in individual dishes.

I like this with a spoonful of softly whipped cream on top; heavy cream or a chilled vanilla custard sauce would also be nice.

◆———◆———◆

EXOTIC FRUIT SALAD

SOUTH AMERICA

I like to use a can of pink guavas as the basis of this salad because they're such a beautiful color and they give the mixture a rather exotic appearance and flavor. Kiwi fruit, or Chinese gooseberries, are quite easy to get these days—they sometimes appear in my local supermarket and are about the size of a large egg with a brown, slightly furry-looking skin. When you cut them open they're an amazing, gorgeous green and enhance any fruit salad mixture. But if you can't get them, just use extra pineapple or banana or a small can of mangoes instead—or a fresh mango if you can get it. *Serves 6.*

1 can (14½ ounces/435 g) guavas
1 ripe pineapple

2 large ripe bananas
2–3 kiwi fruit

Put the syrup from the guavas into a bowl. Cut the pieces of guava into halves or quarters, then add these to the bowl of syrup. Slice the leaves and prickly skin off the pineapple and dice the flesh, removing the hard center core. Peel and slice the bananas. Using a sharp knife, peel the skin off the kiwi fruit—like peeling an apple—then slice the fruit into thin rounds. Mix all the fruits together and chill the salad before serving. If you need more liquid, add a little fresh orange juice.

This salad is nice served with crisp coconut cookies.

FRESH FRUIT SALAD

ITALY

This mixture of fresh figs, with their exotic-looking purple and red flesh, oranges, peaches, and plums, makes an Italian-style fruit salad reminiscent of hot sun and blue seas. If you can't get fresh figs you could use canned ones or substitute something like black grapes or strawberries instead. *Serves 6.*

1 large orange　　　　　　　　　*4 fresh figs*
4 large fresh peaches
6 ripe, fresh plums; or 1 can
　(16 ounces/480 g) plums,
　drained

Cut the peel and pith from the oranges and then separate the segments of flesh, leaving the membranous skin behind. Do this over a bowl to catch any juice. Put the orange segments into the bowl. Peel the peaches as you would tomatoes, by covering them with boiling water, leaving for 1 minute, then draining; slip the point of a knife under the skin and ease it off. Cut the peaches into small pieces, discarding the pits. Halve, pit, and cut up the plums, and slice the figs. Add them all to the bowl and mix everything gently together, stirring in a little extra orange juice to moisten if necessary. Chill thoroughly before serving.

VARIATIONS

A fruit salad makes such delicious dessert, and of course the mixture of fruits can be varied according to what's available. Another summer version would be peaches, melon, oranges, or strawberries; in the autumn, those sweet, crisp green grapes, oranges, apples and plums. In the winter, oranges, pineapples, and black grapes are delicious; in the spring, sweet juicy pears, oranges, apples, and green grapes.

You can make fruit salad more substantial if you want to by serving it with crisp wafers or lady fingers, some whipped cream or chilled egg custard, or brandy snaps filled with cream.

FRUITY MUESLI

SWITZERLAND

Most people think of this as a breakfast dish consisting mainly of oats and other cereals. But when Dr. Bircher-Benner invented it for his patients in his clinic in Zurich at the turn of the century, it was really a fruit dish and as such it makes a delicious dessert, light and nourishing. If you use condensed milk, which is the type Dr. Bircher-Benner used, it gives the *muesli* a delectable, almost jellied consistency and sweet taste. *Serves 4.*

4 tablespoons sweetened
   condensed milk
4 tablespoons lemon juice
4 level tablespoons rolled oats

4 large eating apples
4 tablespoons chopped or grated
   hazelnuts or almonds

Put the condensed milk and lemon juice into a large bowl and mix them until they're smooth; then stir in the oats. Wash the apples and grate them fairly coarsely (unpeeled); then add them to the bowl. If the mixture seems rather stiff, add a little cold water or orange juice. Spoon the *muesli* into individual bowls and sprinkle the nuts over the top.

For a less sweet version of this dessert you can use plain yogurt instead of the condensed milk, but the consistency will not be quite the same.

GOOSEBERRY FOOL

ENGLAND

It's up to you whether you strain or purée the gooseberries for this fool. If you strain them you'll get a very smooth mixture; if you just purée them it will be more lumpy, but I think this texture is rather nice. I like it best made with half yogurt, which gives a pleasant sharpness, and half cream, but you could use all yogurt for a more dietetic version. It's nice made with other fruits, too: cooked rhubarb, apples, dried apricots, blackberries, or fresh raspberries or strawberries. *Serves 4.*

1 can (15½ ounces/465 g) gooseberries	*⅓ cup (80 ml) plain yogurt*
2 tablespoons water	*⅓ cup (80 ml) heavy cream*
½ cup (125 ml) sugar	*Chocolate sprinkles or a few roasted hazelnuts*

Wash the gooseberries, then "top and tail" them with a small sharp knife. Put the gooseberries into a medium-size heavy-bottomed saucepan with the water and cook them gently with a lid on the saucepan until they're tender—10–15 minutes. Drain off the liquid, which you won't need for this recipe. Strain or purée the gooseberries. Stir in the sugar, then leave them to one side to cool.

Mix the yogurt into the cooled gooseberry purée. Beat the cream until it's standing in soft peaks, then fold it gently but thoroughly into the gooseberry mixture. Spoon the fool into individual glass dishes and chill the mixture in the refrigerator until needed. Sprinkle a few sprinkles of chocolate or some chopped, roasted nuts on top just before serving. This fool is nice with macaroons.

Don't make the mistake I made while testing recipes for this book: On a hot July day I served chilled cucumber soup for a first course and gooseberry fool for dessert—the two mixtures looked almost the same!

RICE FLOUR AND ROSEWATER PUDDING

TURKEY

The traditional way of making this pudding involves simmering the milk for a long time to reduce it and thicken the mixture, so my method, using evaporated milk, is a shortcut, but it gives a lovely creamy result. I know the rosewater flavoring is not to everyone's taste, but I love it. You can usually find it in specialty shops. This is a useful dish because it's rich in protein. *Serves 4–6.*

5 tablespoons (75 ml) cornstarch
  or rice flour
1 can (14½ ounces/435 g)
  evaporated milk
¼ cup (60 ml) sugar

2 tablespoons rosewater
A little red food coloring
A few pistachio nuts, shelled—
  or a little chopped angelica

Put the rice flour into a small bowl and mix it to a paste with a little of the milk. Put the rest of the milk into a saucepan with the sugar and bring to the boil. Pour a little of the boiling milk into the rice-flour paste and mix; then pour this into the saucepan of milk. Put the saucepan over a gentle heat and stir for 4–5 minutes, until it has thickened and will coat the spoon fairly heavily.

Take the saucepan off the heat and stir in the rosewater and enough red coloring to tint the mixture a pale pink; then pour it into one large bowl or 4–6 individual dishes—glass ones are nice if you've got them. Leave the pudding to cool, then chill it in the refrigerator. Just before serving, decorate the top with the pistachio nuts or angelica.

LEMON WHIP

HOLLAND

This is a very light, delicious dessert, just right for serving after a substantial main course that's filled you up. Although it tastes so airy, it's rich in protein. It sounds a bit complicated to make, but really it isn't. *Serves 4–6.*

2 large lemons or 3–4 smaller ones
½ cup (125 ml) superfine sugar
4 eggs, separated

A few slivered almonds, toasted
  in the oven until golden brown,
  and cooled

To make this pudding you will need a double boiler or a china or glass bowl set over a saucepan of water. Put the water on to heat while you prepare the mixture. Scrub the lemons thoroughly in hot water to get rid of any residue from sprays with which they may have been treated, then grate the rind into the top of the double boiler or the bowl. Halve the lemons, squeeze out the juice, and put it in with the rind, together with the sugar. Add the egg yolks to the lemon mixture. Put the whites into a clean bowl and leave them to one side for the moment.

Stir the egg yolks, sugar, and lemon over the simmering water. Gradually this will thicken to a shiny golden sauce (like lemon curd) that will coat the back of a spoon thickly. This takes about 10 minutes. Remove from the heat. Beat the whites until they are stiff and standing in peaks, then gradually beat in the lemon sauce. Spoon the whip into individual glasses and put it into the refrigerator to chill. Serve it sprinkled with the nuts.

Crisp wafers or lemon thins are nice served with this dessert.

MONT BLANC

FRANCE

Actually this dessert is found in both France and Italy. It's very simple and, I think, very delicious, a "mountain" of soft chestnut purée topped with a snowy cap of whipped cream. You could use fresh chestnuts, but I must admit I use canned chestnut purée. Get the sweetened kind if you can; if not, beat unsweetened purée with ½ cup (125 ml) confectioners sugar, form it into a ball, wrap it in foil, and put it in the fridge for several hours to chill and firm up, and then push it through a food mill as described in the recipe. *Serves 6.*

1 can (15½ ounces/465 g)	*½ cup (125 ml) heavy cream*
sweetened chestnut purée	*1 tablespoon kirsch or brandy*

Put the chestnut purée into a food mill (a *Mouli-légumes*) fitted with a fairly fine blade; hold this over the flat dish from which you intend to serve the dessert and then push the chestnut purée through. The chestnut purée will fall into a mountain shape; don't attempt to shape it at all; let it stay as it is.

You can do this a few hours in advance and keep it carefully in a cool place. Whip the cream with the kirsch or brandy until it's in soft peaks, then spoon this gently on top of the chestnut mountain just before serving.

This is quite a rich, filling dessert, lovely after something like spinach *gnocchi.*

FRESH ORANGE SALAD

ITALY

This is one of the most refreshing desserts imaginable, and I find it just the thing for serving after a more substantial main course. *Serves 4.*

6 large oranges   *2 tablespoons sugar or honey*
A little extra orange juice if
  necessary

First of all wash one of the oranges and then shave off some thin slices of peel, or zest—I find a potato peeler good for this. Then, using kitchen scissors, snip the zest into shreds and put them into a large bowl. Next, cut the peel and pith off all the oranges. Do this with a sharp knife and a 'round-and-'round sawing action (like peeling a whole apple when you want to make a long curl of peel) and hold the oranges over the bowl as you do so to catch every drop of juice. Again with a sharp knife, cut the individual sections of orange away from the white skin and add them, along with any remaining juice in the skin, to the bowl. Add the sugar or honey to the bowl and chill.

For a Middle Eastern-style orange salad, served after, say, *hummus* followed by stuffed vine leaves or pilaf, add a tablespoonful of orange-flower water or rosewater to the mixture and garnish with a scattering of toasted almonds.

PASHKA

RUSSIA

This traditional Easter dish from Russia makes a beautiful dessert, and it's useful when you're planning a grain-based or vegetable meal because it's rich in protein. In Russia it's made in a special tall pyramid-shape mold and decorated with the initials "XB" for "Christ Is Risen." I use a 6-inch (15 cm) clay flower pot that I scrubbed and baked in a hot oven and now keep in my kitchen cupboard. *Pashka* needs to be prepared several hours before you want to eat it, to allow time for the liquid to drain away through the hole in the flower pot, leaving the mixture firm enough to unmold. It's nice served with macaroons, lady fingers, or slices of Madeira cake. *Serves 6.*

2 egg yolks
⅓ cup (80 ml) sugar
½ teaspoon vanilla extract
4 tablespoons light cream
3 cups (750 ml) cottage cheese
½ cup (125 ml) unsalted butter,
   softened

¼ cup (60 ml) chopped candied
   fruits
½ cup (125 ml) chopped almonds
A little chopped glacé fruit

Beat the egg yolks, sugar, and vanilla together until they're pale and foamy. Put the cream or milk into a small saucepan and bring it just to the boil, then pour it over the egg yolks and sugar. Pour the whole lot back into the saucepan and stir over a gentle heat until it has thickened—this won't take a moment, so watch it carefully. Leave to one side to cool.

Beat together the cottage cheese and butter; add the candied fruits and nuts and finally the cooled custard. Line your flower pot with a double layer of dampened cheesecloth, spoon in the *pashka* mixture, and smooth the top. Fold the ends of the cheesecloth over the top, cover with a saucer and a weight, and leave in a cool place or the fridge itself for several hours, preferably overnight. Some moisture will seep out of the hole in the base of the flower pot, so stand it on a plate or in a bowl.

To serve the *pashka,* invert the flower pot onto a serving dish, unmold it, and carefully peel off the cheesecloth. Decorate with the glacé fruit.

FRESH PEACH SALAD

ITALY

This is a luscious salad that's very refreshing after a substantial main course. I make it with orange juice instead of a sugar syrup; this is healthier and also adds its own delicious flavor. The salad is lovely accompanied by crunchy macaroons. *Serves 6.*

8 large ripe peaches   *⅔ cup (160 ml) orange juice*

Put the peaches into a bowl and cover them with boiling water. Leave the peaches for 1 minute, then drain them and cover them with cold water. Strip the skins off using a small sharp-pointed knife. Cut the peaches in half, remove the pits, and then slice the flesh fairly thinly. Put the slices into a serving dish—a pretty glass bowl is ideal. Cover them with orange juice and chill until needed.

STUFFED PEACHES

ITALY

In this recipe peaches are stuffed with macaroon crumbs and baked until tender. It's a curiously pleasant blend of flavors and a good way of using peaches that are not quite as luscious as they might be. *Serves 4.*

4 large peaches   *1 egg yolk*
About 3 macaroons

Preheat the oven to 350° F (180° C). Cut the peaches in half and carefully remove the pits; then scoop out a little of the peach flesh to make a larger cavity for the stuffing. Crush the macaroons with a rolling pin; mix the macaroon crumbs with the chopped, scooped-out peach flesh and the egg yolk. Spoon the mixture into the peach cavities and place the two halves of each peach together again. Put the stuffed peaches into a buttered ovenproof dish—a nice one that you can take to the table is best—and bake them for 45–60 minutes, or until they're tender when pierced with a knife. They're good with light cream or chilled vanilla custard.

PEARS BAKED IN WINE

FRANCE

One of the nicest things about this dish is its appearance: shapely whole pears, richly and deeply stained and flavored with wine. A large bowl of them always goes over well. The only trouble is that they take about 4 hours to cook in a lowish oven, so they're only really worth doing if you can justify the oven heat by baking a fruit cake, casserole, or even meringues at the same time.

Serve the pears with a big bowl of light, fluffy whipped cream and some homemade shortbread or macaroons for a special-occasion dessert. *Serves 4.*

2 pounds (900 g) small, hard pears   ½ cup (125 ml) granulated sugar
2 cups (500 ml) sweet red wine

Preheat the oven to 325° F (160° C). Peel the pears, keeping them whole and leaving their stalks on. Put them into a shallow ovenproof casserole and add the wine and sugar. Place the casserole in the oven and bake (uncovered) for about 4 hours, until the pears feel very tender when pierced with the point of a knife. Turn the pears over once or twice during the cooking time so that they bake evenly.

When the pears are ready, pour the liquid off into a small saucepan and bubble it over a high heat for about 10 minutes, until it has reduced in quantity and looks syrupy. Arrange the pears in a serving dish and pour the syrupy liquid over them. Serve them warm or chill them in the refrigerator.

PINEAPPLE SHERBET

ITALY

If you've got a blender or food processor, this is very easy to make. It turns out a beautiful pale yellow and has a lovely, sweet, true pineapple flavor, very refreshing after a filling meal. Because the pineapple is naturally sweet, you don't need to add much sugar. *Serves 4–6.*

1 large ripe pineapple	*2 egg whites*
¼ cup (60 ml) sugar	

Turn the refrigerator to its coldest setting. Slice the pineapple into quarters and then cut off the leafy top and all the prickly skin; also any hard core. Cut the pineapple into rough chunks, put them into your blender with the sugar, and blend them to a smooth creamy-looking purée. Pour this purée into a container that will fit into the freezing compartment of your refrigerator; freeze until it's solid 'round the edges.

Beat the egg whites until they stand in soft peaks. Break up the pineapple mixture with a fork and gradually add it to the egg whites, still beating. Put the mixture back into the freezer until it's solid.

Turn the refrigerator back to its normal setting. The sherbet tastes best when it's not too cold and iced so it's a good idea to move it from the freezer itself to one of the shelves about 30–45 minutes before you sit down for your first course. It's nice with shortbread fingers, and I must admit I also like some whipped cream with it.

PRUNE DELIGHT

NORWAY

In Norway this is called *sviskeblancmange*, which means prune blancmange, but if I call it this I find it tends to put people off and so I refer to it as prune delight, which I think describes it better. I know that to some people the thought of prunes can never be de-lightful, but if you like them, as I do, then I think you will enjoy this dessert. *Serves 4–6.*

2 cups (500 ml) water	*Slivered almonds*
2 tablespoons cornstarch	*Whipped cream*
Grated rind of ½ lemon	*A little ground cinnamon*
About ¼ cup (60 ml) sugar	

Put the prunes into a good-size bowl, cover them with boiling water, and leave them to soak for several hours if possible. Then transfer them to a saucepan and simmer them gently until they're tender. Drain the prunes but keep the liquid. Using a small sharp knife, remove the pits. Put the prunes into your blender with 1½ cups (375 ml) of the liquid in which they were cooked, and blend until smooth; or put the prunes through a *Mouli-légumes* and then mix them with the liquid.

Put the cornstarch into a small bowl and mix it to a smooth paste with a little of the prune purée. Bring the remaining purée to the boil in a medium-size saucepan and then add a little of it to the cornstarch; when it is blended pour all of this cornstarch mixture in with the rest in the saucepan and stir it over a gentle heat for a couple of minutes to cook the cornstarch. Take the mixture off the heat and let it cool slightly; then add the lemon rind and sugar to taste. Pour into individual dishes and leave to cool; chill in the refrigerator.

Sprinkle the top of each serving thickly with almonds and serve with whipped cream; or pipe or spoon some cream on top of each portion and sprinkle with cinnamon. Shortbread fingers go well with this.

I think this pudding would be delicious for a special occasion if you soaked the prunes in sweet white wine or cider instead of water, with maybe a dash of brandy added to the mixture after cooking.

PUMPKIN IN ORANGE SYRUP

SOUTH AMERICA

If you don't tell people what this is, they may well think it's some exotic fruit they're eating! *Serves 4.*

About 3½ (1½ kg) pumpkin　　　*1 orange*
1¼ cups (310 ml) water　　　*Orange liqueur (optional)*
½ cup (125 ml) sugar

Remove the peel and seeds from the pumpkin and slice the flesh into pieces. Put the water and sugar into a medium-size saucepan and bring to the boil over a gentle heat. Scrub the orange under hot water and then cut off 3 thin ribbons of peel, or zest—a potato peeler is good for doing this. Add the peel and the pumpkin to the sugar syrup in the saucepan and let it all simmer gently for about 10 minutes, until the pumpkin is tender. Remove the pumpkin and orange peel with a slotted spoon and put them into a bowl. Boil the syrup in which the pumpkin was cooked until it has reduced to just 2–3 tablespoonfuls and is very thick. This will take just a few minutes over a high heat without a lid on the saucepan. Pour the syrup over the pumpkin in the bowl and leave it to cool.

Serve the pumpkin chilled. A tablespoonful of orange liqueur is lovely added to the syrup if you really want to be impressive. Another variation is to cover the cooked, drained pumpkin with orange juice instead of the syrup—a fresh-tasting, lower-calorie version!

RED FRUIT PUDDING

DENMARK

I think this is an extremely delicious dessert, and it makes a little fruit go a long way. My version is unusual in that I hardly cook the fruit; I think this gives a particularly fresh-tasting result. Serve in individual glass bowls, if possible, to show off its rich ruby-red coloring. *Serves 4.*

*½ pound (240 g) fresh ripe fruit—
  red currants, raspberries, or
  strawberries, or a mixture*
2½ cups (625 ml) water
¼ cup (60 ml) cornstarch

½ cup (125 ml) superfine sugar
A few slivered almonds
Whipped cream (optional)
Ladyfingers

Wash the fruit and remove any little bits of stalk. Put the fruit into your blender jar with all the other ingredients and purée. Pour this purée into a saucepan and stir over a gentle heat until it thickens. Cook for a couple of minutes, then take off the heat and pour into 1 large or 4 smaller dishes. Let the pudding cool, then chill it if you wish. Decorate the top with a sprinkling of slivered almonds, and some cream if you like, and serve with ladyfingers.

RHUBARB COMPOTE

NORWAY

I think this pretty, pink, slightly jellied compote is one of the nicest rhubarb desserts. It's light and refreshing, delicious with crisp, crumbly shortbread or ladyfingers. *Serves 4.*

1 pound (450 g) fresh rhubarb	2 tablespoons cornstarch or
1¼ cups (310 ml) water	arrowroot
½ cup (125 ml) superfine sugar	Shortbread cookies or ladyfingers
A vanilla bean or a few drops of	Lightly whipped cream (optional)
vanilla extract	

Wash and trim the rhubarb, cutting off the leaves and scraping off tough fibers if necessary; then cut the stalks into 1-inch (2.5 cm) lengths. Put the water, sugar, and vanilla into a medium-size saucepan and bring to the boil. Add the rhubarb and simmer very gently, with a lid on the saucepan, until the rhubarb is almost tender. This takes 5–15 minutes, depending on the age and type of rhubarb. Remove the vanilla bean.

Mix the cornstarch or arrowroot to form a paste with a little cold water and add to the rhubarb, stirring constantly. Simmer for 2 minutes, until thickened. Pour into 4 individual serving bowls; cool, then chill. Serve with the shortbread or ladyfingers and cream.

RICE AND ALMOND PUDDING

DENMARK

This is luxurious and rich-tasting and guaranteed to appeal even to people who think they don't like rice pudding! In Denmark it's served at Christmastime. You will notice that I use ordinary white rice for this recipe. If you're very strict about eating largely unrefined foods you might not approve of this, but I haven't found brown rice satisfactory, and the amount is so small anyway. *Serves 4–6.*

FOR THE PUDDING:

2½ cups (625 ml) milk
¼ cup (60 ml) white rice
3 tablespoons sugar

½ cup (125 ml) slivered almonds
1 teaspoon vanilla extract
½ cup (125 ml) heavy cream

FOR THE SAUCE:

1 package (10 ounces/300 g)
  frozen raspberries
A pinch of sugar

1 tablespoon cherry brandy or
  kirsch (optional)

Wash the rice and put it into a pie dish with the milk and sugar. Bake in a lowish oven for 2–3 hours, to make a rice pudding. The temperature isn't crucial: 300°–325° F (150°–160° C) is best, but if necessary the pudding can cook near the bottom of a hotter oven. As the skin forms stir it into the pudding—this gives a nice creamy result. When the rice is soft and the pudding thick, take it out of the oven and leave it to cool; then beat it and add the almonds and vanilla. Whip the cream until it stands in soft peaks, then fold it into the rice mixture. Chill.

To make the raspberry sauce, strain the raspberries, sweeten them with just a little sugar, and flavor with the cherry brandy or kirsch if you like. Serve the pudding in small bowls and spoon the sauce attractively over the top.

◆———◆———◆

TRIFLE

ENGLAND

Proper trifle, made with egg custard and topped with whipped cream, is a delicious dessert; light, not too sweet, and excellent served after a grain- or vegetable-based main course or to round off a salad buffet meal. *Serves 6–8.*

1 8-inch sponge cake or 1 package
  (3 ounces/90 g) ladyfingers, or
  sponge fingers, (see page 265)

3 tablespoons raspberry jam
4 tablespoons sherry

FOR THE CUSTARD:

3 eggs
¼ cup (60 ml) superfine sugar

¼ teaspoon vanilla extract
2½ cups (625 ml) milk

TO FINISH:

1 cup (250 ml) heavy cream
¼ cup (60 ml) toasted slivered
    almonds

Split the sponge cake and spread with the jam, or sandwich the fingers together in pairs and then cut them up into smaller pieces. Put the pieces of sponge cake into the bottom of a serving dish—a pretty glass one is nice—and pour the sherry over them. Leave to one side while you make the custard.

Beat the eggs, sugar, and vanilla together in a bowl; put the milk into a saucepan and bring it just to the boil, then pour it over the egg mixture and beat again. Strain the mixture back into the saucepan and stir over a gentle heat for just a minute or two until it thickens. Don't let it overcook or it will separate. (If this does happen I've found if I put it in the blender for a moment and blend it at a high speed, amazingly, it seems to be all right again.) Pour the custard over the sponge pieces and leave to one side to cool. To finish the trifle whip the cream until it's softly thickened, then spoon it over the top of the trifle. Chill the trifle and then sprinkle the almonds over the top just before you serve it, so that they're still crisp.

VANILLA ICE CREAM

ITALY

Homemade ice cream sounds like hard work but it isn't really all that much effort, and the result is so delicate and creamy that it's well worth it. My recipe is a fairly modest, economical one, but I think you'll find the flavor and texture pleasing. Actually, home-made ice cream isn't really extravagant when you consider what a useful source of protein it is and plan the meal accordingly. It's excel-

lent, for instance, after a simple pasta-, rice- or vegetable-based meal.
Serves 4.

2 eggs or 4 egg yolks
1¼ cups (310 ml) milk
⅓ cup (80 ml) sugar

½ teaspoon vanilla extract
1 cup (250 ml) heavy cream

Turn the refrigerator to its coldest setting. Beat the eggs in a medium-size bowl. Put the milk and sugar into a heavy-bottomed saucepan and bring just to the boil, then slowly add it to the eggs, stirring constantly. Pour the eggs and milk back into the saucepan and return to the heat, stirring for just a minute or two until the mixture thickens—this happens very suddenly and the custard soon goes lumpy and curdled if you're not careful. Don't worry too much if it does; I've found that this doesn't affect the ice cream. Cool.

Beat the cream until it has thickened and is standing in soft peaks, then fold it gently but thoroughly into the cooled egg custard. Pour the mixture into a suitable container (don't cover with a lid) and freeze until it's setting well 'round the edges. Then scrape the ice cream into a bowl and beat it thoroughly. Put the ice cream back into the container and freeze it until it's firm.

It's a good idea to put the ice cream into the main part of the refrigerator at the beginning of the meal so that it can soften a little. Don't forget to turn the fridge setting back to normal.

◆——◆——◆

YOGURT

MIDDLE EAST

Chilled and served in small bowls, yogurt makes a delicious, refreshing dessert. It's particularly good for a special occasion if you use evaporated milk or even light cream or a proportion of light cream. Also used in a number of other recipes in this book, yogurt is particularly useful in salad dressings. It's not difficult to make; all you need is a suitably warm place in which to put the yogurt while it sets. I stand my yogurt on the gas stove by the pilot light; alternatively you can use a cupboard or find a corner near a radiator. *Serves 4–6.*

2½ cups (625 ml) milk
2 rounded tablespoons instant
  nonfat dry milk

1 teaspoon plain yogurt
A little brown sugar or honey

Put the milk into a saucepan and bring to the boil; reduce heat and leave it to simmer, without a lid on the saucepan, for 10 minutes. This reduces the milk a little and makes the yogurt thick and creamy. Take the saucepan off the heat and leave it until it has cooled to lukewarm. While you are waiting for the milk to cool, select a bowl or two jars big enough to contain the milk and sterilize them by swishing them out with warm water mixed with some household bleach; then rinse them thoroughly again in very hot water.

Beat the milk powder and yogurt into the milk and pour into your clean sterilized bowl or jars; cover with foil and leave in a warm place for a few hours or overnight until it's firm. Cool and then put the yogurt into the refrigerator where it will firm up even more and be thick and creamy to eat. To serve, spoon the yogurt out into individual dishes and sprinkle with sugar just before taking the yogurt to the table. You may wish to use honey instead.

If you prefer, you can make the yogurt directly into little individual dishes, as you would egg custards.

SWEET PASTRIES, COOKIES, AND CAKES

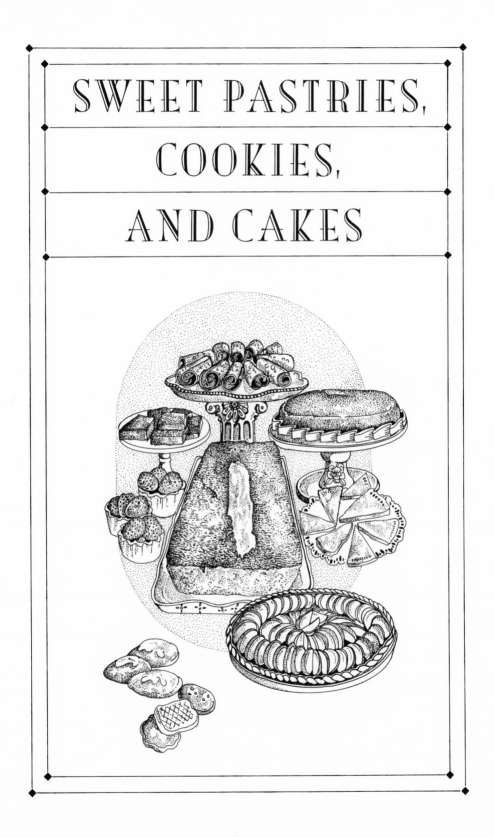

Apple Tart
Brandy Snaps
Cheesecake
Honey Cheesecake
Chocolate Brownies
Coconut Cookies
Dundee Cake
Linzertorte
Macaroons
Madeira Cake
Miniature Meringues
Parkin
Pumpkin Pie
Raisin Sour Cream Pie
Shortbread Fingers
Sponge Fingers
Strawberry Tartlets
Yogurt Tart

THIS IS QUITE A VARIED COLLECTION OF GOODIES. There are some mouth-watering pastries—such as the apple tart from France, the cheesecake and raisin sour cream pie from the USA, the yogurt tart from Greece, and *linzertorte* from Austria—which all make delicious desserts after a light main course or salad. Then there are a few cakes, such as Madeira cake and Dundee cake, which are particularly good as a snack with coffee or tea; slices of Madeira cake are delicious with fools and fruit salads.

Also good as accompaniments to various desserts are the numerous cookies included here: a little dish of crumbly homemade shortbread, crunchy coconut cookies, or crisp macaroons provide the final touch when you're serving a special fruit salad or compote, and they're not difficult to make.

As you will have gathered by now, I am keen on using whole-wheat flour and some of the recipes are made entirely with whole-wheat flour while in others I suggest using a mixture of whole-wheat flour and white flour (try to get unbleached white flour). You can of course use almost any flour you prefer; but the proportions I've suggested in the recipes are the ones I recommend, bearing in mind the sometimes conflicting aims of nutrition on the one hand and taste and appearance on the other!

◆——◆——◆

APPLE TART

FRANCE

This tart looks very appetizing with its glossy golden rings of apple slices on a crisp pastry base. If you have time, bake the pastry before you add the topping; this ensures the pastry will be lovely and crisp, a delicious contrast to the soft apple slices and moist, golden apricot glaze. I make this tart on one of those big round ceramic pizza dishes measuring 12 inches (30 cm) across, but any big, flat, ovenproof plate or pan would do. If you use a 10-inch tart pan, your crust will simply be a bit thicker. *Serves 6.*

FOR THE PASTRY:

2 cups (500 ml) plain
  whole-wheat flour
2 teaspoons baking powder

4 tablespoons soft margarine
4 tablespoons shortening
2 tablespoons water

FOR THE TOPPING:

2 pounds (900 g) apples—
  Bramleys or Golden Delicious

FOR THE GLAZE:

1½ cups (375 ml) apricot jam   *2 teaspoons cornstarch*
4 tablespoons water

First preheat the oven to 400° F (200° C); then make the pastry. Measure the flour into a large bowl. With your fingertips, rub the fats into the flour until the mixture looks like bread crumbs, then add the cold water and form the dough. Turn the dough onto a floured board and roll it out to fit your plate or pan. Turn under the edges of the pastry to make it fit the dish neatly and then decorate the edge by pressing it with the prongs of a fork. Prick the pastry all over and bake it in the preheated oven for 15 minutes, until it's golden brown. Remove the pastry but leave the oven on.

While the pastry is cooking, prepare the apples. Cut them into quarters, then remove the skin and core with a sharp knife and cut the apples into thin slices. Arrange these slices on the pastry base, overlapping them a bit to achieve a nice even pattern. When the apples are all arranged, put the tart into the oven and bake it for 30 minutes, until the apples feel tender when pierced with the point of a knife.

Toward the end of the cooking time, prepare the apricot glaze. Heat the apricot jam in a small saucepan with 2 tablespoons of the water. Mix the remaining 2 tablespoons with the cornstarch in a small bowl or cup. When the jam is boiling, pour some of it over the cornstarch mixture, stir, then return it to the saucepan and stir over the heat for about 2 minutes until it has thickened. Take the saucepan off the heat and pour the glaze evenly over the top of the hot tart; try to make sure that all the apple is covered with the lovely shiny apricot glaze, then leave it to cool slightly before serving. We like it best hot, but you could equally well serve it cold.

BRANDY SNAPS

GREAT BRITAIN

Crisp brandy snaps with their filling of brandy-flavored whipped cream are really sheer indulgence and a very French-tasting British contribution. This is an easy recipe for brandy snaps because it doesn't contain Golden Syrup and so you have more time to get the brandy snaps off the baking sheet and curl them up before they harden. They are really quite easy, and lovely for serving for a special occasion, perhaps to accompany a fruit salad or compote. You can also keep them flat and serve them without cream as crisp cookies, or roll them up tightly into "cigarettes." Served in this way, they're good with gooseberry fool. *Makes 12.*

4 tablespoons soft margarine
¼ cup (60 ml) soft brown sugar
½ cup (125 ml) all-purpose flour
   —I use white for these

¼ teaspoon ground ginger

TO FINISH:

⅔ cup (160 ml) heavy cream
A little confectioners sugar

1–2 teaspoons brandy

Cream the margarine and sugar in a mixing bowl, then sift in the flour and ginger and mix to a smooth dough. If you've got time to cover the bowl and leave it to one side for an hour or so before continuing, I've found this helps the brandy snaps to cook better.

When you're ready to cook them, preheat the oven to 375° F (190° C). Butter a large baking sheet. Roll teaspoons of the brandy snap mixture into balls and place them well apart on the baking sheet. You will probably have to cook them in two batches. Bake the brandy snaps for about 15 minutes, until they're golden brown in the middle, deeper brown at the edges. Take the baking sheet out of the oven and let it stand for 2 minutes, then ease the brandy snaps off the baking sheet with a small spatula. (As there is quite a lot of margarine in the mixture, it's not difficult to get them off the tray, and I find I don't have to butter it again between batches.) Roll the brandy snaps around the handle of a wooden spoon and leave them to cool. As they cool they will get crisp. Keep them in an air-tight container until you want them.

Whip the cream until it's standing in soft peaks. Stir in the confectioners sugar and the brandy to taste and whip again. Then spoon or pipe the cream into the brandy snaps. Serve them as soon as possible after this, while they're still crisp.

CHEESECAKE

U S A

This cheesecake looks most impressive if you make it in an 8-inch (20 cm) springform pan so that you get a good deep layer of the lovely white creamy mixture above the crumb base.

I've experimented a good deal to find the right combination, and I think this mixture of low-fat cottage cheese and sour cream gives the best result—light but creamy. If you prefer a richer cheesecake you could use cream cheese or half cream cheese and half cottage cheese. On the other hand, you can make a very good low-fat cheesecake by using cottage cheese or skim milk *ricotta* with plain low-fat yogurt instead of the sour cream. *Serves 8–10.*

1½ cups (375 ml) graham cracker crumbs
1 tablespoon sugar
6 tablespoons unsalted butter, softened
12 ounces (350 g) low-fat ricotta or cottage cheese

3 eggs
1 teaspoon vanilla extract
½ cup (125 ml) sugar
1 tablespoon lemon juice
⅔ cup (160 ml) sour cream

Preheat the oven to 300° F (150° C). Put the graham crackers on a board and crush them with a rolling pin, then mix them with the sugar and butter. Press the mixture evenly into the base of your springform pan. Leave to one side while you make the filling. To do this, if you've got a blender or food processor, just blend everything else for a minute until smooth. Otherwise, push the cottage cheese through a strainer into a large bowl, or just put the *ricotta* straight into the bowl, then add the eggs, vanilla, sugar, lemon juice, and sour cream and beat thoroughly to a smooth, creamy consistency. Pour the mixture into the pan on top of the crumbs.

Bake the cheesecake on the bottom rack of the oven for 1½ hours, or until it looks set and feels firm to a very light touch. Cool, then chill.

Slip a knife round the sides of the cheesecake and unclip the spring on the pan. Stand the pan on something like a jam jar and carefully slip the sides of the pan down, leaving the cheesecake standing clear.

If you want to top your cheesecake with fruit you'll need 1 pint (500 ml) fresh strawberries and 6–8 tablespoons of red currant jelly. Wash and dry the strawberries and then arrange them on top of the chilled cheesecake. Melt the jelly in a small saucepan and then pour it evenly over the strawberries to glaze them. Leave to set before serving.

To my mind, an even nicer topping is made by simply spreading another ⅔ cup (160 ml) sour cream over the surface of the cooled cheesecake, chilling the lot for several hours before serving. Divine!

HONEY CHEESECAKE

GREECE

I think this cheesecake, like the one from the USA, is best made in one of those deep springform pans (8-inch/20 cm in diameter), because this gives a nice thick, luscious layer of filling. *Serves 6.*

FOR THE CRUST:

1½ cups (375 ml) flour—use
   whole-wheat or half
   whole-wheat and half white
8 tablespoons unsalted butter
1 egg yolk

½ cup (125 ml) sugar
¾ cup (180 ml) honey
2 eggs
1 teaspoon ground cinnamon
1 egg white

FOR THE FILLING:

2 cups (500 ml) low-fat ricotta or cottage cheese

First preheat the oven to 375° F (190° C) and then prepare your pan by greasing it lightly with butter. Next make the pastry. Sift the flour into a bowl, then rub in the butter until the mixture looks like fine bread crumbs. Add the egg yolk and knead the mixture gently to form a dough. Turn the dough out onto a lightly floured board, knead it a little until it's smooth, then roll it out and gently ease it into your springform pan. I find the best way to do this with the crumbly whole-wheat pastry is to tip the pastry straight from the board to the pan, holding the board with one hand and easing the pastry into the pan with the other. Leave to one side while you make the filling.

The easiest way to make the filling is to put everything into the blend jar except the egg white and purée until it's smooth. Alternatively, push the cottage cheese through a strainer (no need to strain *ricotta*), then gradually beat in all the other ingredients except the egg white. Beat the egg white until it's stiff and fold it in, then pour the mixture into the pastry shell and smooth the top gently. It may be necessary to trim the pastry a little so that it's practically level with the filling. Put the cheesecake into the oven to bake for 30 minutes; then turn the oven down to 325° F (160° C) and cook for another 50 minutes.

Let the cheesecake cool before serving. It should be served chilled—this firms the cheesecake up and makes the filling luscious and creamy to eat. This is an ideal dessert to serve after one of the low-protein stuffed vegetable main courses.

CHOCOLATE BROWNIES

U S A

These chocolate brownies are quick and easy to make and don't need any icing as they're already lovely and gooey. I like them particularly because you can use brown sugar and whole-wheat flour to make them, and they're all the better for it. You can use other nuts instead of pecans if you like; walnuts are probably the obvious substitute, but I think hazelnuts are especially good. *Makes 18.*

1 cup (250 ml) butter or margarine	*¾ cup (180 ml) whole-wheat flour*
¼ cup (60 ml) cocoa	*½ teaspoon baking powder*
1 cup (250 ml) firmly packed brown sugar	*½ teaspoon vanilla extract*
2 eggs	*½ cup (125 ml) chopped pecans —or walnuts or hazelnuts*

Preheat the oven to 350° F (180° C). Lightly grease a cake pan (7 by 11 inches/18 by 28 cm). Put the butter or margarine into a saucepan with the cocoa and sugar and heat gently until melted. Remove from the heat and cool to lukewarm, then beat in the eggs one by one.

Measure the flour and baking powder into the mixture and mix well; stir in the vanilla extract and nuts. Pour the mixture into the prepared pan, pushing it into the corners. Bake in the center of the oven for about 30 minutes, until the mixture springs back when touched lightly in the center.

Allow the brownies to cool in the pan, then cut them into 18 squares.

◆———◆———◆

COCONUT COOKIES

SOUTH AMERICA

These crunchy coconut cookies are lovely with creamy desserts and fruit salads, especially the exotic fruit salad that also comes from South America. *Makes 24.*

4 tablespoons butter, softened	*1 teaspoon baking powder*
⅓ cup (80 ml) sugar	*1 egg, beaten*
¾ cup (180 ml) whole-wheat	*½ cup (125 ml) flaked coconut*
flour	*Extra coconut to finish*

Preheat the oven to 350° F (180° C). Put the butter and sugar into a bowl and sift the flour and baking powder on top. Add the beaten egg and coconut and just mix everything together to a soft dough. Sprinkle a board with the flaked coconut and turn the dough out onto this; knead the dough lightly into a long sausage shape, then flatten the sausage a bit. Cut ¼-inch (6 mm) slices off the sausage to make roughly finger-shaped cookies; place these on a greased and floured baking sheet. Don't put them too close together, as they will almost double in size.

Press a little more coconut onto the top of each cookie and bake them for 15–20 minutes, until they're golden brown. Let them cool for a few minutes on the baking sheet and then transfer them to a wire cooling rack.

◆———◆———◆

DUNDEE CAKE

I've included a recipe for this traditional Scottish cake partly because it's irresistible, with its luscious fruit inside and its topping of crunchy almonds, and also because it makes a very acceptable dessert after a salad lunch or supper. *Makes one 9-inch (23 cm) cake.*

2 cups (500 ml) whole-wheat
   flour
Pinch of salt
1 teaspoon baking soda
1 teaspoon mixed spice—
   cinnamon, nutmeg, cloves,
   ginger, etc.
12 tablespoons soft butter or
   margarine
¾ cup (180 ml) soft firmly packed
   brown sugar

3 eggs
Grated rind of 1 lemon
3 cups (750 ml) mixed dried fruit
   —raisins, sultanas, currants,
   apricots, etc.
½ cup (125 ml) chopped mixed
   peel
½ cup (125 ml) glacé cherries,
   rinsed and halved
A little milk
¼ cup (60 ml) slivered almonds

Line an 9-inch cake pan with a double layer of greased waxed or brown paper. Preheat the oven to 325° F (160° C). Measure the flour, salt, and baking soda into a bowl; leave to one side. Cream the butter or margarine with the sugar until light and fluffy; add the eggs one at a time, beating well after each addition. Gently fold in the flour, grated lemon rind, and mixed fruit, adding a little milk if necessary to make a moister consistency. Spoon the mixture into the prepared pan and smooth the top level. Sprinkle with slivered almonds and bake for 2½ hours, until a skewer inserted into the center comes out clean. Cool for a few minutes in the pan, then turn the cake out onto a wire cooling rack and gently peel off the paper.

LINZERTORTE

This light, flaky tart is delicately flavored with spices and lemon rind and melts in your mouth. I experimented many times with this recipe until I came up with this version, which I think is just right.

With one of my later efforts, my husband said he liked the flavor but the tart wasn't thick enough to get his teeth into, so I increased the amount of pastry to the present quantity. If you'd like to make a thinner tart, you could try using only 1 cup (250 ml) of flour, almonds, and butter and 2 tablespoons sugar, or use a larger dish. *Serves 6.*

1½ cups (575 ml) whole-wheat flour	3 tablespoons sugar
1 teaspoon ground cinnamon	12 tablespoons butter
Pinch of ground cloves	1 egg yolk
1 cup (250 ml) ground almonds	¾–1 cup (180–250 ml) raspberry or black-currant jam
Grated rind of ½ lemon	A little confectioners sugar

Measure the flour, cinnamon, and cloves into a bowl. Mix in the almonds, lemon rind, and sugar, then rub the butter into the dry ingredients. Gently mix in the egg yolk to make a soft dough. Wrap the dough in a piece of foil or plastic and chill it in the refrigerator for 30 minutes or so. If you have time for this, the dough will be easier to roll out, but this step isn't essential if you're in a hurry.

Preheat the oven to 400° F (200° C). On a lightly floured board roll out three-quarters of the dough to fit a 9-inch (23 cm) fluted quiche dish—one of those pretty porcelain ones is ideal for this recipe. Spread the jam evenly over the pastry. Roll out the rest of the pastry and cut it into long strips; arrange these strips in a lattice over the jam, then fold the edges of the pastry down and press them in to make a sort of rim around the edge of the tart. Bake the tart for 25–30 minutes, until it's slightly risen and golden brown.

You can serve the tart hot, cold, or—my choice—warm. Sprinkle a little confectioners sugar over the top of the tart before taking it to the table; the red jam looks very appetizing glistening underneath this snowy topping. It's nice with light cream.

MACAROONS

FRANCE

Crisp macaroons are lovely for serving with cold, creamy desserts. Although they might seem a bit extravagant, they are in fact rich in protein and so not completely frivolous. *Makes 12.*

1 egg white
¾ cup (180 ml) ground almonds
½ cup (125 ml) superfine sugar

Rice paper
12 whole blanched almonds

Preheat the oven to 350° F (180° C). Put the egg white into a good-size bowl and beat lightly, just to break it up. Stir in the ground almonds and sugar and mix to a paste. Lay the rice paper on baking sheets and put spoonfuls of the macaroon mixture on it, leaving room for them to spread a little. Smooth the macaroons with the back of a spoon dipped in cold water and place an almond in the center of each. Bake for 15–25 minutes.

Transfer the macaroons to a wire rack, tearing the rice paper roughly; trim off the remaining paper when the macaroons have cooled.

◆——————◆——————◆

MADEIRA CAKE

ENGLAND

This cake used to be served in England to accompany a glass of Madeira wine, but I think it is a nice accompariment to other desserts, especially the Russian *pashka*. But really it's such a beautiful, delicately flavored, smooth-textured cake that it's useful on all sorts of occasions. In my family it has formed the basis of a number of birthday cakes ranging from an enchanted house to a teddy bear, which I literally carved out of an oblong block of cake. Normally I just bake the cake in a loafpan and serve it unadorned except for the pieces of peel baked into the top. I like to use a loaf pan as it is easier for cutting and you can arrange the peel all down the center so that everyone gets some on top of their slice. *Makes one.*

1½ cups (375 ml) flour—half
　whole-wheat, half white is best
　for this
2 teaspoons baking powder
12 tablespoons unsalted butter,
　softened

⅔ cup (160 ml) superfine sugar
1 tablespoon grated lemon rind
3 eggs
3 tablespoons milk
Several pieces of citrus peel

Preheat the oven to 325° F (160° C). Line the loaf pan with a strip of waxed or brown paper and brush with softened butter, then sprinkle with a little flour.

Sift the flour and baking powder into a large bowl or the bowl of your mixer, adding the residue of bran left in the sieve and all the other ingredients except the citrus peel. Stir everything together thoroughly to make a light, fluffy mixture. Spoon the batter lightly into the prepared pan and level the top. Place in the oven and bake for 45 minutes; then, without taking the cake out of the oven, very carefully lay the citrus peel along the top of the cake, and bake it for another 40–45 minutes.

Cool the cake for a few minutes in the pan and then turn it out onto a wire rack to cool completely. Remove the paper when it's cooled.

◆———◆———◆

MINIATURE MERINGUES

FRANCE

Crisp little meringues make a very nice accompaniment to smooth fools and ice creams. They're also a pretty garnish to use on a trifle or an egg custard if you don't want to use cream. *Makes about 24.*

2 egg whites   *½ cup (125 ml) superfine sugar*

First prepare a couple of baking sheets by covering them with parchment paper and brushing the paper with cooking oil. Or use non-stick baking paper.

Beat the egg whites until they're very stiff. Add half the sugar and quickly beat it into the mixture; then fold in the remaining sugar.

The best way to put the meringues onto the baking sheets is to use a pastry bag fitted with a ½-inch (1 cm) shell nozzle, but if you haven't got one a teaspoon will do. Pipe or spoon the mixture onto the baking sheets, leaving a little space between the meringues, as they will spread slightly and I find they bake best if they are not too close together. Put the meringues into the oven and set it at its lowest temperature—225° F (110° C).

They will take about 1½ hours to dry out. Test one by taking it off the baking sheet and tapping it on the base to see if it feels and sounds firm and dry. Let the meringues cool on the trays, then take them off and store them in an air-tight container. In theory they keep well for a week or so, but in practice I find they never get the chance to do so!

PARKIN

ENGLAND

This is one of those cakes in which you can use whole-wheat flour, brown sugar, and molasses without any problems at all, and the result is delicious as well as nutritious. It's moist and gooey, particularly if you wrap it in foil and keep it for a few days before you eat it. *Makes 15–18 pieces.*

8 tablespoons butter or margarine
1 cup (250 ml) molasses
½ cup (125 ml) firmly packed
   dark brown sugar
1 cup (250 ml) whole-wheat flour
1 teaspoon baking powder
1 teaspoon ground ginger

1 teaspoon mixed spice—ground
   ginger, nutmeg, cinnamon,
   allspice, etc., to taste
1½ cups (375 ml) rolled oats
6 tablespoons milk
1 egg

Preheat the oven to 325° F (160° C). Put the butter or margarine into a small saucepan with the molasses and sugar and heat gently until melted, but don't let the mixture boil. Cool. Measure the flour, baking powder, and spices into a bowl and stir in the oats. Make a well in the center of the dry ingredients and pour in the molasses mixture and the milk; then add the egg and mix everything until smooth. Brush an 8-inch (20 cm) square pan with softened butter or margarine and then pour in the parkin and put it in the oven.

Bake it for 55–60 minutes, or until it has shrunk away from the sides of the pan and feels firm to the touch. Cool in the pan, then cut into slices.

PUMPKIN PIE

U S A

An American friend gave me this recipe, which I've adapted to give the right quantity for a 9-inch (23 cm) pie dish. It makes a lovely autumn dessert, smooth and warmly spiced. I think it's best when it's hot but you can also serve it cold; it's nicest with cream. Sometimes I scatter some roughly chopped walnuts over the top of the pie, which makes it look especially interesting and is a pleasant variation. *Serves 6.*

FOR THE PASTRY SHELL:

1½ cups (375 ml) whole-wheat flour
1½ teaspoons baking powder

4 tablespoons butter
4 tablespoons shortening
1 tablespoon cold water

FOR THE FILLING:

2¼ pounds (1 kg) fresh pumpkin, unpeeled; or 2 cups canned pumpkin
4 tablespoons water
½ cup (125 ml) firmly packed soft brown sugar

½ teaspoon ground ginger
½ teaspoon ground cinnamon
A little grated nutmeg
Pinch of cloves
⅔ cup (160 ml) light cream
2 eggs

Preheat the oven to 400° F (200° C). Measure the flour and baking powder into a bowl. Rub in the fats until the mixture looks like fine bread crumbs; then add the water and mix to form a dough. Roll the pastry out on a lightly floured board and put into a 9-inch (23 cm) pie dish. Prick the base, then bake the crust in the oven for about 15 minutes, until it's browned and crisp. Take it out of the oven and let it cool slightly while you make the filling. Reduce the oven setting to 350° F (180° C).

Peel the pumpkin and remove the seeds. Cut the pumpkin into even-size pieces, put them into a heavy-bottomed saucepan with the water, and cook gently, with a lid on the saucepan, until the pumpkin is tender—about 10 minutes. Put the pumpkin into a colander and drain it very well indeed, pressing gently with a spoon to extract as much water as possible. Put the pumpkin into a bowl and add the sugar, spices, cream, and eggs. Mix well, then pour into the pastry shell and bake in the preheated oven for about 50 minutes, until it's set.

◆——◆——◆

RAISIN SOUR CREAM PIE

U S A

The friend in the USA who kindly gave me this recipe serves it as an alternative to pumpkin pie at Thanksgiving. I think it also makes an excellent alternative to mincemeat pie at Christmas because of its spicy, festive flavor. It's a nourishing, protein-rich dessert with the whole-wheat flour, eggs, and nuts. If you can't get pecans you can use walnuts instead—or slivered almonds, which I like best of all; and an alternative to the sour cream is plain yogurt. *Serves 6.*

*1½ cups (375 ml) raisins or
   sultanas
⅔ cup (160 ml) sour cream
¼ teaspoon ground cloves
¼ teaspoon grated nutmeg*

*1 teaspoon cinnamon
2 eggs
¼ cup (60 ml) soft brown sugar
¼ cup (60 ml) pecans, walnuts, or
   slivered almonds*

FOR THE PASTRY CRUST:

*1 cup (250 ml) whole-wheat flour
1 teaspoon baking powder
4 tablespoons butter or soft
   margarine*

1 tablespoon cold water

First start making the filling by putting the raisins or sultanas into a bowl with the sour cream and the spices; mix well, then leave to one side while you make the pastry shell.

Preheat the oven to 400° F (200° C). To make the pastry, measure the flour and baking powder into a bowl. Rub in the fat until the mixture looks like bread crumbs; then mix in the water and gently press the mixture together to form a dough. Roll out the dough on a lightly floured board and use to line a 9-inch (23 cm) pie dish. Trim the edges and prick the dough; bake it in the oven for about 15 minutes, until it is set and golden brown. Take the pastry out of the oven and reduce the temperature to 350° F (180° C).

Finish making the filling: beat the eggs and then add them to the sour cream and fruit mixture, together with the sugar and nuts. Mix everything together well, then pour the filling evenly into the pastry shell—it doesn't matter if this is still warm—and smooth the top gently with a knife or the back of a spoon. Bake the pie in the oven for 35–40 minutes, until the filling is set. You can serve the pie hot or cold, but I think it's nicest hot.

SHORTBREAD FINGERS

SCOTLAND

These crisp little cookies melt in your mouth and are perfect for serving with fruit salads, fools, and creamy puddings. *Makes 18–20.*

1 cup (250 ml) whole-wheat flour	*⅓ cup (80 ml) superfine sugar*
1 cup (250 ml) all-purpose flour	*14 tablespoons butter, softened*
2 teaspoons baking powder	*Sugar to finish*

Preheat the oven to 325° F (160° C). Sift the flours and baking powder into a large bowl or the bowl of your mixer, and tip in any residual bran from the sieve too. Add the sugar and butter, then beat everything together to form a soft dough. Turn the dough out onto a floured board and knead it a little; then roll the dough out to a thickness of ¼ inch (6mm) and cut it into fingers. Put these on a lightly floured baking sheet, prick them all over with a fork, and bake them for about 20 minutes, until they're golden brown.

Let them cool on the baking sheet, as they're fragile while they're still hot. Sprinkle them generously with sugar before serving them.

SPONGE FINGERS

FRANCE

These are good for serving with fools and creamy puddings when you want something crisp but not as rich as shortbread. You really do need an electric mixer for these, and they're best made the day you want to eat them. *Makes 12–15.*

1 egg	*6 tablespoons all-purpose flour*
3 tablespoons sugar	*Extra sugar for sprinkling*

Preheat oven to 375° F (190° C). Prepare a baking sheet by covering it with a piece of parchment paper and brushing it with oil. Put the egg and granulated sugar into the bowl of your mixer and beat at top speed until the mixture is very thick and pale and able to hold its shape. Gently sift the flour over the top of the egg mixture and carefully cut and fold it in with a metal spoon. Pipe or spoon thin fingers of the mixture onto the prepared baking sheet, allowing space for them to spread—they will roughly double in width. Sprinkle the tops of the fingers thickly with sugar, then bake them for about 12 minutes until they're golden brown and firm to a light touch. Let the fingers cool slightly, then carefully ease them off the baking sheet and put them on a wire rack to finish cooling.

◆——◆——◆

STRAWBERRY TARTLETS

FRANCE

The combination of crisp pastry, creamy filling, and shiny strawberries makes these little tartlets very delicious. You can vary the flavor of the filling; I like it with rose essence or rosewater as a change from vanilla. The tartlets are also good made with other fruit toppings: I particularly like them with those little green seedless grapes or halved and seeded black grapes, with lemon-flavored filling and apricot jam to glaze. *Makes 12.*

FOR THE PASTRY CREAM:

¼ cup (60 ml) all-purpose flour	*2 tablespoons sugar*
1 egg yolk	*3 tablespoons butter*
1 cup (250 ml) milk	

FOR THE PASTRY:

1½ cups (375 ml) whole-wheat flour—or you could use a mixture of white and whole-wheat	*1½ teaspoons baking powder*
	6 tablespoons (90 ml) butter or margarine
	1–2 tablespoons cold water

1½ cups (375 ml) small ripe   2 tablespoons water
   strawberries   ½ teaspoon cornstarch
½ cup (125 ml) red currant jelly

First make the pastry cream. You can do this a day or two in advance if you like because it will keep perfectly in a covered container in the refrigerator. Put the flour into a small bowl with the egg yolk and enough milk to make a smooth paste. Put the rest of the milk and the sugar into a small saucepan and bring to the boil, then pour it over the egg and flour mixture, stirring. Pour the mixture back into the saucepan and stir over a moderate heat. It will go lumpy, but go on stirring hard (try a wire whisk) and after a few minutes you will have a thick, smooth sauce. Take the saucepan off the heat, turn the mixture into a small bowl, and add a little vanilla extract or any other flavoring you fancy to complement the fruit. Dot the butter over the top of the mixture—this will prevent a skin from forming—cover with a piece of foil, and leave to one side. When the pastry cream is cool, store it in the fridge until you need it.

Next make the tartlet crusts. Preheat the oven to 400° F (200° C). Sift the flour and baking powder into a bowl. Rub the fat into the flour using your fingertips and then mix to form a dough with the cold water. Roll the dough out on a lightly floured board so that it lines 12 tartlet tins. Prick each crust lightly with a fork, then bake them in the preheated oven for about 15 minutes, until they're golden brown. Leave to one side to cool.

When you're ready to fill the tartlet shells, beat the pastry cream to blend in the butter and make the mixture smooth and light, then put about a teaspoonful of pastry cream in each tartlet. The exact amount will depend on how deep the tartlets are; you may find you don't need quite all the pastry cream. Hull and wash the strawberries and halve or quarter them unless they're really small. Arrange the strawberries on top of the pastry cream.

To make the glaze, melt the red currant jelly with 1 tablespoonful of the water. Mix the cornstarch to a paste with another tablespoonful of water and add this to the red currant jelly in the saucepan, stirring until you have a smooth, slightly thickened glaze. Spoon the glaze over the strawberries on the tartlets and leave them to cool. Eat them the same day.

◆——◆——◆

YOGURT TART

GREECE

In this tart the combination of creamy, fresh-tasting filling and crisp whole-wheat pastry is delicious, and it couldn't be simpler to make, as the filling is uncooked. *Serves 6.*

FOR THE PASTRY:

1½ cups (375 ml) whole-wheat   *4 tablespoons butter*
  flour   *1 tablespoon cold water*
1 teaspoon baking powder

FOR THE FILLING:

8 ounces (225 g) low-fat ricotta or   *1 tablespoon honey*
  cream cheese   *1 tablespoon sugar*
⅔ cup (180 ml) plain yogurt   *A few chopped walnuts*

Preheat the oven to 400° F (200° C). Measure the flour and baking powder into a bowl. Rub the fat into the flour and then mix to form a dough with the cold water. Roll the pastry out on a lightly floured board and fit it into a 9-inch (23 cm) pie dish; trim the edges and prick the base. Bake the pie for about 15 minutes, until it's set and golden brown. Leave to one side while you make the filling.

Put the *ricotta* or cream cheese into a bowl and break it up with a fork; gradually beat in the yogurt, honey, and sugar until you've got a light, creamy mixture. Spoon the mixture into the pastry shell and smooth the top. Chill for 1–2 hours, then scatter a few chopped nuts over the top just before serving. The filling will be fairly soft at first, but it will firm up as it chills.

BREADS, SCONES, AND SANDWICHES

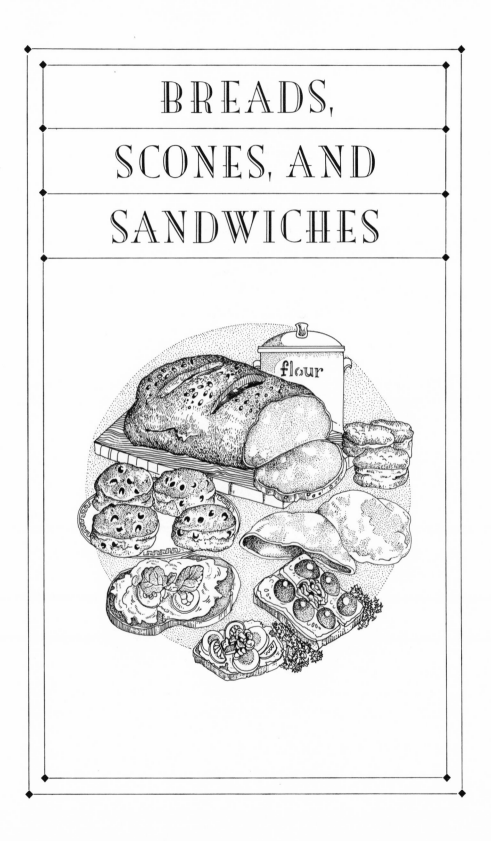

Chapatis
Cheese Scones
Christmas Fruit Loaf
Danish Pastries
Garlic Bread
Melba Toast
Oatcakes
Open Sandwiches
Pear Bread
Pita Bread
Soda Bread
Tortillas
Tostadas
Whole-Wheat Bread
Whole-Wheat Rolls

Y̶OU WILL SEE I SUGGEST WHOLE-WHEAT FLOUR
for most of these recipes; as I'm convinced of the value of whole-wheat
flour I was determined to try to make good whole-wheat versions of
some of the traditional international breads and scones. I'm particularly
pleased with the whole-wheat version of pita bread, which we think is
nicer than the type you can buy in the grocery. If you want to use
white flour instead, you can of course do so. As whole-wheat flour
absorbs less water than white, you will probably need to add a little
extra liquid to the recipes where you make this substitution.

For the yeast recipes, I suggest dried yeast because that's what I
normally use—mainly because I can keep a large drum of it in my
cupboard and it's one less thing to have to remember to buy, or, with
me, forget to buy! You can certainly use fresh yeast for the recipes,
though, if you prefer; simply use double the amount and crumble it
into the liquid without adding the ½ teaspoonful of sugar; then continue with the recipe as described.

These breads and scones can be the basis of very nourishing meals;
a bowl of lentil soup and whole-wheat rolls, or some lovely hunks of
homemade whole-wheat bread with cheese and fruit may be simple
to prepare but they contain as many nutrients as a cooked meal and
always seem to be popular.

◆——◆——◆

CHAPATIS

INDIA

These circles of unleavened bread are delicious with any curry dish;
they can also be rolled around salad fillings or stuffed and baked in a
similar way to the tortillas in the pasta and crêpes section of this
book. *Makes 12.*

2¼ cups (560 ml) whole-wheat   1 teaspoon sea salt
   flour   About ⅔ cup (160 ml) cold water
1½ teaspoons oil, melted butter, or
   ghee

Measure the flour into a bowl. Mix in the fat, salt, and water to make
a firm dough. When the dough has formed, turn it out onto a very

lightly floured board and knead it for about 5 minutes. Then cover it with a damp cloth and leave it to rest for 2–3 hours before kneading it again.

Divide the dough into 12 pieces, form each into a ball with your hands, then roll them out with a rolling pin so that they are 6–8 inches (15–20 cm) across. Fry the chapatis both sides in an ungreased skillet. Pile them up on a plate as they're done and cover them with a piece of foil to prevent them from drying out.

If you like, you can brush them over with a little oil, melted butter, or *ghee* before serving them.

CHEESE SCONES

SCOTLAND

Light and savory, cheese scones are delicious both with creamy dips and with hot soups, especially if the scones have come straight from the oven. As they're quick and easy to make, it's not difficult to mix up a batch while the soup is finishing cooking. They really make soup or salad into a meal, with just some fruit to follow. *Makes about 12.*

2 cups (500 ml) whole-wheat flour, or use half whole-wheat and half white
2 teaspoons baking powder
½ teaspoon dry mustard
½ teaspoon sea salt

4 tablespoons softened butter or soft margarine
1 cup (250 ml) finely grated Gruyère or Cheddar cheese
⅓–½ cup (80–125 ml) milk

Preheat the oven to 400° F (200° C). Sift the flour, baking powder, dry mustard, and salt into a large bowl, adding any residue of bran left in the sieve. Using your fingertips, rub the fat into the flour until the mixture looks like fine bread crumbs. Lightly mix in the grated cheese, then enough of the milk to make a soft but firm dough. Turn the dough onto a lightly floured board and knead briefly; roll it or press it out to a thickness of about ½ inch (1 cm). Use a plain 2-inch (5 cm) pastry cutter to cut the dough into rounds. Place the rounds on a floured baking sheet and bake in the preheated oven for about 10 minutes, or until the scones are risen and golden brown.

Cheese and walnut scones are delicious. Add ¼ cup (60 ml) chopped walnuts to the mixture with the grated cheese.

CHRISTMAS FRUIT LOAF

DENMARK

The candied fruits make this a pretty, jeweled loaf. It's nice for Christmas because it's festive without being too rich. If ground cardamom is hard to come by where you live, the best way to get it is to buy some cardamom pods and crush them with a mortar and pestle or with the back of a spoon—the seeds will come out of the pods as you crush them, and you keep the seeds and discard the pods. Cardamom is a useful flavoring for curries and spicy rice dishes, too. *Makes 1 large loaf.*

½ cup (125 ml) lukewarm milk
½ teaspoon superfine sugar
1 package active dry yeast
4 cups (1 liter) flour—I use half whole-wheat, half white for this recipe
Pinch of salt
¼ cup (60 ml) firmly packed soft brown sugar

7 tablespoons softened butter or margarine
½ teaspoon crushed cardamom
2 teaspoons vanilla extract
Zest of ½ lemon
1 cup (250 ml) mixed candied fruits, chopped—try to get a nice variety of colors
2 eggs, beaten

First butter a 9-by-5 inch (23-by-13 cm) loaf pan. Then put the milk into a small bowl, stir in the sugar and yeast, and leave to one side to ferment. Meanwhile mix together the flour, salt, and sugar and rub in the butter or margarine; add the cardamom, vanilla, lemon, fruit, and eggs. Make a well in the center and pour in the yeast mixture. Mix to a soft dough, adding a little more flour if necessary, then knead for 10 minutes. Put the dough into an oiled bowl, cover with a clean damp cloth, and leave it in a warm place until doubled in bulk—about 1 hour.

Punch the dough down, knead it again lightly, form into a loaf shape, and put into the prepared pan. Cover the loaf with the cloth again and leave in a warm place for about 30 minutes to rise. Preheat the oven to 350° F (180° C). When the loaf has risen up to the top of the pan, bake it until it's golden and crisp. The loaf should sound hollow when turned out of the loaf pan and tapped on the bottom. Leave on a wire rack to cool. It's nice served with a rich dessert, like *pashka or crème brûlée*, or sliced and buttered with coffee or tea.

◆——◆——◆

DANISH PASTRIES

DENMARK

Light, crisp and not too sweet, Danish pastries are ideal for serving with coffee on a special occasion. They take time to make but are not difficult. They freeze well, but leave the final icing until just before serving. *Makes 15.*

10 tablespoons butter, softened	3 tablespoons butter
1 cup (250 ml) warm water	2½ cups (675 ml) whole-wheat
1 teaspoon sugar	flour
1 package active dry yeast	1 egg

FOR THE FILLINGS:

½ cup (125 ml) mixed dried fruit	nutmeg, cinnamon, ginger,
3 tablespoons superfine sugar	allspice, etc., to taste
1 teaspoon mixed spices—ground	4 ounces (125 g) marzipan

TO FINISH:

Beaten egg for glaze	¼ cup (60 ml) slivered almonds
Glacé icing made from 1½ cups (375 ml) confectioners sugar and a little water	

Beat the butter and spread it out into an 8-inch (20 cm) square. Place it in the refrigerator to get really hard while you prepare the dough.

Put the water into a small bowl and stir in the sugar and yeast; leave to one side for 10 minutes to ferment. Rub the 3 tablespoons of butter into the flour, then make a well in the center, pour in the frothy yeast mixture, and add the egg. Mix everything together to make a soft dough; knead it until it feels smooth and pliable. Wrap the dough in waxed paper and leave it in the refrigerator to rest for 15 minutes. Roll the dough ¼ inch (6 mm) thick into an 8 by 12 inch (20 by 30 cm) oblong. Place the square of butter on the dough, covering two-thirds of it.

Fold the remaining third of the dough over the butter-covered part and then fold the remaining pieces of butter-covered dough over so that you have the unbuttered piece in the center.

Seal the edges by pressing with a rolling pin; chill the dough in the fridge for 15 minutes. Roll the dough into an oblong again and fold in three as before; chill in the fridge for 15 more minutes. Repeat the rolling and folding 3 or 4 times more, then roll the dough out to a thickness of ½ inch (1 cm) and cut into 3 pieces.

Roll one of these pieces into an oblong the same size as the first one you made. Sprinkle the dried fruit, sugar, and spices over the top of the dough and press it in lightly with a rolling pin. Roll up the dough from the long side, jelly-roll fashion. Cut the roll into 6 even-size pieces, then make two deep cuts in each piece and open them out slightly. Place them on a baking sheet.

Cut both the remaining pieces of dough into 6 pieces. Roll each piece into a 4-inch (10 cm) square. Cut the marzipan into 12 pieces. Form 6 of the pieces of marzipan into 1 by 4 inch (2.5 by 10 cm) strips. Place a strip of marzipan at the top edges of 6 of the squares of dough. Roll the dough over and make cuts all down the length, almost through to the edge. Curl the dough around to make a circle. For the remaining pieces of dough, fold the corners to the center and press down. Form the remaining marzipan into rounds. Place one round in the center of each piece of dough.

Brush all the pastries with beaten egg. Preheat the oven to 425° F (220° C). Place the pastries on top of the stove to benefit from the heat of the oven as it warms up. When the pastries are puffy, after about 20 minutes or so, place them in the oven and bake for 20 minutes. Cool the pastries on a wire rack, then ice them and sprinkle with toasted slivered almonds. I think they're best warmed through before serving.

To freeze Danish pastries, open-freeze the cooled pastries. When they're firm, store them in a plastic bag. When you're ready to serve them, put them on a wire rack to defrost—allow about 2 hours for this—then ice them as usual.

GARLIC BREAD

Hot bread oozing with melted butter and garlic is a wonderful accompaniment to soups and creamy dips, particularly those containing lentils and beans. French bread is, of course, the type that is normally used for garlic bread, and there's no doubt that this is delicious, with a crisp crust and tender center, but whole-wheat bread can also be used very usccessfully. Although the loaf is a different shape, you treat it in just the same way, but allow a little longer for it to heat through. For quick whole-wheat garlic bread for just one or two people, you can spread slices of whole-wheat broad with garlic butter, lay them out individually on a baking sheet or broiler pan without any foil covering, and heat them in the oven or under the broiler until the butter has melted and the bread is just crispy around the edges. *Serves 4–6.*

1 French loaf or 1 small	*Salt*
whole-wheat loaf	*8 tablespoons butter, softened*
3–4 cloves garlic	

Preheat the oven to 400° F (200° C). Slice the French loaf almost through into chunky pieces—they should just hold together at the base. If you're using the whole-wheat loaf, cut right through into slices—don't make them too thick. Make the garlic butter by peeling the garlic and crushing it, then mixing it into the butter. Spread this butter on both sides of the slices of bread. Pile the whole-wheat bread back into the loaf shape. Wrap whichever loaf you've chosen in foil and place it on a baking sheet in the oven. Bake it for about 20 minutes, until it's heated right through and crisp on the outside. Serve at once.

MELBA TOAST

Whole-wheat Melba toast is delicious, crisp, and nutty-tasting. This is the method I've found to be most successful for making Melba toast with whole-wheat bread. *Serves 4.*

8 thin slices whole-wheat bread

Preheat the oven to 400° F (200° C). Cut the slices of bread as thin as you can; it helps if the bread is a couple of days old. Lay the slices on baking sheets and place in the oven. After about 7 minutes turn the bread over and bake it for another 7–10 minutes, or until lightly browned. As soon as the bread comes out of the oven, cut it diagonally across, then cool the slices on a wire rack—they'll crispen as they cool. Melba toast is particularly good with creamy dips.

OATCAKES

SCOTLAND

Oatcakes are easy to make, and crisp and nutty-tasting to eat. Try them for breakfast or tea with butter and clear honey, or serve them with a creamy dip or Scottish cream cheese. *Makes 24–28.*

2 cups (500 ml) rolled oats	*6 teaspoons hot water*
½ teaspoon baking powder	*Extra oats to finish*
½ teaspoon salt	
2 tablespoons butter or margarine, melted	

Preheat the oven to 400° F (200° C). Put the oats into a bowl with the baking powder, salt, and butter or margarine. Mix them together lightly, then stir in enough warm water to make a dough—you'll need about 6 teaspoonsful.

Sprinkle some oats on a board and turn the dough out onto this, kneading lightly; roll the dough out to a thickness of about ¼ inch (6 mm), sprinkling the surface with extra oats if necessary to prevent it from sticking. You can either roll the mixture into a circle and then cut it into wedges, or cut it into rounds using a pastry cutter. Transfer the oatcakes to a baking sheet and bake them for about 15 minutes, until firm and lightly colored. Let them cool on the sheet for a few minutes, then transfer them to a wire cooling rack. Or serve them straight from the oven, all warm and crumbly.

OPEN SANDWICHES

A tray of colorful open sandwiches looks really mouth-watering and is a surprisingly practical way of feeding a large group of people. If you want to make the meal more substantial, serve mugs or bowls of soup as well with a choice of different desserts laid out on a separate table for people to help themselves. Medium-size plates and forks will be needed for eating the sandwiches, and plenty of paper napkins are advisable.

It's fun to make the open sandwiches and not difficult to make them look pretty. I think the easiest way to do them is to prepare a really good assortment of different ingredients and spread them all out in front of you so that you can create different combinations as you go along.

FOR THE BASE:

Whole-wheat bread, rye bread, or pumpernickel

Butter
Crisp lettuce leaves

FOR THE TOPPINGS:

Finely grated cheese mixed to a paste with mayonnaise, cream, or milk
Sliced hard-boiled egg
Chopped hard-boiled egg mixed with mayonnaise or low-fat ricotta
Peanut butter

Cottage cheese
Ricotta or cream cheese
Any of the dips on pages 33–42 (hummus, mock caviar, Liptauer cheese, and avocado dip are particularly good)
Cold bean or lentil salads are also excellent

FOR THE GARNISHES:

Slices of lemon, tomato, avocado (tossed in lemon juice), onion, red and green pepper, cooked beets, cucumber, radishes, scallions
Sprigs of parsley, mint, or watercress
Chopped chives
Pineapple cubes or rings
Chopped apple, sliced banana tossed in lemon juice

Raisins, dates, chopped dried apricots
Black or green grapes
Ripe or green olives
Chopped walnuts and slivered almonds
Chopped preserved ginger
Mango chutney
Olive oil
Mayonnaise
Paprika

Butter the bread fairly generously and place it on the tray from which it will be served. Cover each piece of bread with a lettuce leaf, pressing it down so that the butter sticks it onto the bread. Now arrange your toppings and garnishes on the lettuce leaf, covering each as generously as possible whilst making them practical to eat. Here are some ideas for different combinations:

- Avocado (dipped in lemon juice), watercress, a spoonful of mayonnaise, *ricotta* or cottage cheese, chopped walnuts
- Peanut butter, coarsely grated carrot, green pepper rings, sliced onion
- *Ricotta* or cottage cheese, pineapple rings, black grapes, toasted slivered almonds
- Sliced cooked beets, onion rings, chopped walnuts, cream cheese or *ricotta*
- Cold lentil salad, mango chutney, chopped apple, parsley
- *Hummus*, onion rings, paprika, sliced tomato, parsley
- Mock caviar or eggplant and sesame paste, sliced tomato, onion rings, olive oil
- Liptauer cheese, tomato, ripe olives, parsley sprigs
- Feta cheese and herb spread, sliced cucumber, and radishes
- Avocado dip, coarsely grated carrot, sliced tomato, chopped walnuts
- Cubes of cold spicy fritters, mango chutney, tomato, onion rings, garlic mayonnaise
- *Ricotta* or cream cheese, apple, chopped preserved ginger, walnuts

PEAR BREAD

SWITZERLAND

Slices of this pear bread, *birnbrot,* are lovely served warm with coffee, or if you serve it hot with light cream it makes a very good dessert. I think it is good after a fondue because it's sweet without being rich. You can leave out the kirsch and wine, but they do give beautiful flavor for a special occasion. You will probably be able to get dry pears easily enough; they're also nice in fruit compotes. *Makes 1 large loaf.*

5 tablespoons lukewarm milk
¼ teaspoon sugar
1 package active dry yeast
1¼ cups (310 ml) whole-wheat
flour
1¼ cups (310 ml) all-purpose
flour

Pinch of salt
4 tablespoons butter or soft
margarine
¼ cup (60 ml) firmly packed
brown sugar
1 egg, beaten

FOR THE FILLING:

⅔ cup (160 ml) dry, pitted prunes
1 cup (250 ml) dry pears
⅓ cup (80 ml) raisins
Zest and juice of ½ lemon
¼ cup (60 ml) firmly packed
brown sugar

A little ground cinnamon
Grated nutmeg
1 tablespoon each of dry red wine
and kirsch (optional)
1¼ cups (310 ml) water

FOR THE GLAZE:

A little beaten egg

Butter a large baking sheet: leave to one side. First make the dough. Put the milk into a small bowl and stir in the sugar and yeast. Leave in a warm place for the yeast to ferment. Put the flours and salt into a large bowl; rub in the butter or margarine and add the sugar. Make a well in the center and pour in the yeast and milk, together with the beaten egg. Mix everything together to make a smooth, soft dough, adding a little flour if necessary. Turn the dough onto a floured board and knead it for 10 minutes; then put the dough into a clean, oiled bowl and cover it with a damp cloth. Put the bowl in a warm place for about an hour, or until the dough has doubled in bulk.

While this is happening make the filling. Put the water, prunes, pears and raisins into a small pan and heat gently until soft, thick, and dry. Finely chop or purée the mixture, then add the lemon and sugar and some cinnamon and nutmeg to taste—about ¼ teaspoon of each—Add the wine and kirsch if you are using them. Don't make the mixture too moist—it should hold its shape.

To assemble the pear bread, take the risen dough and knead it for a minute or two, then put it onto a lightly floured board and roll out into a large 15-inch (38 cm) square not more than ¼ inch (6 mm) thick. Spread the fruity filling over the square to within about 1 inch (2.5 cm) of the edges. Fold the edges over to enclose the filling, then roll it firmly like a jelly roll and put it onto the prepared baking sheet. Prick the pear bread all over, cover it with a clean cloth, and put it into a warm place for 30 minutes to rise. About 15 minutes before the pear bread is ready, preheat the oven to 350° F (180° C). Then brush the bread with beaten egg and bake it in the center of the oven, for about 35 minutes, or until it's golden brown and crisp. Serve warm.

PITA BREAD

MIDDLE EAST

These thin bread "pockets" are very popular with my children who irreverently refer to them as "Arabs' feet" on account of their shape! They're no more trouble to make than rolls, and fun to eat because you can fill them with lots of crunchy salad, dips, cottage cheese, etc., when they make a delectable lunch or supper. You will need one or two large baking sheets to cook them on, as they take up rather a lot of space. *Makes 12.*

1¼ cups (310 ml) lukewarm
   water
½ teaspoon sugar
1 package active dry yeast

4 cups (1 liter) whole-wheat flour
2 teaspoons salt
1 teaspoon sugar
1 tablespoon oil

Put the water into a jug and stir in the yeast and the ½ teaspoon of sugar; leave to one side to ferment. Meanwhile put the flour, salt, the sugar, and the olive oil into a bowl and mix together. Add the yeast mixture and mix to a dough. Knead for 5 minutes until smooth. Put the dough into an oiled bowl, cover with a damp cloth, and leave it in a warm place for 1 hour to rise. When the dough has doubled in size, punch it down and knead it lightly. Preheat the oven to 450° F (230° C).

Divide the dough into 12 pieces and roll each into an oblong about 3 by 7 inches (7 by 18 cm). Put the pieces onto oiled baking sheets and leave them in a warm place or on top of the stove for 15 minutes to rise a bit.

Put them in the oven and bake them for 5 minutes; then turn the oven heat down to 400° F (200° C) and bake for another 10 minutes or so, until the pita breads are golden brown. When they come out of the oven they'll be light and puffed up; cool them on a wire rack and make them into pouches by inserting the point of a sharp knife into one of the long edges and sliding it along.

That's proper pita bread, but when I was working out this recipe I made a batch that I rolled out rather longer and thinner and baked for a bit longer at the higher temperature. They came out thin and very crisp and that is how my children always ask me to make them now.

SODA BREAD

IRELAND

Soda bread is quick to make, an ideal standby when the bread bin is empty and there is no time to make yeast bread. It only takes about 40 minutes from start to finish and is delicious served slightly warm. It's particularly good with honey. Although I'm very much a whole-wheat bread fan, I think this particular recipe is best made with half whole-wheat and half all-purpose flour. Interestingly enough, an Irishman I met while writing this book told me that, although no one ever made bread like his mother, he thought the most authentic-tasting loaf was made with scofa flour and buttermilk. *Makes 1 loaf.*

4 cups (1 liter) whole-wheat and all-purpose flour mixed
1 teaspoon salt
1 rounded teaspoon baking soda
2 tablespoons butter or margarine

1¼ cups (310 ml) buttermilk, sour milk, or milk warmed with a tablespoon of cider vinegar or lemon juice to sour it

Preheat the oven to 425° F (220° C). Flour a baking sheet. Sift the flour, salt, and baking soda into a large bowl. With your fingertips, rub in the fat until the mixture resembles fine bread crumbs. Make a well in the center and pour in the milk, then gradually mix everything together to make a dough. Turn the dough out onto a floured board and knead it lightly, then form it into a round loaf. Put the loaf on the prepared baking sheet and, using a sharp knife, cut a cross shape in the top. Bake the loaf for 30–35 minutes, or until it's risen, golden, and crusty; leave it to cool on a wire rack.

Soda bread doesn't keep well; it's really best eaten the same day.

TORTILLAS

MEXICO

In Mexico tortillas are eaten as we would eat bread. They're easy to make and versatile. You can eat them as they are, with butter or other toppings; you can roll them round salad mixtures such as cottage cheese, lettuce and tomato or mixed bean salad, watercress, and onion to make a kind of hearty rolled sandwich. If you fry them in hot oil they became crisp like *poppadums* and can be served with creamy salad dips. They can also be treated like crêpes, filled with savory mixtures, covered with a well-flavored sauce and baked; for the two recipes for this see pages 190 and 193. *Makes 12.*

1 cup (250 ml) masa harina—
  or use whole-wheat flour
*1¼ cups (310 ml) whole-wheat
  flour*

1 teaspoon sea salt
About ⅔ cup (180 ml) water

Measure the flour into a bowl, then stir in the salt and enough water to make a dough that's soft but not sticky. Turn the dough onto a floured board and knead it slightly to make it smooth; then divide it into 12 pieces. Roll each piece into a ball and then use a rolling pin to roll each into a thin round, 6–8 inches (15–20 cm) in diameter.

Heat a skillet without any fat in it and fry the tortillas in this, one at a time: keep the heat fairly low. When the underside is set, turn the tortilla over and cook the other side. Put them on a plate when they're ready and cover them with a piece of foil because they quickly become dry and brittle.

Serve the tortillas instead of bread with salads. A pile of freshly cooked tortillas and bowls of spicy avocado dip, sliced tomatoes, quarters of hard-boiled egg, grated cheese, red kidney bean salad, and shredded lettuce makes a lovely easy-going buffet lunch or supper.

TOSTADAS

MEXICO

A *tostada* is a tortilla that has been fried in oil so that it becomes crisp, like a *poppadum*. *Tostadas* are particularly good with creamy dips and salads because their crispness is such a pleasant contrast. *Makes 12.*

12 *tortillas—see page 282*
Oil for shallow frying

Make the tortillas as described—this can be done in advance if more convenient. Heat a little oil in a skillet and fry the tortillas until they're crisp on one side; then turn them over and fry on the other side. Drain them well on paper towels.

Tostadas make an excellent "edible plate" for a salad—allow one *tostada* for each person and arrange the salad on top, making it as colorful and mouth-watering as you can. Lettuce makes a good foundation, but make sure it's well dried so that the *tostada* remains crisp. Suggested toppings: sliced tomato, grated carrot, red kidney bean salad, grated cheese, cottage cheese or *ricotta*, watercress and scallion, piled up well and finished off with a generous dollop of spicy avocado dip or mayonnaise.

WHOLE-WHEAT BREAD

ENGLAND

So many recipes for making bread start off by telling you how easy it is—and it really is—but still many people say they find the prospect daunting! I must admit that what recipes should say is that making bread is easy when you do it often. If you make bread twice a week or so, you learn a lot about the behavior of the yeast and the dough and the effect of heat on the mixture. But for everyone there has to be a first time, and so I'm going to try and put down all the things I've discovered and I hope this will be helpful and make it as easy as possible for you.

If you're baking for a family, or have a deep-freeze, I don't think it's worth making up small amounts. You can use all whole-wheat flour, or, if your family isn't used to whole-wheat flour you might find it best to use a proportion of strong white bread flour (preferably unbleached) —half and half is a good mixture to start with.

I use active dry yeast, largely because it's handy—one of those large tubs lasts ages and so I don't have to keep remembering to buy it; also it's more predictable and, I think, easier when you're learning. But it is important that the yeast not be stale, so buy it from a shop that has a quick turnover and, unless you know you're going to make a lot of bread, it's best to buy a small quantity to start with.

If you've got a warm place like an airing cupboard you can put the bread there to rise; I stand mine near the pilot light on my gas stove. But the bread will rise just as well—but more slowly—standing on the counter in the kitchen; you don't especially need to put it in a warm place, and it's important not to let it get too hot. *Makes two loaves.*

4 teaspoons active dry yeast	*2 teaspoons salt*
2½ teaspoons sugar	*1 tablespoon soft butter, or*
3 cups lukewarm water	*margarine*
8 cups (2 liters) whole-wheat flour	

Put the yeast into a small bowl with ½ teaspoon of the sugar and 1 cup of the water. Mix lightly and leave to one side for 10 minutes to ferment. In a large bowl mix the flour with the remaining sugar and the salt; using your fingertips, rub in the fat. Make a well in the center and add the frothy yeast mixture and the remaining 2 cups of water. Mix together with your hands until soft but firm dough forms. If you've got a dough hook on your mixer—and I must say it's since I got one that I've managed to make our bread regularly—you can now let the hook knead the dough for 5 minutes. Otherwise, turn the dough out and knead it by hand, pushing and pummeling, folding and refolding it, for 10 minutes. As you knead the dough, you'll feel it change from a coarse, lumpy and slightly sticky texture to a beautiful smooth, supple, silky one.

Put the dough back in its bowl, cover it with a damp cloth, and then stand the bowl in a warm place until double in size. I find this takes an hour, perhaps slightly longer if the bowl is just standing on the counter, and up to 2 hours if the kitchen is cold.

Now punch down the dough with your fist and knead it again a little—just 1–2 minutes this time, to wake the yeast up again. Cut the dough in half and shape the two lumps to fit the loaf pans (9 by 5 inches/23 by 13 cm)). I find the best way to do this is to flatten each piece with the palm of my hand, then gently roll it up and pop it into the pan with the fold underneath. Put the loaves on top of the stove or in a warm place, cover with the damp cloth again, and preheat the oven to 475° F (240° C). (If you put the loaves on top of the stove, the heat of the oven as it warms up will help them to rise.)

They'll take about 30 minutes to rise: as soon as the dough is just peeping over the tops of the pans, put them into the oven. Don't let them over-rise or they'll collapse in the oven: if there is still some rise left in them the heat from the oven will give them a final boost and they'll have a lovely domed crust.

After 10 minutes turn the heat down to 400° F (200° C) and bake the loaves for another 35 minutes. When done, turn the loaves out of their pans right away—they should sound hollow when you tap them on the bottom—and leave them on a wire rack to cool.

WHOLE-WHEAT ROLLS

ENGLAND

Warm homemade rolls are useful for serving with so many dishes and they're really not difficult to make. *Makes 24.*

1 cup (250 ml) lukewarm water
1 package active dry yeast
½ teaspoon sugar
6 cups (1.2 liters) whole-wheat
*   flour*
2 teaspoons salt

1 tablespoon sugar
4 tablespoons butter
1 cup (250 ml) milk
1 egg, beaten
A little extra flour to finish

Put the water into a small bowl and stir in the yeast and the ½ tea-spoon of sugar. Leave to one side for 10 minutes to ferment. Mean-while put the flour, salt, and the 1 tablespoon of sugar into a bowl and rub in the butter. Pour the frothed-up yeast into the center of the flour and add the milk and egg; mix together to make a firm but pliable dough. Turn the dough out and knead it for 10 minutes, then put it back into the bowl, cover with a damp cloth, and leave until it's doubled in size. This takes about an hour in a warm place, and 1–2 hours just standing on a counter, depending on how warm the room is.

When the dough has risen, preheat the oven to 425° F (220° C). Punch down the dough, knead it again lightly, and then divide it into

24 pieces. Form the pieces into rounds, flatten them with the palm of your hand, and place them on greased baking sheets, allowing room for them to spread. Cover them with a damp cloth and leave in a warm place for 20–30 minutes to double in size—I put mine on top of the stove so that they get the benefit of the heat of the oven as it warms up. Sprinkle the rolls with a little flour and then bake them for 15 minutes. Cool on a wire rack.

INDEX

fruity *muesli*, 232
gooseberry fool, 232–33
lemon whip, 234–35
little coffee custards, 226
mont blanc, 235
pashka, 236–37
pears baked in wine, 239
pineapple sherbet, 239–40
prune delight (*sviskeblancmange*),
    240–41
pumpkin in orange syrup, 241–42
red fruit pudding, 242
rhubarb compote, 243
rice and almond pudding, 243–44
rice flour and rosewater pudding, 233–
    34
stuffed peaches, 238
trifle, 244–45
vanilla ice cream, 245–46
yogurt, 246–47
dips and spreads, 34–42
    aïoli with *crudités*, 35–36
    avocado (*guacamole*), 37–38
    bean, 38–39
    cream cheese and sour cream, 39–40
    eggplant and sesame cream (*baba
        ghannooj*), 36–37
    feta cheese and herb, 40
    hummus, 40–41
    liptauer cheese, 41–42
    mock caviar, 42

eggplant:
    bake, 98
    paste, with sesame cream (*baba
        ghannooj*), 36–37
    stuffed, *à la duxelles*, 120–21
    stuffed, in Béchamel sauce, 118–19
    stuffed with cheese, 119
eggs:
    baked stuffed, 151–52
    curried stuffed, 154–55
    omelette, 158–59
    pipérade, 159–60

fats, xv
fennel, baked with cheese, 80
flour, xvi
fritters:
    banana, with lime, 223
    corn, 178
    spicy, 177–78
fruit compote, dried, 229–30
fruit pudding, red, 242

fruit salads, 230–32
fruity *muesli*, 232

garlic bread, 276
gazpacho, 11
ghee, 133–34
Glamorgan sausages, 169–70
gnocchi:
    alla Romana, 138–39
    fried (*bombolini*), 170–71
    in mushroom sauce, 171–72
    ricotta, 172–73
    spinach, 174
gooseberry fool, 232–33
gougère:
    cold, with cream cheese filling, 157–58
    with mushrooms, onions, and red wine
        sauce, 155–57
gravy, 26–27
green peppers:
    pizza, 213–14
    stuffed, 124–25
    and tomato stew, 101
green salad, 55–56

herbs, xvii
hummus, 40–41

ice cream, vanilla, 245–46

khitchari, 140
kidney beans:
    salad, 63–64
    with tomatoes, onions, and cumin,
        101–2
    see also red kidney beans

leek:
    pie, 208–9
    quiche, 206–7
    soufflé, 161–62
lemon whip, 234–35
lentils, xvii
    khitchari, 140
    pasta with, 195–96
    salad, 57–58
    soup, 12–13
    spicy fritters, 177–78
    stew, with red pepper, 102–3
linzertorte, 258–59

macaroni, *see* pasta
macaroons, 259–60
mayonnaise, 27–28

mushroom, 209–10
onion, 210–11

Rose Elliot, a self-proclaimed vegetarian since the age of three, is one of England's most popular cookbook authors. Her bestselling titles include Simply Delicious, Not Just a Load of Old Lentils, *and* The Bean Book. *She contributes widely to newspapers and magazines in England and appears on both radio and television. Born and educated in England, she lives in Hampshire with her husband, Anthony, and her three daughters, Katy, Margaret, and Claire. She is now at work on a gourmet vegetarian cookbook.*